Activities for Teaching Science as Inquiry

FIFTH EDITION

Merrill
Prentice Hall

Upper Saddle River, New Jersey
Columbus, Ohio

Activities for Teaching Science as Inquiry

ARTHUR A. CARIN
Professor Emeritus, Queens College

JOEL E. BASS
Sam Houston State University

Library of Congress Cataloging-in-Publication Data
Carin, Arthur A.
  Activities for teaching science as inquiry/Arthur A. Carin, Joel E. Bass—5th ed.
    p. cm.
  Rev. ed. of: Guided discovery activities for elementary school science. 4th ed. c1997.
  Includes bibliographical references.
  ISBN 0–13–021281–4
    1. Science—Study and teaching (Elementary)—Activity programs—Handbooks,
  manuals, etc   I. Bass, Joel E.   II. Carin, Arthur A. Guided discovery activities for
  elementary school science   III. Title.

LB1585.C267 2001
372.3'5044—dc21   00-041883

Vice President and Publisher: Jeffery W. Johnston
Editor: Linda Ashe Montgomery
Editorial Assistant: Jennifer Day
Production Editor: Mary Harlan
Design Coordinator: Diane C. Lorenzo
Photo Coordinator: Sandy Lenahan
Cover Design: Ceri Fitzgerald
Cover Photo: FPG
Text Design: Kate Nichols Design Studio
Illustrations: Carlisle Graphics
Production Coordination: Betsy Keefer
Production Manager: Pamela D. Bennett
Director of Marketing: Kevin Flanagan
Marketing Manager: Amy June
Marketing Services Manager: Krista Groshong

This book was set in Goudy by Carlisle Communications, Ltd. It was printed and bound by R. R.
Donnelley & Sons Company. The cover was printed by Phoenix Color Corp.

Previous editions, entitled *Guided Discovery Activities for Elementary School Science*, © 1997, 1993,
1989, 1980.

10 9 8 7 6 5 4 3 2
ISBN 0-13-021281-4

Preface

THE FIFTH EDITION of *Activities for Teaching Science as Inquiry* introduces prospective and experienced teachers to inquiry activities necessary to teach science in contemporary ways. Inquiry is both a way to teach and a way for students to investigate the world. Doing inquiry means asking simple but thoughtful questions about the world and engaging students to answer them. Inquiry incorporates the use of hands-on and process-oriented activities for the benefit of knowledge construction. Inquiry encourages students to connect their prior knowledge to observations and to use their observations as evidence to increase personal scientific knowledge. In this instructional environment, teachers act as facilitators of learning rather than "bankers" who have stored knowledge that they transfer into students' heads.

New to the Fifth Edition

Prodigious efforts of the American Association for the Advancement of Science (AAAS), the National Research Council, and other groups in the 1990s have provided a coherent vision and a research-based framework for a new era of science education. As a result, the *National Science Education Standards* (NSES) were created to coordinate the goals and objectives for science instruction. The *National Science Education Standards* provide directives not only for the setting up of district-wide science programs but also for the science concepts that are to be covered in inquiry activities at each grade level. These standards are not rigid but rather provide you, and the school system in which you teach, concrete guidelines for exposing students to science experiences throughout their schooling. As you become familiar with the *National Science Education Standards* you will be able to incorporate the activities provided in this text into your lesson plans and curricular goals for your school science program.

Significant changes within this edition include:

- *Practical suggestions for building learning communities* include guidelines for the development of cooperative group strategies. Members of cooperative groups encourage the exchange of ideas among students during inquiry experiences.
- *Instructional models for continuing professional development are illustrated in Video Case Studies.* Nine elementary and middle school teachers reflect on their growth as science teachers as they work with science mentors and explore how they could teach science better.
- *The Companion Website* identifies how to utilize technology while learning how to teach science effectively.

The Video Case Studies

Your professor will have copies of several exemplary Video Case Studies. These cases illustrate the professional development of classroom teachers in their search to become more effective at teaching science. When reviewing the Video Case Studies, it is important to explain how to get the most out of using them to advance your own learning.

The Value of Video Cases. In their practical guide *Designing Professional Development for Teachers of Science and Mathematics*, Susan Loucks-Horsley, Peter Hewson, Nancy Love, and Katherine Stiles (1998) identified the case study method as one of the most important strategies for professional development. The process of observing and reflecting on teachers' actions, and on students' learning and thinking, can lead to changes in the knowledge, beliefs, attitudes, and ultimately the practice of pre-service and in-service teachers. You and your colleagues can use classroom discussions about the Video Case Studies to:

- extend and apply knowledge presented in the chapters,
- formulate questions and ideas,
- learn from one another,
- become aware of alternative perspectives and strategies,
- reflect on real problems faced by practicing teachers, and
- increase your science knowledge, as more than 30 science topics are taught in the case studies.

The Annenberg Case Studies. The Video Case Studies are available free to your professor, and are part of the professional library developed by ▲ Annenberg. In the cases chosen to accompany your study of this text, ten video cases depict nine different teachers in three videos in Annenberg's Case Studies in Science Education series. Each video case is divided into three segments: An Introduction to the Case, Trying New Ideas, and Reflecting and Building on Change. The three parts of each Video Case Study enable you to look in on a teacher and his or her students at intervals throughout the school year. From one segment to the next, in each case you will see how the teacher undergoes professional changes in approaching science teaching. The changes reflect the real life experiences of teachers who see a need to improve the way they teach, meet with a teaching mentor to gather ideas, and implement ways to improve their science teaching practice. As a result of this work you will witness not only a teacher's growing confidence and capability in science teaching but also a growing involvement of students in their own science learning.

For optimum benefit while watching the video segments, you as a participant have an opportunity to "share a commitment to improve your teaching practice, a willingness to share and critically discuss aspects of practice and curiosity about important assumptions that underlie teaching and learning" (Loucks-Horsley et al., 1998, pp. 108–109). A knowledgeable and experienced facilitator can enhance the case discussions. The role of the facilitator is to help participants

- understand the situation and issues in the case,
- focus on the thinking of students in the video classrooms,
- examine the approach taken by the teacher,
- reflect on the theoretical foundation for the teachers' actions, and
- consider alternative actions and their consequences (Loucks-Horsley et al., 1998).

Although these Video Case Studies are not intended to replace actual classroom visits, they can provide a more focused picture of specific aspects of teaching and learning than might be obtained from real-time observations of classes.

The Companion Website

A Companion Website designed for student and professor use accompanies this text. The Syllabus Manager allows professors the opportunity to place the class syllabus online. This enables students to also see a course calendar, chapter assignments and course changes as they are posted. In addition, content information is organized as chapter-by-chapter features and provides you with study guide questions and self-assessment tests so you can check your own understanding of teaching science in an ongoing way. Links on the website navigation bar can transport you to

- focus questions you can use as a study guide,
- online quizzes that are self-pacing and self-evaluating, with scores e-mailed to professors if desired,
- Web destinations and links to wonderful science resources on the Internet, and
- a Message Board where you can engage in meaningful discourse about science teaching and learning issues with others taking the course.

Unique to this Companion Website are virtual classroom experiences. Although they are linked more directly to the ninth edition of the core text, *Teaching*

Science as Inquiry, the video essays depicted in certain Website chapters will let you see how well you understand the components of good science teaching. Videostreaming on the video essays illustrates the various teaching strategies of classroom teachers teaching properties of air in grade 1, balance beams in grade 4, and pendulums in grade 8. As you begin to understand the components of good science instruction, test yourself on the strategies that exemplify effective science teaching. You should also see opportunities for improving each science lesson. As you become more familiar with the rudiments of effective science instruction, you may choose to revisit these virtual sites and reassess your understanding of science teaching and learning.

Acknowledgments

To be meaningful, educational visions have to be practically implemented in teacher education and staff development programs, and most important, in our nation's classrooms. Our goal in writing and revising this textbook has been to present the new vision of science education and provide you with specific help, guidelines, and examples as you prepare to teach science in a new millennium.

The reviewers for the third edition of this text, as well as those who read and commented on the chapters in the fourth edition, have been very perceptive and insightful and have offered many comments and suggestions that, hopefully, have led to significant improvements. We acknowledge and express our gratitude to the following reviewers: Carol Brewer, The University of Montana; Rosemarie Kolstad, East Texas State University; Mark R. Malone, The University of Colorado; Richard H. Moyer, The University of Michigan–Dearborn; Michael Odell, The University of Idaho; William A. Rieck, The University of Southwestern Louisiana; Joseph D. Sharpe, Tennessee Technological University; Leone E. Snyder, Northwestern College; M. Dale Streigle, Iowa State University; and Dana L. Zeidler, The University of South Florida–Tampa.

We thank editor Linda Ashe Montgomery at Merrill Education who has provided substantive, as well as editorial assistance throughout the writing and revision efforts. She has a great sensitivity to education issues, not only in science but in other specialized fields as well. We wish to acknowledge her contributions to this text and convey our appreciation to her.

We also wish to thank Kathy Deselle, copyeditor; Kate Nichols, designer; Mary Harlan, production editor; and Betsy Keefer, project coordinator.

Reference

Loucks-Horsley, S., Hewson, P., Love, N., and Stiles, K. (1998). *Designing professional development for teachers of science and mathematics.* Thousand Oaks, CA: Corwin Press.

From Art Carin

I am certain you will find this text a valuable resource as you become an even more competent, confident decision maker. I strongly encourage you to adapt the strategies in this text and appeal to you to apply the concepts in ways that are meaningful to you and your students. It is my hope that it will empower you confidently to teach science to your students in your unique classroom situations. I wish you much success as you experience the joy of seeing your students construct and broaden their science knowledge and grow in their appreciation of this marvelous world.

I wish to personally thank the continued support and encouragement I receive from my wife and family, who urged me to write this book. I was forcefully reinforced and motivated when I visited my grandson's primary classroom, and Andy said, "I hope my teacher gets a copy of your book so we can do these fun science things together." I want all the Andys out there to enjoy the wonders of science that you can offer in the classroom. Hopefully this book will help you accomplish that.

From Joel Bass

As a teacher, you exemplify science for your students. I encourage you to portray science as a way of inquiring into the wonders of our world. This book contains a wealth of activities that you will find useful in heightening the interest and curiosity of young students and guiding them as they investigate how the world works. The pages in this book reflect a great deal that my own students have taught me about science, children, and teaching. Thanks to each and every one of you for what you have taught me, for responding to my teaching, and for your continued friendship. Thanks also to my own teachers and colleagues for their guidance and friendship.

I would also like to express my special appreciation for the support and encouragement of my wife, Helen, and our two sons, Randy and Ricky. Helen is a creative teacher who is now using her multiple talents in staff development for the implementation of social studies standards in our state. I am grateful to her for enlarging my own view of science and culture, particularly as it relates to American history. In our mutual quest to understand the first Americans, we have trudged down canyons, explored ancient ruins, gazed in wonder at rock art, meditated at sacred sites, and danced in tribal powwows. Helen, thanks for your love, companionship, care, and concern in the day-to-day life of raising a family and balancing professional and other concerns and responsibilities.

With sincere gratitude to all,

Art Carin
Joel Bass

Contents

x

III   Life, Ecology, and Environmental Science Activities A-104

IV Earth and Space Science Activities A-193

Activities for Teaching Science as Inquiry

I

Using Activities for Inquiry

NSES *Science as inquiry is basic to science education and a controlling principle in the ultimate organization and selection of students' activities. Students at all grade levels and in every domain of science should have the opportunity to use scientific inquiry and develop the ability to think and act in ways associated with inquiry, including asking questions, planning and conducting investigations, using appropriate tools and techniques to gather data, thinking critically and logically about relationships between evidence and explanations, constructing and analyzing alternative explanations, and communicating scientific arguments. (National Research Council, 1996, p. 105)*

The fifth grade classroom teacher opened the science lesson holding up a poinsettia leftover from the holiday season. "Is this living or dead?" she said.

Because the plant had sometimes been watered and sometimes ignored for long periods of time, the question presented a dilemma for the fifth graders. Did the teacher mean was it living at one time or could it still be living?

The neglected twig-like structure, sitting atop the foil-wrapped pot, was not intended to be an enigma. The classroom teacher had simply needed a motivation strategy to open the lesson and remembered the plant on the windowsill. Two students tentatively raised their hands. "Alive?" queried the student who was called on. "Correct," the teacher said.

The next 30 minutes were more routine. The class read, in round-robin fashion, 11 pages in the science textbook that discussed environmental communities and ecological niches. Thirty minutes later, after skipping the activity page and ensuring that the 30 boldfaced vocabulary words were noted, the teacher concluded the lesson. "Good job," she said. "We got through that lesson in 30 minutes. That was a lot of science! Now, clear off your desktops and line up for lunch."

Unfortunately, this science lesson was not observed 30 years ago, when round-robin reading was considered an acceptable way to teach every content area covered in school, including science. The science lesson described here happened in a suburban elementary school in a middle-class neighborhood late last spring. Perhaps it mirrors classroom science experiences you have had. How can you plan science lessons that really engage and motivate students? Hopefully, you have learned that science learning is meaningful only when students are able to actively participate in constructing their own knowledge through exploration and inquiry. That is the message of the *National Science Education Standards*. And it is the message of this text.

Engaging Students in Inquiry

This text is about inquiry. It is about engaging students in explorations designed to stimulate their interest, pique their curiosity, and encourage them to seek answers to new questions. It is about teaching students a way to structure inquiry and develop questioning strategies.

> Inquiry should not be taught in isolation but as a tool for finding answers to questions about the world in which we live. In addition, science teachers should very clearly and consistently emphasize students' conceptual development of scientific explanations, as opposed to step-by-step methods that too often characterize the nature of scientific inquiry. (DeBoer and Bybee, 1995, p. 73)

Inquiry in school classrooms is supposed to mirror the acts of practicing scientists. This does not mean following a scientific method but rather engaging in activities characteristic of scientists:

- Ask questions about objects, events, and systems.
- Make observations and measurements to obtain data and seek evidence.
- Blend logic and imagination.
- Strive to make sense of observations of phenomena by inventing explanations consistent with currently accepted scientific principles.
- Use observations to make predictions that evidence past theories and speculate events of the future.
- Identify and avoid bias.
- Reach conclusions or *not*. (AAAS, 1989, 27–28)

As you engage your own students in science activities, consider how you might encourage students to behave as scientists.

Use Well-Designed and Proven Activities

The activities in this text, although not a comprehensive list, will provide you with a good base for science teaching. The structure of well-designed classroom activities, whether from this text or other sources, have several factors in common, including the following:

1. A materials list that is complete and includes safe and easily obtainable items appropriate for the grade level of students in individual classrooms.

2. Measurable amounts of specific materials that are accurately prescribed.
3. Activities that are possible to do within the confines of a classroom or outside on school grounds.
4. Clearly written procedures that explain the safe use of materials and the order in which they can be used. In addition, illustrations are visually accurate and precise.
5. Activities that have been field-tested.

The activities in this text have all been field-tested by teachers and students in preschools, elementary schools, and middle or junior high schools. Neither the teachers nor the students were given any special preparation or training in science, outside of their own prior experiences, before doing any of the activities. After testing the activities in class, the teachers evaluated each activity and students identified concerns they had with procedures and materials. The activities were then rewritten to incorporate the suggestions and then re-tested.

Because many other sources for effective activities are available, it would be advantageous to your success in science teaching to look for more. Searching the Internet is a good place to begin. Appendixes C and I will also lead you to reliable resources.

Look for acronyms that identify sources recognized for their long-standing efforts to provide teachers and students with relevant and motivating classroom activities. Try FOSS, ESS, GEMS, GLOBE, AIMS, and BSCS.

Planning for the Use of Activities

Try It Out! Before you introduce an activity to students or demonstrate one for students, try it out. Then you can anticipate questions and ensure that the activity will work. Finding out in the middle of a lesson that you don't have enough materials or you can't get the equipment to work properly can discourage you or your students. It can also thwart the excitement that generally comes when students handle concrete materials and discover science phenomena for themselves.

Allow for Flexibility. It is important to note that although activities from reliable sources are generally tested in actual classrooms, no teacher can be certain that a class will respond "according to plan." So, be flexible in your expectations and encourage findings that align with the prior knowledge of your students and expand their knowledge base. Also, be aware that you do not have to follow the activities exactly. The ideas presented are intended only as a guide. Modify the activities to meet the diverse needs of your learners including their learning styles, interests, and abilities.

Don't Give Away the "Answer." To advance the inquiry process, tell students very little about the purpose of an activity or what can be expected to happen before they begin. You want students to make observations, discuss what they observe, and have a chance to make predictions or inferences from their observations. Otherwise, they are likely to discover exactly what you have told them they will discover. Part of the joy of exploring is not knowing what to expect! It is the wonder of science that keeps us all kids at heart.

Listen for Students' Conceptions and Misconceptions. As students exchange ideas with you or with their classmates, listen to how they have conceptualized what they think. Often, they will be wrong because they have developed erroneous beliefs about how something "works." Misconceptions are difficult to change. Simply pointing out misconceptions will not generally change what students believe. Sometimes, students' ideas are naïve, and they just need to grow cognitively. Often though, students will confront inconsistencies in their beliefs with new observations, and yet they will not be deterred from their original ideas. If you hear students voice inaccurate explanations, you can employ several strategies that have been identified by researchers to help students see that their current way of thinking is contradictory or inadequate to explain what they are observing. These strategies include:

- Asking questions that challenge students' current beliefs.
- Presenting phenomena that students cannot adequately explain within their existing perspectives.
- Engaging students in discussions of the pros and cons of various explanations.
- Pointing out, explicitly, the differences between students' beliefs and "reality."
- Showing how the correct explanation of an event or phenomena is more plausible or makes more sense than anything students themselves can offer. (Roth and Anderson, 1988; Ormrod, 1999.)

Hold Off on Presenting Science Vocabulary. Don't give students the vocabulary words that will describe what they observe *before* they do the activity. Let students engage in the inquiry and experience the phenomena they observe. You will recognize when they need the science labels to explain what they see. Concrete experiences will capture students' attention. Attending triggers cognitive processes and the capacity for students to store knowledge in long-term memory (Ormrod, 1999). It is after exploration that science vocabulary will have more meaning for students. Inquiry activities engage students in witnessing the evidence of important science concepts that memorizing boldfaced terms cannot do.

Appropriate Instruction. Bransford, Brown, and Cocking (1999, p. 11), suggest that a common misconception regarding inquiry teaching is that teachers should never tell students anything directly but, instead, should always allow them to construct knowledge for themselves. However, although it is the child who must do the knowledge construction work, teachers must be ready to assist in the process. Thus, teachers can and should be very active agents in children's inquiry processes. It is appropriate for teachers to supply vocabulary terms, invent relevant concepts and principles, and give hints and even complete explanations to children. But, always follow this principle: Tell only after student inquiry.

Appropriate Sequencing of Activities. The activities in this text need not be taught in the exact order in which they are presented. Rather, as you develop science lesson plans and the instructional objectives to accompany those lessons, determine how the sequence of a series of activities will support the development of conceptual understanding.

Sequencing Science Instruction and Inquiry

A great deal of thoughtful planning and organization is needed to prepare meaningful inquiry lessons and activities. Activities done in isolation of a purposeful lesson and instructional objectives will have little relevance for students. Rather, a number of considerations should be entertained such as:

What do I want my students to explore?

What activities will support the concepts and principles I want and need to teach?

What sequence of activities will help students develop science understanding?

Begin with State or Local Curriculum Guidelines

The science concepts you teach will probably be dictated by your local or state curriculum guidelines. These guidelines will likely reflect the *National Science Education Standards*. Organizing instruction and activities around the *Standards* means beginning with ideas that unify concepts and principles such as those embodied in systems, order, and organization; evidence, models, and explanation; change, constancy, and measurement; evolution and equilibrium; and form and function. For example, to demonstrate patterns of change, you might develop a series of lessons that illustrates cycles such as the metamorphosis of insects, egg development, seasons, or weather changes. Experiences with simple patterns of change can help students understand more complex patterns they may encounter in the photos, data, and graphs that scientists often provide from their research.

The *National Science Education Standards* also recommend that teachers teach *science as inquiry*, which means to engage students in understanding scientific concepts so they can appreciate how we know "what we know"; understand the nature of science; learn the skills necessary to make independent inquiries; and have the disposition to use the skills, abilities, and attitudes associated with science (National Research Council, 1996, p. 105). A science program that provides students with concrete experiences in inquiry in the classroom rather than only reading about science facts and concepts will advance scientific literacy.

Core to the *Science Standards* are activities that address:

- *Physical science* including concepts and principles of matter and energy.
- *Life science* including concepts and principles of living things, genetics, ecology, and adaptations and changes over time.
- *Earth science* including concepts and principles related to geology, meteorology, astronomy, and oceanography.

Go to http://www.prenhall.com/carin for a link to the complete text of the *National Science Education Standards.*

Also important and noted in the *National Science Education Standards* are concepts and principles that expose students to:

- *Science and technology* to establish connections between the natural and designed worlds and to create opportunities for decision making linked to technology.
- *Science in personal and social perspectives* as a means to understand and act on personal and social issues.
- *History and the nature of science* that sees science as a changing human endeavor.

Once you or other educators (such as grade level teachers) who are involved in curriculum decision making decide the science content you want students to explore, use the *National Science Education Standards* to review the fundamental concepts and principles that cover that content. See Table I-1 as an example of the fundamental principles and concepts appropriate to introduce physical science for grades K–4. Remember, it is not your responsibility to ensure that students understand each of these principles. It is your responsibility as a curriculum planner to see that

TABLE I-1 NSES CONTENT STANDARDS

Physical Science: Grades K–4

Properties of Objects and Materials	Position and Motion of Objects	Light, Heat, Electricity, and Magnetism
• Objects have many observable properties, including size, weight, shape, color, temperature, and the ability to react with other substances. Those properties can be measured using tools, such as rulers, balances, and thermometers. • Objects are made of one or more materials, such as paper, wood, and metal. Objects can be described by the properties of the materials from which they are made, and those properties can be used to separate or sort a group of objects or materials. • Materials can exist in different states—solid, liquid, and gas. Some common materials, such as water, can be changed from one state to another by heating or cooling.	• The position of an object can be described by locating it relative to another object or the background. • An object's motion can be described by tracing and measuring its position over time. • The position and motion of objects can be changed by pushing or pulling. The size of the change is related to the strength of the push or pull. • Sound is produced by vibrating objects. The pitch of the sound can be varied by changing the rate of vibration.	• Light travels in a straight line until it strikes an object. Light can be reflected by a mirror, refracted by a lens, or absorbed by the object. • Heat can be produced in many ways, such as burning, rubbing, or mixing one substance with another. Heat can move from one object to another by conduction. • Electricity in circuits can produce light, heat, sound, and magnetic effects. Electrical circuits require a complete loop through which an electrical current can pass. • Magnets attract and repel each other and certain kinds of other materials.

Source: National Science Education Standards, 1996, National Research Council, Washington, DC: National Academy Press.

students in grades K–4 are given opportunities to experience, investigate, and think about phenomena so that they can begin to understand these principles in the world in which they live.

Next, find a series of activities, such as those in this text, that supports the learning of the science principles and concepts you want your students to understand. Physical, life, and earth science activities are included in this text. Although some of these activities will cross over, you may want to seek others that explore standards in science and technology, science in personal and social perspectives, and the history and nature of science.

Finally, your role in planning for inquiry is to create a lesson plan or a series of lesson plans that provide activities that sequence exploration for student discovery and conceptual understanding. The following is an example of such a lesson. Note how the *Science Standards* are integrated into this lesson.

Lesson Plan: An Inquiry into Pendulums

This lesson, which is appropriate for students in grade 5 and above, provides opportunities to develop understandings aligned with the physical science standard on Position and Motion of Objects, the unifying concepts and processes standard on Constancy, Change, and Measurement; and the standard on science as inquiry. Specifically, the lesson involves the following fundamental concepts, processes, and abilities identified in the *Science Standards*:

* An object's motion can be described by tracing and measuring its position over time.
* Changes in systems can be quantified through measurement.
* Mathematics is essential for accurately measuring change.
* Rate involves comparing one measured quantity with another measured quantity, such as *20 swings in 15 seconds*.
* Understanding the nature of science requires the ability to use scientific inquiry and to think and act in ways associated with inquiry.

Getting Started

Equipment and Supplies

* Watch with a second hand for each group or clock with a second hand for the whole class
* Paper clips
* Pennies
* Ball of string
* Tongue depressors or pencils (to support the pendulums)
* Masking tape (to tape the pendulum support to a desk)

Adapted from ESS, *Pendulums: Investigating Physics with Swinging Objects*, New York: McGraw-Hill, Inc.

- 20 cone-shaped paper cups or 20 clean, empty soup cans (for making salt or sand pendulums)
- 1 box of salt or 1 bag of clean, fine-grained sand
- Dark-colored construction paper or poster board (to set beneath a salt or sand pendulum)
- Dowels, yardsticks, or metersticks (to support y-shaped pendulums)

Preparation

- Tie a paper clip to one end of several pieces of string and insert one or more pennies into each paper clip to make the pendulum bobs (as in the drawing). Trim the strings to various lengths between 10 cm and 70 cm. Wedge the string into the slit of a tongue depressor, or tie a loop in the free end of the pendulum and insert a pencil in the loop, as in the drawing.
- Determine where teams of students can set up pendulums that can swing freely. To support the pendulums, students should tape or hold the tongue depressor or the pencil securely on the edge of a table.

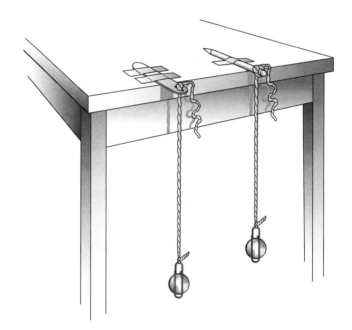

Conducting the Scientific Inquiry

Engage: Ask a Question About Objects or Events in a Phenomenon.

1. Show students a pendulum using the paper clip and pennies as a pendulum bob and a tongue depressor or pencil as a support. Start the pendulum swinging. Ask: *How does a pendulum move? How many ways can you think of to change the motion of the pendulum?* Write your questions on the board or on chart paper.
2. Allow students time to talk with partners or classmates about answers to the questions.
3. Tell students they are going to find out the answers to these questions and other questions by investigating how pendulums move.

Explore: Design and Conduct an Investigation Using Simple Equipment to Gather Data.

1. Help each team of students construct and find a place to support their pendulum.
2. Invite students to explore with their pendulums by asking: *What can you find out about the motion of a pendulum?*
3. After about 10 minutes of open exploration, stop students and ask them what they have discovered. After students share some ideas, invite them to suggest questions they might investigate. Such questions should help students focus on independent investigations.

    Possible questions include:

    ◆ If you pull the pendulum back and let it go, how far will it swing to the other side? Encourage students to think and predict before they observe.
    ◆ How long does it take for a pendulum to stop swinging? Does the time depend on how far you pull the pendulum back before you let it swing?
    ◆ Which will swing farther from the release point, a pendulum with one penny, two pennies, or three pennies wedged in the paper clip?
    ◆ How can you measure how fast a pendulum swings? (Lead the students to count the number of swings in 15 seconds. Explain that this is called the rate of swing of the pendulum. Define a swing as one complete back-and-forth *cycle*.)
    ◆ How can you get a pendulum to swing faster (more times in 15 seconds)?

4. After some discussion, ask students to focus on these three separate, measurable variables or factors that might make a pendulum swing faster or slower:

    ◆ the weight or number of pennies that make up the pendulum bob
    ◆ the length of the pendulum, and
    ◆ the angle at which the pendulum is released.

5. Instruct students to write down a separate question about each variable (i.e., *"How does the rate change when the weight of the pendulum bob is changed?"*). Then tell them to design and conduct investigations to answer the questions they have asked. Ask the students to record what they do and what they find out.
6. When students are ready, help the class to standardize the way they measure weight, length, angle, and rate (number of back-and-forth swings in 15 seconds). Introduce the use of data tables to help them keep track of their data.

Pendulum Length and Rate of Swing

Length (cm)	Rate (number of swings in 15 seconds)
10	24
20	17
30	14
40	12
50	11
60	10
70	9

Weight of Pendulum Bob and Rate of Swing (length fixed at 50 cm)

Weight (pennies)	Rate (number of swings in 15 seconds)
1	11
2	11
3	11

Explain: Use Data to Construct a Reasonable Explanation.

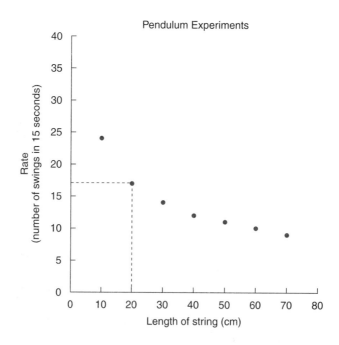

Students often have great difficulty in controlling variables while investigating. For a dramatic example of this problem, see the video clip and essay about designing pendulum investigations for seventh grade students in Chapter 3 of the Carin and Bass web site:
http//www.prenhall.com/carin.

1. Explain to students how to use their data tables to answer their questions.
2. If students have changed more than one variable at a time (for example, length and weight), discuss with them the importance of experimental design. Ask: *Why must you change only one variable at a time when investigating? Why must other variables be kept constant?* (So you can be sure which of the variables really made a difference.)
3. Guide students to use their data to arrive at these conclusions:
   ◆ The rate of swing decreases as the length of the pendulum increases.
   ◆ The rate of swing is not affected by changes in the angle of release.
   ◆ The rate of swing is not affected by changes in the weight of the pendulum bob.
4. Help students realize that they can use the data tables to predict future events as well as to record their observations and arrive at conclusions. (Once they have recorded the number of swings per 15 seconds for string lengths of 15 cm, 30 cm, 45 cm, and 60 cm, for example, they should be able to predict the number of swings each 15 seconds for a pendulum that is 40 cm or 70 cm long.)
5. Using data from the whole class and an overhead transparency of a grid (or a computer graphing program and LCD projector), show students how to construct a graph of *rate* versus *length* for pendulums. Rate (the number of swings in 15 seconds) should be graphed on the y-, or vertical, axis. Length should be graphed on the x-axis. Explain to students that scientists conventionally graph the *independent* variable (the variable deliberately *manipulated*) on the x-axis and the *dependent* variable (the variable *responding* to the deliberate manipulation) on the y-axis.

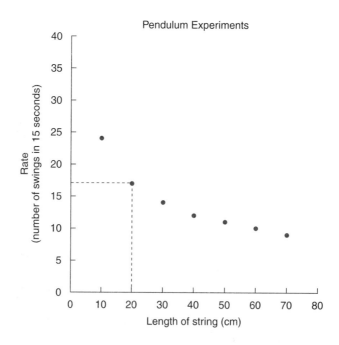

6. Explain to students that the graph visually depicts the *pattern of changes* in rate that occur when the length of the pendulum is changed.

7. Lead students to use the pattern of change represented by the graph to predict the rate for a pendulum length that is between two measured lengths (for example, between 30 cm and 45 cm) and the rate for a pendulum length that is greater than any length shown on the graph (an 80-cm length pendulum, for example).

8. Ask students to test their predictions by making pendulums of the designated lengths and measuring the rate of swing for each one (the number of swings in 15 seconds).

Elaboration: Building on Fundamental Concepts, Processes, and Abilities.

1. Introduce the salt or sand pendulum. Make a salt pendulum by suspending a conical cup or soup can from a pendulum string as in the illustration. Based on their previous findings about the motion of pendulums, ask students to predict the trail the salt will leave as the pendulum swings back and forth, in a circle, and in other configurations. Have them draw their predicted responses.

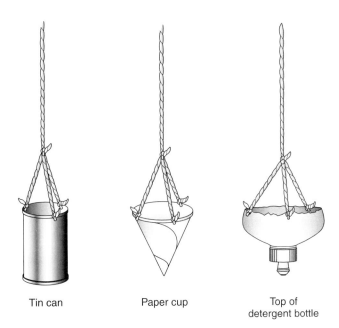

Tin can   Paper cup   Top of detergent bottle

2. Set the salt pendulum in motion and have students observe the path the salt traces. Make sure you place dark-colored construction paper under the salt pendulum. Invite students to compare their drawings with the salt path.

3. As the salt spills out of the cup, the pendulum bob gets lighter. Ask: *What changes in rate can you expect as the salt pendulum swings?* (The rate should be constant, because it does not depend on the weight of the pendulum bob.)

4. Introduce the y-shaped pendulum (see drawing). Ask students to predict, draw, and then explore the patterns of change in the salt trail for different ways of releasing the y-shaped pendulum, such as parallel or perpendicular to the support rod. After students work with regular and y-shaped salt pendulums, they should be able to design interesting patterns of the salt from different motions.

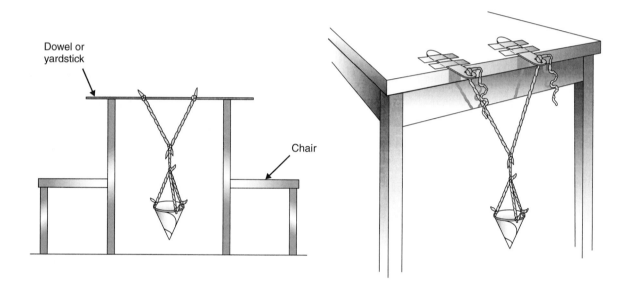

Dowel or yardstick

Chair

5. Encourage students to notice pendulums in the world around them. Grandfather clocks, swings, and trapezes are all forms of pendulums.

Evaluate: Communicate Investigations and Explanations of New Phenomena to Demonstrate Understanding.

1. Set up the following performance task for teams or individual students.
   ◆ Create a pendulum that swings from one extreme to the other in one second (7.5 complete back-and-forth swings in 15 seconds).
   Encourage students not just to work empirically but to try to predict the appropriate length (100 cm). Students can use data from their previous investigations and gather additional data as needed. Remind students of the data tables and graph created previously.
2. Bonus Question: How would you fix a grandfather clock that was running too fast? too slow? (Students should realize that the pendulum must be lengthened for the clock to slow down and shortened for the clock to run faster.)

Note that, consistent within this lesson model for inquiry, the roles of the teacher and the students are different than in traditional science lessons. See Tables I-2 and I-3 to identify these roles.

TABLE I-2 APPLYING THE 5-E INSTRUCTIONAL MODEL

Stage of the Instructional Model	What the TEACHER does	
	that is consistent with this model	that is inconsistent with this model
Engage	• Creates interest • Generates curiosity • Raises questions • Elicits responses that uncover what the students know or think about the concept/topic	• Explains concepts • Provides definitions and answers • States conclusions • Provides closure • Lectures
Explore	• Encourages students to work together without direct instruction from the teacher • Observes and listens to students as they interact • Asks probing questions to redirect students' investigations when necessary • Provides time for students to puzzle through problems • Acts as a consultant for students	• Provides answers • Tells or explains how to work through the problem • Provides closure • Tells students that they are wrong • Gives information or facts that solve the problem • Leads students step-by-step to a solution
Explain	• Encourages students to explain concepts and definitions in their own words • Asks for justification (evidence) and clarification from students • Formally provides definitions, explanations, and new labels • Uses students' previous experiences as the basis for explaining concepts	• Accepts explanations that have no justification • Neglects to solicit students' explanations • Introduces unrelated concepts or skills
Elaborate	• Expects students to use formal labels, definitions, and explanations provided previously • Encourages students to apply or extend the concepts and skills in new situations • Reminds students of alternative explanations • Refers students to existing data and evidence and asks: "What do you already know?" "Why do you think . . .?" (Strategies from Explore apply here also.)	• Provides definitive answers • Tells students that they are wrong • Lectures • Leads students step-by-step to a solution • Explains how to work through the problem
Evaluate	• Observes students as they apply new concepts and skills • Assesses students' knowledge and/or skills • Looks for evidence that students have changed their thinking or behaviors • Allows students to assess their own learning and group-process skills • Asks open-ended question, such as: "Why do you think . . .?", "What evidence do you have?", "What do you know about x?", "How would you explain x?"	• Tests vocabulary words, terms, and isolated facts • Introduces new ideas or concepts • Creates ambiguity • Promotes open-ended discussion unrelated to the concept or skill

Source: Teaching Secondary School Science, 7th ed., (p. 249), by Leslie Trowbridge and Rodger Bybee, © 2000, Merrill/Prentice-Hall, Inc. Used by permission.

TABLE 1-3 APPLYING THE 5-E INSTRUCTIONAL MODEL

Stage of the Instructional Model	What the STUDENT does	
	that is consistent with this model	that is inconsistent with this model
Engage	• Asks questions, such as: "Why did this happen?", "What do I already know about this?", "What can I find out about this?" • Shows interest in the topic	• Asks for the "right" answer • Offers the "right" answer • Insists on answers or explanations • Seeks one solution
Explore	• Thinks freely, but within the limits of the activity • Tests predictions and hypotheses • Forms new predictions and hypotheses • Tries alternatives and discusses them with others • Records observations and ideas • Suspends judgment	• Lets others do the thinking and exploring (passive involvement) • Works quietly with little or no interaction with others (only appropriate when exploring ideas or feelings) • Plays around indiscriminately with no goal in mind • Stops with one solution
Explain	• Explains possible solutions or answers to others • Listens critically to one another's explanations • Questions one another's explanations • Listens to and tries to comprehend explanations offered by the teacher • Refers to previous activities • Uses recorded observations in explanations	• Proposes explanations from thin air with no relationship to previous experiences • Brings up irrelevant experiences and examples • Accepts explanations without justification • Does not attend to other plausible explanations
Elaborate	• Applies new labels, definitions, explanations, and skills in new, but similar, situations • Uses previous information to ask questions, propose solutions, make decisions, design experiments • Draws reasonable conclusions from evidence • Records observations and explanations • Checks for understanding among peers	• Plays around with no goal in mind • Ignores previous information or evidence • Draws conclusions from thin air • Uses in discussions only those labels that the teacher provided
Evaluate	• Answers open-ended questions by using observations, evidence, and previously accepted explanations • Demonstrates an understanding or knowledge of the concept or skill • Evaluates his or her own progress and knowledge • Asks related questions that would encourage future investigations	• Draws conclusions, not using evidence or previously accepted explanations • Offers only yes-or-no answers, memorized definitions, or explanations as answers • Fails to express satisfactory explanations in his or her own words • Introduces new, irrelevant topics

Source: *Teaching Secondary School Science*, 7th ed. (pp. 248), by Leslie Trowbridge and Rodger Bybee, © 2000, Merrill/Prentice-Hall, Inc. Used with permission.

Cooperative Learning

Cooperative learning plays a vital role in inquiry. Glenn T. Seaborg, 1951 Nobel prize winner in chemistry and now the principal investigator for Great Explorations in Math and Science (GEMS), a science curriculum project, reminds us that cooperation is the norm in science.

> In the case of all great "discoveries" it must be remembered that science is a group process. When we devise experiments and research today, we do so on the basis of an enormous body of knowledge contributed by people from all over the world over thousands of years. . . . Research effort is above all a team effort. (Seaborg, 1991)

Working cooperatively is important for students also. Children have a special way of communicating with one another that enables them to work well together. According to Baloche (1998), when students engage in peer discussions they exchange and interpret one another's ideas. This social transmission implies that a child understands the information being transmitted, and because children are often able to describe things to each other in ways that adults cannot, interaction is important in social transmission (Baloche, 1998).

Qin, Johnson, and Johnson (1995) state that cooperative learning results in better performance in problem solving for both clearly defined and ill-defined problems. Their research indicates that cooperative efforts result in better performance in problem solving than competitive efforts do. This is true in every subject, at all grade levels, and particularly when higher-level thinking skills are required (Johnson, Maruyama, Johnson, Nelson, and Skon, 1981).

Johnson, Johnson, and Holubec (1993) indicate that advantages to cooperative learning are interwoven in five basic principles: 1) positive interdependence, 2) simultaneous interaction, 3) individual responsibility, 4) interpersonal and small-group learning skills, and 5) reflection and planning. Cooperative learning provides opportunities for diverse groups of learners to build trust, empathy, and respect for one another. You can encourage the growth of these skills by grouping your students as they engage in inquiry.

In this context, cooperative learning is a process that asks students to work together and support one another's learning. It entails students working collaboratively in small groups to

- consider a problem or assignment together,
- verbalize what they know and what they want to find out,
- plan investigations,
- collect and compare the data,
- consider the multiple viewpoints of group members, and
- come up with group solutions to the problem.

The goal of cooperative learning for science inquiry is to build learning communities and positive interdependence by maximizing the learning of all group members. This can be accomplished when group members take on the responsibility of learning both for themselves individually and collectively as a group. Your role will be to assign or otherwise ensure that specific work goals are undertaken and accomplished by the group. Furthermore, as you set up groups of students who will work together, be sure that they have opportunities and obligations to learn and use interpersonal skills which will be necessary to get the work done. Setting up some standard rules or guidelines for working in a group should be established before the groups meet for the first time each school year. Classroom guidelines for working together in groups will help students build and maintain effective peer relationships. Finally, group members should have opportunities and obligations to reflect both on what they learned and how well the group members interacted (Johnson, Johnson, and Holubec, 1992).

"The discipline of using [formal cooperative groups] begins with the careful structuring of positive interdependence" (Johnson, Johnson, and Holubec, 1993, 49). Strategies for building that interdependence might include:

- Assigning group roles.
- Making students responsible for their own learning as well as for that of their other group members.
- Helping students develop interpersonal small-group skills.
- Interacting with groups as needed.

A Cooperative Learning Group Model

In the 1960s, Martha Piper developed a cooperative learning group (CLG) model to assist teachers in effectively managing the use of activities in the science classroom. She and other recognized leaders in the field, Roger and David Johnson, Robert Jones, and the Biological Sciences Curriculum Study (BSCS) group then built on the original and developed variations that are widely used today.

The CLG model consists of classroom group techniques for facilitating and guiding students to do inquiry activities. CLGs are especially useful in classrooms

Figure I-1 Alternative cooperative group roles.

Source: From Cooperative Learning: Where Heart Meets Mind, by B. Bennett, C. Rolheiser, and L. Stevahn, 1991, Toronto, Ontario: Educational Connections.

- *Checker:* Ensures that everybody understands the work in progress.
- *Scout:* Seeks additional information from other groups.
- *Timekeeper:* Keeps the group focused on the task and monitors the time.
- *Active Listener:* Repeats or paraphrases what has been said.
- *Questioner:* Seeks information and opinions from all members of the group.
- *Summarizer:* Pulls together the conclusions of the group so that they can be presented coherently.
- *Encourager:* Provides support to members of the group so that they are more enthused about their participation.
- *Materials Manager:* Collects all necessary material for the group.
- *Reader:* Reads material to the group.

where science materials and equipment are limited, cooperative group processes and skill development are desired, and an orderly system is desired to maintain control of the noise level and movement of students while engaged in activities.

The use of CLGs offer teachers many advantages such as:

- Students share limited supplies and science equipment.
- Students assist teachers in classroom management because students become accountable for managing science materials.
- Teachers can manage outdoor activities more confidently.
- Students take responsibility for helping team members create positive and realistic expectations of one another and help each other with assignments and problem solving.
- Students become more positive about contributing to groups because they recognize and understand their role in the group.
- Cooperative learning is fun—students like working together in CLGs.

To make full use of these advantages, you must learn how to set up CLGs, assign roles to student members, and guide the teams in their activities.

Setting Up CLG Teams. Initially, you should assign students to a team, because they tend to gravitate to friends only. For primary grade students, or older students who have not worked previously in CLGs, it is best to start with two students. As students acquire basic cooperative group skills, combine two groups of two as a working team. Generally, CLG teams of three to five are recommended once your classroom is comfortable and knowledgeable about the process.

When you form groups you will want to integrate students with various abilities, disabilities, and cultural backgrounds. Note, however, that you may raise the perceived abilities of some students when they cannot count on the student "known" to be most capable to lead the group. Once you have established a cooperative group routine, keep teams together for at least three to six weeks so teammates have time to learn to work with each other. As a team builder, let each team choose its own name. After three to six weeks, change team membership, so students get to work with other students and learn the differences in team dynamics.

To promote success with the use of CLGs, develop a class procedure for rotating jobs. Post team assignments in a prominent place so all students can see it. Wherever possible, all students should have experiences in all CLG jobs to develop the skills of each. When you first introduce and use CLGs, you will need to take time to explain or perhaps provide written descriptions to students for job assignments and responsibilities.

CLG Job Functions and Assignments. A specific job is assigned to each CLG team member. The names and functions are quite similar in all CLGs. The following are from Robert Jones's Inquiry Task Group Management System (ITGMS).

- *Principal Investigator.* In charge of all team operations including checking assignments, communicating activity directions, asking teacher informational questions, assisting group members, conducting group discussion about activity results, and either directing activity or assigning it to other team members.
- *Materials Manager.* Gets and distributes materials to each team, sets up and operates any activity equipment, and is usually the only student moving around the room without special permission during an activity.
- *Recorder/Reporter.* Collects, records, and certifies data on team work or lab sheets, reports results to whole class orally or in writing on Class Summary Chart posted on chalkboard.
- *Maintenance Director.* Assigns team members to help him clean up and return materials and equipment to their appropriate storage space or container. Directs the disposal of used materials and is responsible for team members' safety.
- *Technical Advisor.* Moves to teams having difficulties and assists; may prepare activity materials for teachers and inspect equipment to ensure that it is ready for activities two or three days before its use. This is a special role for dependable students who work quickly and accurately.
- *Observer.* Acts as a special administrative assistant to the teacher to record and share team problems.

CLG Job Badges. To supply easy identification of team members' jobs and responsibilities, students should wear job badges. It will be easier for you to spot students who should not be straying away from their group's space if you can readily identify the role of each team member during an activity. However, you will need to use your judgment here depending on your students age levels. Younger students will especially enjoy displaying an ID badge. As students get older, they may be reticent about wearing badges unless there is a level of sophistication to their design. You may liken the wearing or possession of such a badge to the security information that adults often use in the workplace.

CLG Job Descriptions. Job description cards may be left at each science activity station for students to use and refer to while performing their assigned part of the activity. Users have found it is best to write direct "you" statements on each card. The cards spell out—with words or pictures—the job responsibilities and limits.

Job description cards should be modified according to team size (two, three, four, five members), students' ages, maturation, learning levels and styles, and any other variables that affect their usage. Often, teachers color-code CLG job description cards according to job description.

Using CLGs in Science Inquiry. So how do you get started using CLGs in your science classroom? Although each classroom situation is unique, several CLG models adhere to the following prototype developed by Martha Piper (1980). Initially, you should follow the specific sequence given here, but with time you'll be able to modify the sequence and the steps themselves as you and your students gain experience and confidence with CLG techniques and science inquiry.

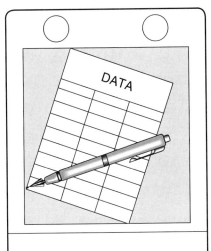

Figure I-2 Cooperative learning group (CLG) job badge.

Source: Reprinted by permission from Robert M. Jones, *Teaming Up! The Inquiry Task Group Management System User's Guide,* LaPorte, TX: ITGROUP, December 1990, 55.

Figure I-3 Cooperative job description card.

Source: Reprinted by permission from Robert M. Jones, *Teaming Up! The Inquiry Task Group Management System User's Guide,* LaPorte, TX: ITGROUP, December 1990, 43.

Step 1: Preparation. The teacher prepares the inquiry activity for whole class or small-group work by:

- Arranging classroom furniture to facilitate inquiry and avoid excessive noise, movement, or confusion. Consider the furniture configuration in the illustration.
- Organizing materials needed by teams in small boxes or bags, or on trays.

Step 2: Engagement. Present an initiating activity designed to engage the students in pursuing the learning objectives.

- Keep the activity open-ended.
- Ask or help the students ask specific questions about the initiating activity. Write appropriate questions on a chart or the chalkboard.
- Tell students they will be exploring this and other related questions.
- Introduce or review pertinent activity information, safety procedures, vocabulary, and such CLG skills such as *"When we begin, move quickly and quietly into your team. Stay with your team at all times. Speak softly, listen and respond to one another, and take turns. Concentrate on your assigned job."*

Figure I-4 CLG classroom furniture arrangement.

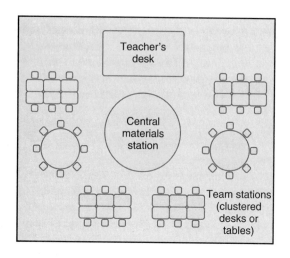

Step 3: Distribution of Science Materials. Do not begin distributing materials until all of Step 1 is completed. Then, have all the Materials Managers collect science materials from the central materials station and deliver them to each team station. Note that this step can make or break the best-planned activity. Make certain that Materials Managers are reliable and know the specifics of their jobs before they begin!

Step 4: Exploration. Each team's Principal Investigator reviews directions with team members to make sure they all understand the procedures to be used. Materials Managers direct the set up of the team's materials while the teacher moves from team to team to ensure the proper distribution of materials has occurred and that teams are practicing safety. Principal Investigators may signal the teacher or Observer if assistance is needed. Recorders/Reporters collect data on data sheets, check with other team results, and post results on the Class Summary Chart.

Step 5: Explanation and Discussion of Results. The teacher conducts a discussion of the results posted on the Class Summary Chart. Then she asks for students' conceptions of ideas and skills learned, discusses the similarities and discrepancies of team data, and notes possible misunderstandings and misconceptions. Appropriate instruction about concepts, principles, and explanations that are relevant to activities takes place at this time.

Step 6: Elaboration. Activities that allow students to apply what they have learned to new and novel situations are suggested by the teacher or the students. The teacher may also have students follow up with readings, worksheets, Internet research, or other individualized reinforcement of inquiry concepts and principles. Principal Investigators lead their teams in inquiring into the new questions. Appropriate class discussion follows.

1. Make certain you have the necessary science equipment and supplies in sufficient amounts to allow your students to participate in the lab activity. Have materials at a central workstation already set up with an adequate number of science materials and equipment for individual or group use.
2. Perform initial steps like boiling water, heating or cooling materials, and double-checking supplies before an activity begins.
3. If any chemicals are used, even diluted vinegar, make sure students wash up immediately following the activity.
4. Whenever possible, substitute plastics for all glassware. However, be certain when using heat that the plastics are able to withstand high temperatures. Whenever students use plastic bags, make sure the bags are too small to fit over their heads.
5. Avoid open flames in the classroom except under absolute necessity. Check your local school policies because the use of open flames in classrooms may be forbidden. Open flames should not be used in primary grade classrooms. Students should NEVER be allowed to use an open flame in any classroom activity. Candles and matches or a Bunsen burner should be used in teacher demonstrations only. If you must use an open flame, be sure a fire extinguisher is available and give instructions for its use.
6. Avoid the use of materials in your classroom that could cause serious damage to classroom facilities such as plaster of Paris. Flushing excess plaster of Paris powder down a sink drain can cause it to harden in the pipes. Check local guidelines before using any science materials to ensure you are aware of school policies regarding their use.
7. Avoid completely the use of electrical house current (110 volts) for student activities. Use dry cell batteries with students who are handling electrical equipment directly.
8. Assemble glass tubing and stoppers yourself and preferably before class. If possible and convenient, store glass tubing and connecting stoppers rather than disassembling and reassembling each time you need them.

Figure I-5   Guidelines for activity preparation and safety (additional safety suggestions are listed in Appendix G).

Step 7: Evaluation. The teacher varies methods for assessing team members' understanding of the inquiry and work of the group as a whole. Performance tests and standardized assessment forms could be used.

Step 8: Team Clean-Up. Maintenance Directors, and any team members they have assigned to help them, return all supplies to designated areas and leave them in a condition where they can be easily reused, inspect the return of all materials and equipment, and ensure that work areas are cleaned. Note that clean up is a team effort. The Maintenance Director is not the "custodian" for the group but rather manages the clean-up operation.

How Text Activities Are Organized

The inquiry activity sections that follow—Physical Science Activities; Life, Ecology, and Environmental Science Activities; and Earth and Space Science Activities—are each organized in the same way to make them predictable to work with. Some activities are labeled Engagement Activities—they can be used as motivating activities to introduce certain science concepts. Most are Exploration Activities and provide a somewhat structured way for students to engage in inquiry. Each activity has questions in the margin. Several of these questions tell you what you need to do to set up the activity and manage it safely. Other questions can be asked of your students as they engage in the activity. The activities are divided into several categories:

1. Problem to be solved: A divergent question.
2. Recommended grade levels: Appropriate within a range.
3. Concepts: What concepts might students construct?
4. Materials: What materials will you need?
5. Questions: What inquiry questions could you ask?
6. Background knowledge: What should you know?
7. Activity steps: What will students do?
8. Applications: How could students apply their new knowledge?

Some activities are conducive for cooperative groups and some for teacher demonstrations. Activities that might be better done as teacher demonstrations are so marked. The most important element in these inquiry activities is that students can discover the joy and wonder of science. And, so can you. Have fun!

REFERENCES

American Association for the Advancement of Science (AAAS). (1989). *Science for all Americans.* Washington, DC: AAAS.

Baloche, L. (1998). *The cooperative classroom: Empowering learning.* Upper Saddle River, NJ: Merrill/Prentice Hall.

Bennett, B., Rolheiser, C., and Stevahn, L. (1991). *Cooperative learning: Where heart meets mind.* Toronto, Ontario: Educational Connections.

Bransford, J. D., Brown, A. L., and Cocking, R. R. (Eds.). (1999). *How people learn: Brain, mind, experience, and school.* Washington, DC: National Academy Press.

DeBoer, G. E., and Bybee, R. W. (1995). Curriculum perspectives: The goal of science curriculum. In R. W. Bybee and J. D. McInerney (Eds.), *Redesigning the Science Curriculum: A Report on the Implications of Standards and Benchmarks for Science Education.* Colorado Springs, CO: BSCS, 73.

Jones, R. M. (1990). *Teaming up! The inquiry task group management system user's guide.* LaPorte, TX: ITGROUP, Dec., 1990.

Johnson, D., Johnson, R., and Holubec, E. (1992). *Advanced cooperative learning: Cooperation in the classroom.* Edina, MN: Interaction Books.

Johnson, D., Johnson, R., and Holubec, E. (1993). *Circles of learning: Cooperation in the classroom.* Edina, MN: Interaction Books.

Johnson, D., Maruyama, G., Johnson, R., Nelson, D., and Skon, L. (1981). Effects of cooperative, competitive, and individualistic structures on achievement: A meta-analysis. *Psychological Bulletin, 89,* 47–62.

National Research Council. (1996). *National science education standards.* Washington, DC: National Academy Press.

Ormrod, J. (1999). *Human learning.* Upper Saddle River, NJ: Merrill/Prentice Hall.

Piper, M. K. (1980). A science activity teaching plan. *School Science and Mathematics 80*(5), 390–406.

Qin, Z., Johnson, D., and Johnson, R. (1995). Cooperative versus competitive efforts and problem solving. *Review of Educational Research, 65*(2), 129–143.

Roth, K., and Anderson, C. (1988). Promoting conceptual change learning from science textbooks. In P. Ramsden (Ed.), *Improving learning: New perspectives.* London: Kogan Page.

Seaborg, G. T. (1991). Some thoughts on discovery. *GEMS network news.* Berkeley, CA: Lawrence Hall of Science, Fall/Winter, 5.

Trowbridge, L., and Bybee, R. (2000). *Teaching secondary school science,* 7th Ed. Upper Saddle River, NJ: Merrill/Prentice Hall.

II

Physical Science Activities

NSES *The National Science Education Standards state that as a result of inquiry in grades K–4, all students should develop an understanding of*

- Properties of objects and materials
- Position and motion of objects
- Light, heat, electricity, and magnetism

As a result of inquiry in grades 5–8, all students should develop an understanding of

- Properties and changes of properties in matter
- Motions and forces
- Transfer of energy

MATTER AND ENERGY

◆ ENGAGEMENT ACTIVITIES

▶ *Where Did the Water Go? (K–2)*

What materials will you need?	Sponges, paintbrushes, dishcloths (This activity should be done on a sunny day, outside the classroom.)
What inquiry questions could you ask?	*What will happen to water if you brush it on different things outside?* *How can you find out?* *From where do you think the water will disappear first? Why?*

What activities could students do?

Invite students to take a paintbrush, dip it in water, and brush it over several places to see what happens. Have them play a game to see whose water disappears first. Have students feel the places from which the water disappeared rapidly and compare them with places from which the water did not seem to disappear as fast. For example, students could compare the feel of sidewalks in the sun and sidewalks in the shade. Have students repeat the activity, but this time have them use sponges and dishcloths instead of brushes. Have them place wet sponges or cloths on different places and determine which ones dry first.

▶ *How Can We Dry Clothes Faster? (K–2)*

What materials will you need?

Paper towels, different pieces of cloth (some that are thin and some that are thick like a towel), sponges, twine, clothespins

What inquiry questions could you ask?

How can we make these things wet?
How can we dry them?

How can we use the twine and clothespins to help them dry?
Where is the best place to put the clothesline? Why?
Which things do you think will dry first?
Which materials dry faster? Why?

What activites could students do?

Have students make a clothesline; then have students dip the various cloths and sponges in water, drain them, and place them on the clothesline with clothespins. Have students try the activity a second time and move the clothesline to another suggested location. Encourage students to predict what will happen.

How could students apply their new knowledge?

How might you use the previous information in choosing your clothes for rainy days? For hot days?

▶ **Why Does Water Roll Off Some Things? (K–5)**

What materials will you need?

Wax paper, paper towels, napkins, typing paper, plastic wrap, medicine droppers, food coloring

What inquiry questions could you ask?

What might happen if you dropped droplets of water on these different kinds of paper and plastic?
How can you find out?
What kind of paper will hold the water the best?
What kinds of paper or plastic will water run off of the easiest?

What activities could students do?

Have students discover which materials soak up **(absorb)** water the best and which absorb the least. Which materials do not absorb, or **repel,** water droplets? Use red and blue food coloring to make different colored water drops. Have students use the medicine droppers to place one red drop and several blue drops of water, at a distance from each other, on wax paper or plastic wrap. Challenge students to maneuver the paper or plastic to try to capture all the blue drops, one at a time, with the red drop.

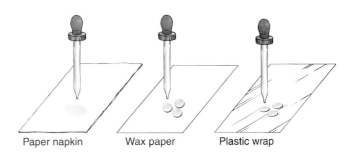

Paper napkin   Wax paper   Plastic wrap

Have students play Water Droplet Race. Show them how to make drop slides of the same lengths and inclinations, as shown in the art. Students can vary the

material they use for each slide. Have three students compete with each other to see on which slides the drops move down the fastest.

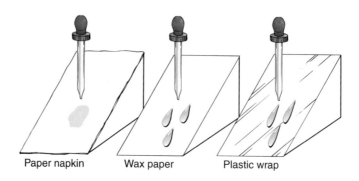

Paper napkin   Wax paper   Plastic wrap

EXPLORATION ACTIVITIES

▶ Why Does Water Appear to Disappear? (K–8)

What concepts might students construct?

A liquid appears to disappear when it changes to an invisible gas when heated. The term to describe this process is **evaporation.**

What materials will you need?

An aquarium, paint jars, and various containers, each filled with water
Measuring cup
Meter- or yardstick and/or a wire coat hanger
Paper clips
3 × 3 × 1 in. sponge
Masking tape and/or marking pens

What inquiry questions could you ask?

Where does the rain in a rain puddle go?
Why do wet things take longer to dry on wet days?
How can we measure how much water a sponge holds?
What are some ways to speed up how fast wet objects dry?

PART I   What Happens to the Water in the Aquarium? (K–2)

What will students do?

1. Using masking tape or marking pens, mark the beginning water levels of some uncovered water containers, such as an aquarium, a paint jar, a water jar used for plant cuttings, and so on.
2. Check the water levels each morning, and, using a measuring cup, add enough water to the containers to bring the water levels back up to the original water level marks you made.

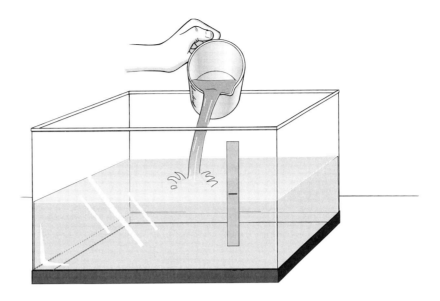

3. Keep a record of how much water was added to your containers each week.
   Where did the water go?
   What caused the water level to change?

PART II   What Happens to the Water in a Wet Sponge? (3–8)

What will students do?   1. Using the meterstick or yardstick, wire coat hanger, and paper clips, build either of the balances shown.

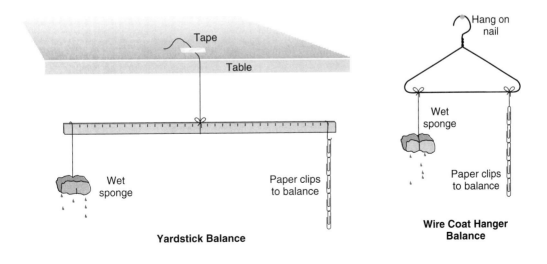

Yardstick Balance

Wire Coat Hanger Balance

2. Soak your piece of sponge until it is dripping water, then hang it with an S-shaped paper clip or string to one end of your balance. Add paper clips to the other end until the balance is level.

   How many clips did it take?

3. Every 15 minutes, check to see if the balance is level.

   What do you see happening after several observations?

   Why do you think the paper clip end of the balance is lower?

   Keep a written record of what happens.

4. At each 15-minute observation, take off and record how many paper clips must be removed to keep the balance level.

5. When the sponge is dry, take your written observations and plot a line graph with the data. Set up your graph like the one below.

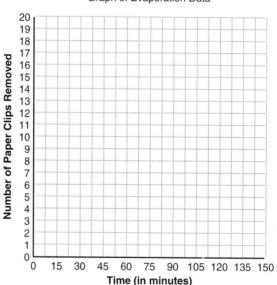

Graph of Evaporation Data

What are some variables that might affect how quickly the water in the sponge evaporates?

How could you set up an experiment to test these variables?

What should you know?

Some of the variables that affect the rate of evaporation are type of liquid, evaporation temperature of the liquid, air temperature, wind velocity, relative humidity, and so on. Guide students in gathering data and in recording and graphing the results in the same way as was done in this activity.

How could students apply their new knowledge?

Why does water evaporate faster from your hands when you vigorously rub them together?

Why does your hair dry faster on a dry day than on a wet one?
Why will a wet towel dry faster if it is spread out rather than crumpled in a ball?

▶ **What Are Water Molecules, and How Do They Affect Each Other? (K–8)**

What concepts might students construct?	The deeper the water, the greater the pressure. A **force** is defined as a push or pull on an object. Molecules of the same substance tend to "stick to" each other because they are attracted by an invisible force. Each molecule of the substance pulls other atoms to it. The force of attraction between molecules of the same kind is called **cohesive force.** Water has cohesive force.

What materials will you need?

12-in. squares of wax paper	Ruler
Medicine dropper	Pennies, paper clips, or marbles
Water (enough to fill containers as desired)	Two 1-gallon plastic milk jugs
Pencil or nail	Masking tape
Glass or plastic tumbler	Large basin or tub
Pan or bowl	

What inquiry questions could you ask?

Why does a drop of water hold together as it runs down a windowpane?
Why are beads of water hemispherical, especially on a well-waxed automobile?
Why can some bugs walk on the top of water?

....

PART I   What Is the Shape of Water Droplets? (K–2)

What will students do?

1. Obtain a 12-inch square of wax paper. Using a medicine dropper, place three or four drops of clean tap water on your wax paper.
   How would you describe the shape of the water droplets?
   What is their color?

2. Push the drops of water around with a pencil point.
   What happens to the water when you push the pencil point into a water droplet?
   What happens when you push several droplets near each other?
   Why do you think this happens?

PART II   Why Does Water Heap in a Cup? (K–2)

What will students do?

1. Obtain a glass or plastic tumbler and place it in a bowl or pan. Fill the tumbler completely full of water, until some water overflows.
   Do you think you can add any more water to the tumbler?
   Can you think of how you might test your hypothesis or guess what will happen?
2. Test your hypothesis or try this test. Holding a medicine dropper no more than ½ inch above the water level of the glass, slowly drop water into the tumbler. (See diagram.)

How many drops of water can you add until the water runs over the rim of the tumbler?
How would you describe the shape of the water above the rim of the tumbler?
   (Hint: Bend down so that you are on eye-level with the rim of the tumbler.)
Why does the water rise above the rim of the tumbler?
At what point does the water run over the rim of the tumbler?
Why do you think the water finally runs over the rim of the tumbler?
*What do you think would happen if you added these things to the glass of water
   instead of water drops: pennies, paper clips, or marbles? Try it.*

PART III   What Affects the Pressure of a Stream of Water? (3–5)

What inquiry questions could you ask?

If the side of a plastic milk jug were punctured with very small holes (one above another) and the jug were then filled with water, what do you think would happen to the water?
How would the water pour out of the holes?

TEACHER DEMO

What will students or a
teacher do?

1. Obtain a clean 1-gallon milk jug.
2. About 1½ inch or 4 centimeters from the bottom of the milk jug, puncture a *very small hole* with a pencil or nail. Puncture three additional small holes ½ inch apart, vertically, above the first hole. Put masking tape over the holes. *Note:* Do not make the holes too large.
3. Fill the container half full with water. Hold the plastic jug over a sink, large basin, or tub, and remove the masking tape as shown.
   What do you notice about the way the water comes out of the holes?
   Why do you think the water comes out of the holes like this?
   If the jug were filled closer to the top with water, do you think there would be a difference in the way the water comes out?

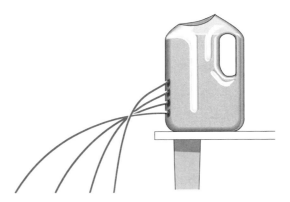

4. Tape over the holes, refill the jug until the water is within an inch of the top, and remove the tape.
   What do you notice about the way the water comes out of the holes?
   What difference did you notice in the way the water came from the holes of the jug when there was less water and when there was more water in it?
   What can you say about how water pressure varies with depth?
   What results do you think you would get if you used a quart, half-gallon, or 2-gallon container? Try it and record your findings.

PART IV   Why Do Streams of Water Cohere Into One Stream? (3–5)

TEACHER DEMO

What will students or a
teacher do?

1. About 2 centimeters or 1/2 inch apart as shown in the diagram, puncture 4 very small holes in a horizontal line about 1/2 inch from the bottom of the second 1-gallon plastic jug. Put masking tape over the holes.
   Note: Do not make the holes too large. Also make the holes very close together.

What do you think will happen when water is poured into this container and the masking tape is removed?

How many jets of water will you get coming out of the holes in the bottom of the plastic jug?

2. Hold the jug over a sink or large tub, pour water into the jug, and remove the tape.

How many jets of water come out?

What could you do to the water pouring out of the bottom of the jug, without plugging any holes, to get only one jet of water?

3. Test your hypothesis.

4. Try this activity using quart or half-gallon milk cartons.

What should you know?

Students should pour water into the plastic jug and pinch the jets of water together with their fingers just as though they were going to pinch someone. The jets will form one stream. If the water comes out in one jet, there must be some kind of force holding the water together. The force that holds similar molecules to each other is called **cohesive force.** Each molecule of water has cohesive force that pulls and holds other molecules of water to it. The diagram represents how molecules of water are held together to form a water droplet due to cohesive force. The pinching of the water brings the jets of water in contact, allowing cohesive force to hold them together. This is true because the cohesive force between two substances increases as the distance between them decreases.

Water molecules held together by <u>cohesive</u> forces

How could students apply their new knowledge?

Why do you think a dam is built with very thick walls at the bottom and thinner walls at the top?

Why do your ears sometimes hurt when you dive deep into a swimming pool? What pushes in on your ears as you go deeper?

Why are the walls of a submarine so thick and strong?

What would happen to water escaping from two holes of a can if you plugged one hole?

What will happen to the water coming out of the bottom hole of the can as the water level gets lower in the can?

Why do many towns have water storage tanks towering high above the city or built on a hill?

THERMAL ENERGY (HEAT)

ENGAGEMENT ACTIVITIES

▶ *What Makes Things Get Hotter? (K–5)*

What materials will you need?
6-in. piece of wire coat hanger, mineral oil, brass button, wool cloth, piece of metal, pencil eraser, notebook paper, ice cubes, newspapers or paper towels, miscellaneous magazines

What inquiry questions could you ask?
How do your fingers feel when you bend a wire hanger back and forth? Why do you think this happens?

What activites could students do?
1. Bend a 6-inch piece of wire hanger back and forth 10 times as shown. Quickly touch the wire at the point where you bent it.
What do you feel? (Heat)
What do you think will happen if you bend the wire more times, for example, 20, 25, 30, 35 times? (Each time the wire gets hotter.)

Safety Precaution!
Caution: Try this activity out first to find out how many bends will make the wire too hot for students to touch.

2. Rub your hands together very fast and hard.
What do you feel?
Try this again but put a few drops of oil or water on your hands first.
How do you think the second rubbing will feel different from the first rubbing?
Now rub different things together and quickly touch them to your upper lip or the tip of your nose (sensitive parts of your body): brass button on a piece of wool, metal on paper, pencil eraser on paper, and so on.

What should you know?
Note: It is recommended that young students go to the bathroom before and after the following activity!

What activities could
students do?

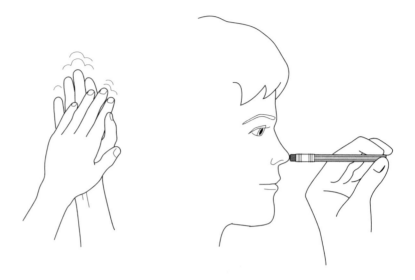

3. Hold an ice cube in your hand over newspapers or paper towels.
   How does your hand feel with the ice cube in it? (Cold)
   What is happening to the ice cube?

Leave an ice cube in a nearby dish and notice the difference between this ice
cube and the one in your hand.
   Why the difference? (Heat from your hand melts the ice cube faster than heat
   from the room melts the ice cube in the dish.)

Which became warmer—your hand or the ice cube you held? (Ice cube; heat moved from hand to ice.)
How is this the same as when you pour a warm soft drink over ice cubes? (The warm drink gets cooler as heat moves to the ice.)

What activities could students do?

4. Students in grades 3–5 can go on a "Heat Hunt" in school and at home. Look for places where heat is produced (school or home furnace, oven and stove, toaster, microwave oven, sunshine through windows). List these places in a booklet or chart and illustrate it with magazine pictures. Then, use these three categories to organize your list of heat producers:
   - Where did you see it?
   - What was heated?
   - How was it heated?

Safety Precaution!

Caution: Remind students not to touch heat-producing appliances or other hot objects.

EXPLORATION ACTIVITIES

▶ *What Is Thermal Energy, or Heat?* (K–8)

Heat is a form of energy.

What concepts might students construct?

When an object is heated, its molecules move faster or vibrate more.
When an object is cooled, its molecules move more slowly.
Heat is a measure of the energy transferred between objects that results in temperature changes of the objects.

What materials will you need?

Baby-food jar with screw top
Sand
Thick towel
Thermometer
12 baby-food jars or clear plastic tumblers

Sugar cubes
Colored cinnamon candies or jelly beans
Tea bags
Pencils
2 Pyrex™ or tin pans

What should you know?   Motion (shaking, stirring, rubbing, etc.) can be a source of heat.
The molecules in liquids are in continuous motion.
Scientists use controlled experiments to test their ideas.
Solids break into smaller pieces (**dissolve**) faster in hot water than in cold water.

PART I   How Can You Heat Up the Sand in a Jar? (K–5)

What inquiry question could you ask?

What do you think will happen to the sand in a baby-food jar if you shake it many times?

What will students do?

1. Fill a baby-food jar three-fourths full of sand, screw on the jar top, and then wrap it with a thick towel.
2. Each person should take a turn doing the following:
   a. Shake the sand vigorously for 5 minutes.
   b. Measure the temperature of the sand.
   c. Write your findings on a record sheet like the one that follows.

Person	Minutes of Shaking	Temperature in °F or °C
1	5	
2	10	
3	15	
4	20	
5	25	

   d. Pass the jar to the next person.

e. When everyone has had a turn, compare the temperature of the sand from the first to the last reading.
How were they different? (The temperature rose higher after shaking.)

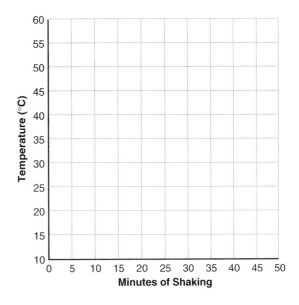

f. Set up a graph like the one above, then graph the data from the record sheets. (*Note:* May be more applicable for students who have been exposed to graphing.)
What was the source of the heat energy added to the sand?

PART II   How Do Molecules Move in a Liquid? (6–8)

What inquiry question could you ask?

How could we set up an experiment to test the effect of heat on molecule movement in a liquid?

What will students do?

1. Fill three baby-food jars or plastic drinking glasses with water to within ½ inch (1 cm) of the top and let them stand until the water is room temperature.
2. Slowly lower a sugar cube into one container, a handful of cinnamon candies or jelly beans into the second, and a tea bag into the third. (See diagram.)

CONTROL: Substances dissolving without stirring

Make certain that the containers are in a spot where they will not be moved or jostled.

3. Set up three more jars/tumblers and materials the same as in Steps 1 and 2, but this time stir the water until the materials dissolve, as shown in the diagram.

EXPERIMENT: Substances dissolving with stirring

The way this experiment was set up is called a **controlled experiment** (fair test) in science. *Why do you think it is called this?*

4. Taking observations every 1/2 hour, record how long it takes for the control containers to look like the experimental containers.
   Which materials do you think will dissolve first? Why?
   Would the results be different if hot water were used? If cold water were used? Why?
   How could we test this?

··

PART III   How Does Heat Affect the Dissolving Time of Substances and the Movement of Molecules in a Liquid? (6–8)

What will students do?

1. Set up two more sets of containers with sugar, cinnamon candies, and tea bags.
2. Place one set of containers in ice-cold water in a pan and the other set in a pan of very hot water.

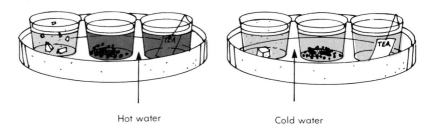

Hot water   Cold water

In which containers—in pans of hot or cold water—will the materials dissolve first? What does the hot water in the pan do to the molecules in the containers?

What should you know?

This activity introduces several new concepts. Students will be helped to see adding heat increases the motion of molecules. In addition, the concept of a control is used as a standard against which scientists check their experimental work. If you think your students are ready, you can introduce the concept of variables. For instance, in Part III, the variable being tested is heat and its effect upon dissolving.

How could students apply their new knowledge?

- Why do you rub a match against the side of a match box?
- Why do matches not catch fire while sitting in a match box?
- When you bend a wire back and forth several times, why does it get warm?
- When you put two pencils together and rub them back and forth several times, what happens to your hands?
- A person tried to strike a match against a piece of glass to light it. The match would not light. Why?
- If you feel the tires of your car before you take a trip and then just after you get out of the car, they will not feel the same. How do you think they will differ? How would you explain the difference?
- A person was chopping wood with an axe. After chopping very hard for about 10 minutes, she felt the axe. How do you think the axe felt and why?

▶ *How Is Heat Transmitted by Radiation, Convection, and Conduction? (3–8)*

What concepts might students construct?

The sun or light bulbs give off radiant heat.
Heat can be transmitted from one body to another by conduction and radiation.
Light objects reflect radiant energy more than do dark objects.
Dark objects absorb more radiant energy than do light objects.
Some objects conduct heat better than others.
Heat can be transmitted within a gas or liquid by convection.

What materials will you need?

3 tin cans of same size	Lamp with 150 to 300 watts
Small can of shiny white paint	Candle
Small can of dull black paint	Matches
2 small paintbrushes	9 thumbtacks
Styrofoam covers for cans	Tripod stand
3 thermometers	Silver or steel knife
4 × 4-in. square of aluminum foil	4-in. length of copper tubing

What should you know?

These activities may be done in groups. For immature or unruly children, the teacher should demonstrate these activities.

....

PART I   How is Heat Transferred Through Radiation? (3–5)

What inquiry question could you ask?

What do you think will happen to the three thermometers in the three different cans after being in the sun or near light bulbs for a while? (See diagram.)

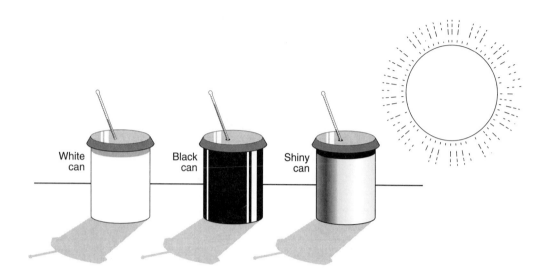

What will students do?

1. Obtain three identically sized cans and remove all labels. Paint one can dull black and another can shiny white; leave the third can unpainted, shiny metal.
2. Fill each can with regular tap water.
3. Put a Styrofoam cover on each can and insert a thermometer through each cover.
4. Set the cans in direct sunlight or at equal distances from a 150- to 300-watt light bulb.
5. Prepare a table for data collection and record the temperature of the water in each can at 1-minute intervals.

What inquiry questions could you ask?

What do you think will happen to the water temperature in the different cans?
If there are different temperatures, how would you explain that?
How would you relate the result of the unequal absorption of heat in the tin cans to different land and water surfaces of the earth?
Knowing what you do about how **radiant** *(light) energy reacts on different surfaces, how would you explain the differences in the three thermometers?*
How might this be related to the microclimates of certain geographic areas?
What color space suits do astronauts wear? Why?

What should you know?

The shiny aluminum of the unpainted can and the shiny white paint of the second can reflect radiant energy, whereas the dull black paint absorbs most of the radiant energy. Dark patches of ground absorb more radiant energy faster than do shiny water surfaces or lighter colored land surfaces.

PART II   How is Heat Transferred Through Connection? (3–5)

What inquiry question could you ask?

Where do you think the warmest and coolest spots are in your classroom? Try this activity to see if you can find the answer.

What will students do?

1. As far away as possible from the room's source of heat, tape three thermometers to a wall at these places: near the ceiling, halfway up the wall, and one near the floor.
2. Make a chart of the thermometer readings once an hour for one day.
3. Using the data collected, graph the results.
   From your data and graph, answer these questions:
   Which thermometer had the highest temperature? The middle temperature? The lowest temperature?
   Why do you think the temperatures were different?

What should you know?

Convection is the transfer of heat by either a gas (air) or a liquid (water). When the air in the room is heated, it expands and becomes lighter per given volume. It then rises because it is lighter. This rising and falling is called a **convection current.**

How could students apply their new knowledge?

When you see "wiggly lines" rising from a parking lot blacktop on a sunny day, how is this the same as the convection current in our classroom?
Why does a "cloud" fall down from a freezer that is above a refrigerator when you open the freezer door?
Why does smoke usually rise up a chimney? Under what conditions would smoke come into the house through the fireplace opening?
Why would a pinwheel start to spin if put over a lit light bulb?

PART III   How is Heat Transferred Through Conduction? (6–8)

Safety Precaution!

Caution: Because of the use of open flame, it is recommended that you supervise students closely. You may wish to demonstrate all or part of the activity.

What inquiry question could you ask?

What do you think will happen to tacks that have been attached with wax to a strip of aluminum foil, to a silver or steel knife, and to a copper tube when the tips of these metals are heated?

What will students or a teacher do?

TEACHER DEMO

1. Obtain a 4 × 4-in. square of aluminum foil, a candle, a match, and nine tacks.
2. Roll the aluminum foil tightly.
3. Light the candle. Drip some wax onto three tacks and the aluminum foil rod so the tacks stick to the foil.

4. Obtain a tripod stand, silver knife, and a 4-in. length of copper tubing.
5. Stick three tacks each to the knife and to the copper tubing as you did with the foil.
6. Place the foil, knife, and copper tubing on a tripod stand as shown in the diagram. Heat the tips of each of these with a candle flame. Have students observe and record what happens.

Why did the tacks not all fall at the same time?

From observing this activity, how do you think the heat affected the three metals?

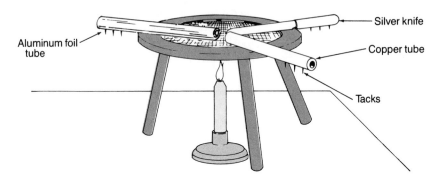

How could students apply their knowledge?

When you stand in front of a fireplace and only the front of you is warmed by the fire, how is the heat transferred?

How does heat or thermal energy come from the sun?

What colors are more likely to absorb heat?

Why do people generally wear lighter colored clothes in the summer?

In the can experiment, what kind of energy did the black surface absorb?

How was the heat transferred from the black surface to the thermometer?

Why is it desirable to have a copper-bottomed tea kettle?

Why would you not want a copper handle on a frying pan?

What metals conduct heat well?

What advantage would there be in having a car with a white top rather than a black top?

Why do many people in warmer climates paint their houses white?

Why would you prefer to put a hot dog on a stick rather than on a wire to cook the hot dog over a camp fire?

▶ What Effect Does Heat Have on the States of Matter? (6–8)

What concepts might students construct?

There are many forms of sugar.
It is possible to obtain carbon from burning sugar.
Sugar may be broken down chemically.

What materials will you need?

Hot plate
Aluminum pie pan
Sugar cube or teaspoon of sugar
Empty, tall glass tumbler
Pot holder or insulated cooking mitt

What inquiry questions could you ask?

Hold up a piece of sugar and ask:

What are some of the properties or characteristics of this piece of sugar?

What should you know?

Students might say the sugar is white, small, made up of crystalline material, sweet, and so on. In its present form, sugar is a white solid. There are, however, ways of changing its appearance. One of the easiest ways is simply to crush the cube, producing sugar in a smaller crystal form. These crystals can be crushed further to make a powdered sugar. Another way to change the cube's appearance is to dissolve it in a cup of water. Once the sugar is dissolved, it cannot be seen, yet the solution will taste sweet. This means that sugar is still present, because some of its characteristics are identifiable. In what ways can sugar be changed so it cannot be identified?

Because of the use of heat, you may wish to demonstrate all or part of this activity.

TEACHER DEMO

What will students or a teacher do?

1. Obtain an aluminum pie pan and place it on top of an electric hot plate. Regulate the burner so the pan is heated slowly.
2. Place 1 teaspoon or cube of sugar in the middle of the pan. (See diagram.)
   What do you think will happen to the sugar when it is heated?
3. Watch what happens to the sugar.
   What happens as the sugar begins to melt?

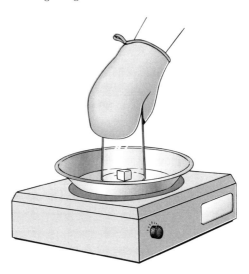

4. Hold a tall, empty glass cup upside down over the bubbling sugar. Use a pot holder or cooking mitt to do this.
   What do you think will appear on the inside of the glass?
5. Observe the inside of the glass very carefully.
6. Lift the glass, wait 10 seconds, then touch the inside of the glass with your fingers.

What do you feel?
What do you think it is? (Water vapor)

7. After the sugar stops bubbling, describe what you see in the pan.
   What do you think this material could be?
   What does it look like?
   Taste this material. (Take this opportunity to remind students that they should *never* taste anything unless you say it is all right.)
   How does it taste?
   Does it have the properties of sugar?

What should you know?   It is probably carbon. Sugar has carbon combined in its molecular structure.
   From what you have learned about sugar, can you explain why a marshmallow
How could students   *turns black when roasted over a fire?*
apply their new   *Why does sugar turn brown as it slowly heats up and melts? (This brown liquid is*
knowledge?   *caramel flavor.)*

AIR PRESSURE

🗣 ENGAGEMENT ACTIVITIES

▶ *What Makes Balloons Grow Bigger and Move Farther? (K–2)*

What materials will you   Balloons, metric tape or meterstick
need?

What inquiry questions   *Which team can get their balloons to go the farthest? How?*
could you ask?

What activities could   Go outside and divide the class into groups of five. Students should blow their bal-
students do?   loons up as much as they can. Do not tie off the ends. Have one student in each
   group release his balloon.

Safety Precaution!   *Caution:* Make sure students do not release balloons into the faces of their classmates.
   Have the second student in each group go to where the first balloon landed, then have
   him release his balloon. This continues until all the students in the team have had a
   turn. The distance is then measured metrically to determine how far their balloons went
   from the starting point. The team whose balloons went the greatest distance wins.

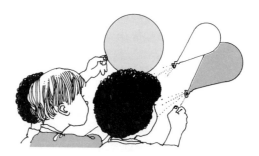

▶ *What's in Your Baggies? How Do You Know? (K–2)*

What materials you will need?

Plastic sandwich bags with plastic ties, sand, buttons, water

What inquiry questions could you ask?

What are some properties of matter?
How do you find out about properties of matter?
How is sand different from buttons?
How is water different from sand?
Can things be real that we cannot see?

What activities could students do?

Take three plastic sandwich bags and half fill them separately with sand, buttons, and water. Twist the top of each bag and tie it with a plastic tie. Take a fourth bag, swish it through the air, quickly close the mouth, twist it tightly, and tie it with a plastic tie. (See diagram below.)

Ask students to respond to these questions by looking at and carefully handling the bags. How are the properties of the objects in the bags the *same*? (They occupy space, have weight, exert pressure on the sides of the bags, can support a weight put on them, etc.) We call these things **properties of matter,** and they show us that the things in the bags are all real—even the air that we cannot see.

How are the properties of the objects in the bags *different*? (They do not all weigh the same, some change shape when you squeeze them, some are solid [buttons and sand], one is a liquid [water], and one is a gas [air] that looks invisible.)

You found out about properties of matter by observation.

What inquiry questions could you ask?

How could you find out if the objects in your bags could be moved from one bag to another?
How could you find out if the objects have a smell?

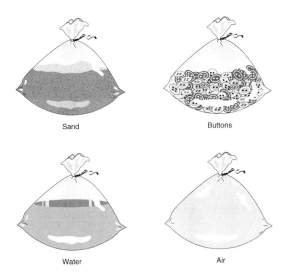

Sand   Buttons

Water   Air

► How Can You Make a Kite and Get It to Fly? (K–2)

What materials will you need?

Plastic such as that used by dry cleaners, paper to cover the kite, small pieces of wood to form the supports, string, transparent tape or glue, cloth for the tail

What inquiry questions could you ask?

How can we make kites?
What will we need?
How should they be constructed?
What shape should they be? Why?

What activities could students do?

Encourage students to plan in small groups how they are going to make their kites before they construct them. Guide them in discussing the properties of air and how it affects kite building and flying. After they have done this, you might bring in some books on kites. Discuss the role of the tail and how it helps to stabilize the kite. Have students experiment with how long the tail should be by flying their kites on windy and calm days. If there is a local kite store, invite students to visit it or invite the owner to your classroom. Discuss some of the dangers of flying kites near power lines.

Safety Precaution!

Caution: Point out that they should *never* use wire instead of string to fly a kite because of the danger involved if the wire hits a power line. Invite students to make several kinds of kites and find out how different cultures use them; for example, have students find out how the Japanese use kites to celebrate certain holidays. *Caution:* Warn students against putting plastic wrapping over heads or on faces.

EXPLORATION ACTIVITIES

► What Is Air? (K–2)

What concepts might students construct?

Air is real.
Air is around us all the time.
Air is found inside solids and liquids.
Air takes up space and has weight.
Air exerts pressure.

What materials will you need?

Piece of cardboard
Commercial-sized mayonnaise jar or aquarium
Drinking glass or plastic tumbler
Food coloring

What inquiry questions could you ask?

What are some of the properties of air?
How can you find out about the properties of air?

TEACHER DEMO

What will students or a teacher do?

1. Swing your hands back and forth.
   What can you feel?
2. Swing a piece of cardboard back and forth.
   What do you feel now?
   What is the cardboard pushing against?
   What do you feel pushing against you when you ride your bicycle down a hill?
   What do you think will happen to a glass if it is turned upside down and pushed straight down under water?
3. Turn a glass upside down and push it *straight* down in a large jar of water or an aquarium, as shown. (Use food coloring to make the water more visible.)

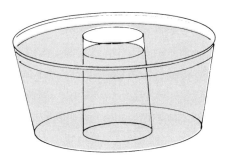

4. Now turn the glass sideways as shown.

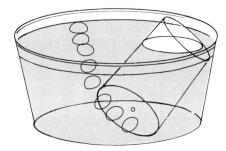

What inquiry questions could you ask?

What happens to the inside of the glass?
What are the bubbles that escape from the glass?
Where did the bubbles come from?

How could students apply their new knowledge?

How can you keep water in a straw by closing the top end with your finger as shown?

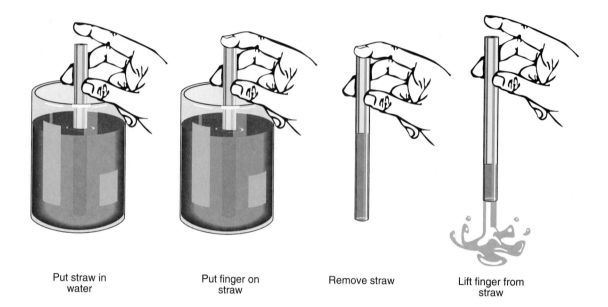

Put straw in water   Put finger on straw   Remove straw   Lift finger from straw

If you fill a paper bag with air and then crush it, what happens and why?
Why does juice flow better from a tin can if you punch two holes instead of one?
Can you push a straw through a potato?
Try this activity:

a. Place a potato on a table and ask a partner to hold it. Raise the straw about 5 inches above the potato and then quickly and forcibly stick the potato, as shown in (a).
   What happened? Why?

b. Repeat Step 4a but this time hold your thumb over the end of the straw as you stick the potato, as shown in (b).

Why is this different than before?

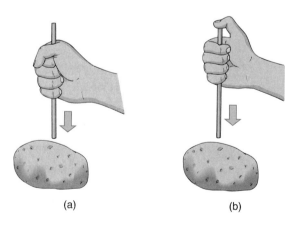

(a)   (b)

What should you know?	The first straw usually bends and only partially penetrates the potato. The second straw does not bend and goes through the potato. Blocking the straw end traps and compresses the air inside the straw, creating greater air pressure. Some of the potato is forced into the straw, further increasing the air pressure.

▶ *How Do the Effects of Moving Air Differ From the Effects of Nonmoving Air? (K–5)*

What concepts might students construct?	The pressure of liquids or gases will be low if they are moving quickly and will be high if they are moving slowly. This principle is called **Bernoulli's principle.**
What materials will you need?	3 pieces of notebook paper Ping-Pong ball Drinking straw Thistle tube or funnel Pop bottle Cylindrical container (oatmeal, salt) Pin with a head Candle Small index card (3 × 5 in.) Matches Thread spool
What inquiry questions could you ask?	Before doing this student inquiry activity, potential energy and kinetic energy should be explained.

PART I   What Happens to the Pressure of the Air Surrounding a Moving Stream of Air? (K–2)

What will students do?	1. Obtain a piece of notebook paper. 2. Make a fold 1-inch wide along the long end of the paper. Make another 1-inch fold at the opposite end as indicated in the diagram. 3. Place the paper on a flat surface. *What do you think will happen if you blow under this folded paper?* 4. Using the drinking straw, blow a stream of air under the paper.

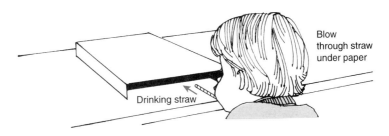

Blow through straw under paper

Drinking straw

What inquiry questions could you ask?	*What do you notice about the way the paper moves?* Describe how the air was circulating under the paper before you blew under it. *What do you know about the air pressure under the paper—when you blow under the paper—as compared with the air pressure exerted on top of the paper?*

PART II   How Can You Use a Bottle and a Piece of Paper to Investigate Bernoulli's Principle? (K–2)

What inquiry question could you ask?

What do you think will happen to a wad of paper placed in the opening of a pop bottle if you blow across the bottle opening?

What will students do?

1. Wad a small piece of paper so it is about the size of a pea (¼-in. or ½-cm diameter).
2. Lay the pop bottle on its side.
3. Place the small wad of paper in the opening of the bottle, next to the edge of the opening. (See diagram.)
4. Blow across the opening in front of the bottle. Make sure you bend down so that *you are level with the bottle.*

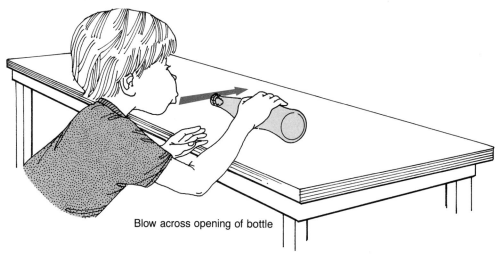

Blow across opening of bottle

What inquiry questions could you ask?

What happens to the wad of paper?

Why is the wad of paper forced to do that?

What do you know about the air pressure in the bottle and the air pressure at the opening of the bottle when you blow across it?

What do you think will happen if you place a wad of paper in the opening of a pop bottle (as before) and blow directly into the bottle?

5. Blow hard directly into the bottle as shown.

Blow directly into bottle

6. Record your observations.
   What do you conclude from your observations?

···

PART III   How Can You Use a Spool and Card to Investigate Bernoulli's Principle? (K–2)

What inquiry question could you ask?	*If a pin with a head is inserted through the center of a card and then into a spool, what will happen when you blow through the other end of the spool?*

What will students do?

1. Place the pin in the center of the index card so that the head is under the card. (See diagram.)
2. Put the thread spool over the pin.
3. Hold the card with one hand and the spool with your other hand.
4. While blowing, let go of the card.

Safety Precaution!

Warning: Instruct students *never to suck in* on the spool.

Blow through here

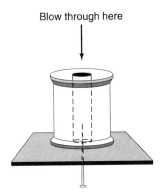

What inquiry questions could you ask?

What happened to the card while you blew through the spool?
What happened when you stopped blowing through the spool?
Why do you think this happened?
What is holding up the card?
Why does the air you blow through the hole not make the card fall?
Why do you need the pin in the middle of the card?

What should you know?

Two variables may affect the outcome: (1) The bottom of the spool must be very smooth (sand it if necessary), and (2) the student must take a deep breath and sustain a long, steady air column down the spool.

PART IV   How Can You Use a Funnel and Ping-Pong Ball to Investigate Bernoulli's Principle? (K–2)

What inquiry question could you ask?

What will happen to a Ping-Pong ball if it is placed in the large end of a thistle tube or funnel and you blow through the small end of the thistle tube or funnel?

What will students do?

Safety Precaution!

1. Hold the Ping-Pong ball in the wide, larger opening of the thistle tube or funnel, put your mouth on the other end, and blow with a long, steady breath. (See diagram.) *Hint:* Get a deep breath before you put your mouth on the tube end to blow. *Caution:* After each person blows through the tube, wash the funnel thoroughly with soap and water and an alcohol wipe, if possible.

Blow here

Thistle tube

Ping-Pong ball

2. While blowing hard and steady through the tube end of the funnel, let go of the Ping-Pong ball.
   Record your observations.
   Why does the ball do what it does?
   Why does the ball spin around in the thistle tube or funnel?

PART V   How Can You Use a Piece of Paper to Investigate Bernoulli's Principle? (K–2)

What inquiry question could you ask?

If you were to hold a piece of paper by each corner and blow across the top of the paper, what would happen to the paper?

What will students do?

1. Hold the lower left corner of a piece of notebook paper with your left hand and the lower right corner with your right hand.
2. Blow hard across the top of the paper. (See diagram.)
   What happens to the paper while you are blowing across it?
   Why does the paper move in this direction?

How could students
apply their new
knowledge?

*Why is it unwise to stand close to the edge of a platform as a moving train is
    coming?*

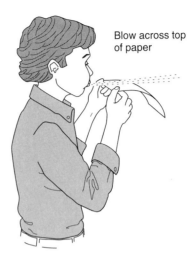

Blow across top
of paper

*When you rapidly pass by another student's desk that has a sheet of paper on it,
    what happens to the paper? Why?*
How would this principle of air pressure work when you fly a kite?
What happens to a girl's skirt if a car speeds close by her?
What would happen if a plane stopped moving in the air? How could this happen?

What should you know?

If a plane is moving fast enough, the upward pressure on the wings is enough to
overcome gravity. The plane must keep moving to stay aloft. If it stopped in midair,
it would glide down immediately.

*Look at the following drawing of an airplane wing. Is the air moving faster at A or
    B? Why?*

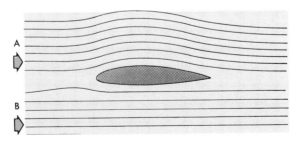

A

B

How do wing slopes vary and why?

PART VI   How Does Air Move Objects? (3–5)

TEACHER DEMO

Safety Precaution!

Because of the use of open flame, it is recommended that you demonstrate all or part of the activity.

What will students or a teacher do?

1. Position a cylindrical container and candle as shown in the diagram and light the candle.

   What do you think will happen to the candle flame if you blow as shown? Why?

2. Blow a deep breath against the front of the container, keeping your mouth even with the candle.

   What happens to the flame?
   Why do you think this happens?

What should you know?

The tendency of a fluid (a liquid or gas) to follow the wall contour of a curved surface is called the **Coanda effect.** In this case, the air (gas) acts like a fluid and follows the contour of the round container. The airstreams meet on the other side, combine, and blow out the candle.

SOUND ENERGY

ENGAGEMENT ACTIVITIES

▶ *What Makes a Drum Louder? (K–2)*

What materials will you need?

Cylindrical oatmeal container, puffed rice or wheat cereal, large balloon or sheet rubber, strong rubber band, pencil with eraser or drumstick.

What inquiry question could you ask?

How can you make a drum sound louder?

What activities could students do?

Stretch the large balloon or piece of sheet rubber over the open end of the oatmeal container and place a strong rubber band around that end to hold the rubber securely in place. This makes a simple drum. Sprinkle puffed rice or wheat cereal on the drum head. Tap the drum head softly with the drumstick or eraser end of the pencil and observe what happens. Now hit it harder.

Ask:

What inquiry question could you ask?

What differences did you notice when you hit the drum softly and when you hit it harder?

Help students to see the patterns formed by the puffed cereal when the drum head is struck softly and how the pattern changes when the drum head is struck harder. Also notice how much higher the cereal moves above the drum head when it is hit harder. Relate more energy (hitting the drum harder) with louder sound from the drum.

▶ *How Can You Make Sounds Less Noisy? (K–2)*

What materials will you need?

Two small battery-operated radios; several different-sized boxes, each of which can fit over one or more of the others and over the radio; cloth; paper; insulating material; cotton balls

What inquiry question could you ask?

How can we deaden the sound of this radio by using these materials?

What activities could students do?

Invite two groups of students to have a "deadening the sound" race, each using a radio with the same volume level and the listed materials. Give the groups a definite time (30–60 minutes) to brainstorm how they can deaden the sound of the radio, set up an experiment, and collect data. Later, discuss how sound can go through objects and what kinds of things deaden sound well. Then ask:

How can what you found in your "deadening the sound" race help to reduce sound in our classroom and make it more comfortable to our ears?

EXPLORATION ACTIVITIES

▶ *What Is Sound, and How Is It Produced and Conducted? (K–2)*

What concepts might students construct?

When an object vibrates, sound may be produced.
Sound may be made by vibrating a number of different objects.
Sound may be conducted by different material objects.

What materials will you need?

As many of the following things as possible should be placed at work stations for groups of four or more students:

Rubber band	Aluminum foil
Fork and spoon	Cotton
6 empty pop bottles	Bell
Alarm clock	Aluminum pie pan
4 feet of string	Toothpicks

What inquiry questions could you ask?

How could you make a sound with a rubber band?
How could you make a rubber band produce a sound? How is the sound produced?

What will students do?

1. The students should stretch a rubber band and cause it to vibrate. They should get the idea that the vibration causes the sound. *Caution:* Point out that students must be careful not to let the stretched rubber bands pop off their hands and that they must not try to snap each other with the rubber bands.

   Can you hear sound by placing your ear against different objects while causing them to make a sound?

2. Try making sounds with the different objects.
   What can you do to stop the sound once it has started?
3. Test your ideas.
4. Determine which materials are better than others for producing sound.
   In what ways are these materials the same or different?

How could students apply their knowledge?

How would you produce a loud sound?
What would you do to make our classroom less noisy?
Why do drapes in a room make sounds softer?

▶ *How Does the Length of an Air Column Affect Sound? (K–2)*

What concepts might students construct?

The higher the pitch of a note, the more rapid the vibrations of the producing body.
Pitch can be varied by adjusting the length of an air column.
The higher the water level in a bottle, the shorter the air column, and the higher the pitch (when blowing across the top of the bottle).

What materials will you need?

8 identical pop bottles
Medium-sized beaker
Drinking straws (wax paper straws work better than plastic)
Scissors

What inquiry questions could you ask?

What might happen if you blew across the openings of pop bottles filled with varying amounts of water?
Would a sound be produced?
If sounds were produced, would they all be the same? If not, which would be the highest? The lowest?

PART I   How Does the Water Level Affect the Pitch of Sound Produced in Bottles?

What will students do?

1. Fill eight identical pop bottles with varying amounts of water.
   What might happen if you blow across the lips of the bottles?
2. Blow across the bottles.

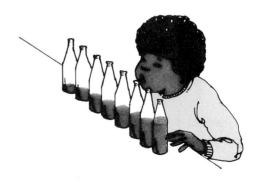

Do all bottles give off the same sound?

Which bottle gives off the highest note? The lowest note?

How could you make a musical scale out of the pop bottles?

3. Arrange the bottles to make a musical scale.
4. After you have made the musical scale, try to make a harmonizing chord.

If you number the lowest note "1" and the highest note "8," what are the numbers of the bottles you used for your chords?

What conclusions can you draw concerning the length of an air column and the sound produced?

What is the relationship between the length of an air column and a note produced by an open tube?

What should you know?   Once a scale is achieved, drop oil from a medicine dropper onto the top of the water in each bottle, just enough to cover the top. This will prevent evaporation and a change in pitch.

PART II   What Affects the Pitch of Sound Produced with a Drinking Straw? (K–2)

What will students do?

1. Give each student a drinking straw and a pair of scissors.
2. Have students cut and pinch the straw to form a reed like the one shown.

Pinch here   Cut a V

Side view   Top view

Why do we cut and pinch the straw?

3. Have students blow on the "V" cut into the straw. (*Note:* They will need to experiment to get the proper lip vibration.)
4. Now cut the straws into different lengths to get different pitches.

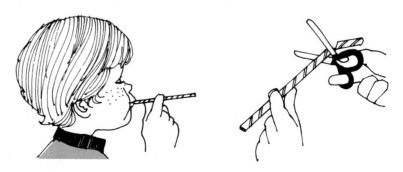

What is the relationship between the length of a straw and the sound it produced?
How can the drinking straws be used to play songs?

How could students apply their new knowledge?

How would the results vary if you put equal amounts of water in bottles of varying sizes?
Does the thickness of the glass in the pop bottle affect the tone produced?
Could you produce the same results using test tubes?
Does the pitch differ when hitting bottles with a spoon or ruler and when blowing over the top of the bottles? Test it.
How can the drinking straws be used to play songs? Experiment to get the straws calibrated in lengths in relation to octave. Try to play simple songs like "Mary Had a Little Lamb."

What should you know?

Once a scale is achieved, drop oil from a medicine dropper onto the top of the water in each bottle, just enough to cover the top. This will prevent evaporation and a change in pitch.

▶ How Do Solids and Liquids Conduct Sounds? (K–5)

What concepts might students construct?

Sound can travel through solid substances.
Sound can travel through liquid substances.
Sound can travel through gaseous substances.

What materials will you need?

Meter- or yardstick	20 feet of copper wire
Pencil	20 feet of steel wire
2 paper cups	Bucket
20 feet of strong cord or nylon fishing line	Water
Buttons	2 rocks

What inquiry questions could you ask?

Have you ever heard people talking when you were in one room and they were in another room next to yours?
How do you suppose you could hear them through the wall and the air?
You know that sound travels, but what substances will sound travel through?

PART I   Does Sound Travel Better Through Solids or Liquids? (K–2)

What will students do?

1. Obtain a meter- or yardstick and a pencil.
2. Hold the meterstick to your ear. Have a partner scratch the other end of the stick with a pencil. What happens?
3. Hold the stick away from your ear and repeat the activity.
   Does sound travel better through a solid or through the air?

PART II   What Affects the Pitch of the Sound Produced by a Vibrating Stick? (K–2)

What will students do?

1. With one hand, hold a meter- or yardstick firmly against a desk. With the other hand, pluck the overhanging part of the stick, causing it to vibrate.
   What causes the sound to be produced?
2. Produce a high-pitched sound by vibrating the stick.
   Produce a low-pitched sound by vibrating the stick.

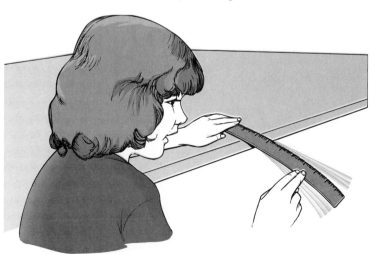

PART III Can Sound Vibration Be Conducted Along a String? (3–5)

What will students do?

1. Get two paper cups and 20 feet of string or nylon fishing line.
2. With a pencil, punch a very small hole in the bottom of the paper cups just large enough to stick the string through.
3. Stick the ends of the string through each one of the paper cups. Tie a button to the ends of the string ending inside the cups so the string will not be easily pulled from the cups. (See diagram.)

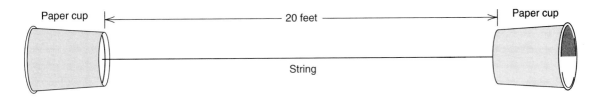

Paper cup ← 20 feet → Paper cup

String

When you talk into one of the cups, what will happen to the other cup? Why?

4. Talk into one cup while another student holds the other cup to her ear and listens.

How can sound best be transferred from one cup to the other? Hint: Make sure the string is stretched very tightly and that nothing is touching the string. Why?

Record what you did to best transmit the sound.

How will the sound be conducted if you use copper or steel wire? Try it.

What happens when you use copper wire?

Is the sound carried better through copper wire than through string? Why or why not?

Why is it important for the string to be tight and not touching anything?

PART IV Does Sound Travel Under Water? (3–5)

What inquiry questions could you ask?

How is sound carried in liquids?
How would you find out?

What will students do?

Obtain a large bucket full of water. Take two pieces of metal or two rocks and hit them together under water. Now hit them together out of water.

Did you hear a sound when you hit the objects together? Why?
What is your conclusion about the ability of a liquid to carry sound?
Which sound was louder—in air or water?

How could students apply their new knowledge?

How far do you think sounds would travel between phones using copper wire, string, and steel wire? Design an experiment to see which conducts sound farther.
How would you use eight rulers to make a musical scale?

Think about what you did to get a low pitch and a high pitch.
What is the purpose of making musical instruments out of wood?
How well do you think liquids other than water conduct sounds?

SIMPLE MACHINES (MECHANICS)

ENGAGEMENT ACTIVITIES

▶ *How Can You Make Balls Roll Faster? (K–2)*

What materials will you need?

Balls of different sizes, including Ping-Pong, golf, tennis, and larger ones; boards to make inclined planes

What inquiry question could you ask?

What things can you do with these balls?

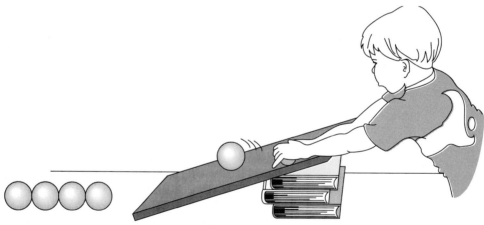

What activities could students do?

Find out which balls roll easiest across the floor, what happens when they are kicked, and which ones will roll the farthest after rolling down an inclined plane. Find out which balls balance best. Throw the balls against the wall at different angles and find out how they bounce off the wall. For example, how should you throw the ball so it will come back to you? Float the balls in water and find out which ones float and which do not. Also, notice how deep they sink in the water. Line up the balls in a vertical line leading from an inclined plane. Roll a ball down the inclined plane so it hits the end of the line. Then roll two balls down so they hit the line one after another. Place all but one of the balls in a close group. Roll another ball into the group and see how the balls scatter. Play croquet with different balls. Construct a tetherball.

▶ *How Do Wheels Help Toys Move? (K–2)*

What materials will you need?

Rollers, small round wheels, buttons, bottle caps, toy cars, small round rocks, oranges, apples, thimbles, boards to make inclined planes, disks cut from poster board, thumbtacks, matchboxes, coat hanger wire

What inquiry questions could you ask?

What can you do with these things?
What kinds of games can you play?
How can you make a toy car using the matchboxes and other things?
Which of the things you see are wheels? Which are not wheels?
How are wheels different from the other things?

What activities could students do?

The students could try seeing how far different things would roll on the floor after rolling down an inclined plane. They could also make toy cars with the matchboxes by tacking the bottle caps or buttons to the sides. The students may also be invited to make toy cars out of a square, small board where axles are made from clothes hangers. These are stapled to the board and then bent at the ends after the button or bottle cap wheels are attached.

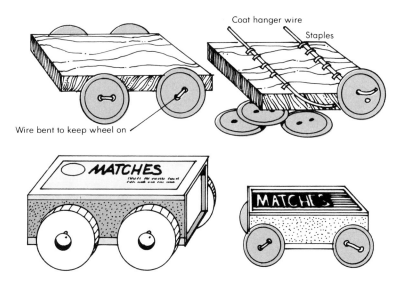

 EXPLORATION ACTIVITIES

▶ *What Is an Inclined Plane, and How Can You Use It? (3–8)*

What concepts might students construct?

Inclined planes are used for moving objects that are too heavy to lift directly. The work done by moving an object up an inclined plane is equal to the weight of the object times the height of the plane.

Weight × height of plane = Effort × length of plane

An **inclined plane** is one example of a **simple machine.**

What materials will you need?

Smooth board 4 ft × 6 in.
Support block 4 × 8 in.
Block with screw eye in one end or a rubber band wrapped around it
Spring scale

What inquiry questions could you ask?

What is an inclined plane?
Why use an inclined plane?
Where are there inclined planes on the school grounds?

What will students do?

1. Take the 4-foot board and place the 4 × 8-inch block under one end so that end of the board is raised 4 inches. Place the block with the screw eye in it on the inclined board as shown in the diagram. Slip the hook of the spring scale through the eye of the block.
   What force do you think will be required to pull the block?
   Will it be greater, equal to, or less than the weight of the block? Why?
2. Slowly and evenly pull the scale and block up the board.

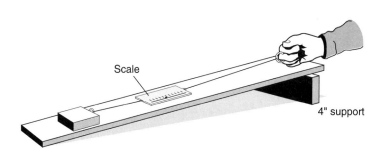

Scale

4" support

3. Record the amount of force needed to pull the block up the board. Do this several times and record your observations.
   Using the data obtained, determine the average force required to pull the weight.
4. Repeat the activity but this time make the inclined plane steeper by changing the support block so its 8-inch dimension is under the end of the board.
5. Again, find the average force needed to pull the weight up the board.
   How do the two forces compare?
6. Lift the block straight up, as shown in the next diagram. Repeat this several times and find the average reading on the scale.

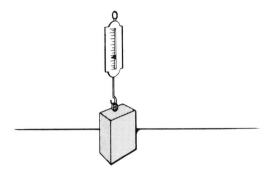

How is the force needed different when lifting the block straight up than when
pulling the block up the board?
Why?

7. The following formula is used to calculate the force needed to move a weight up
an inclined plane:

Weight × height of plane = Effort × length of plane

Use this formula to calculate the force that should have been necessary to move
the weight up the inclined plane.
Why do the experimental results and the calculated results not agree exactly?
What can you say about the amount of force required as an inclined plane becomes
steeper?
What is the advantage of having a long inclined plane rather than a short inclined
plane if both planes are the same height?

**How could students
apply their new
knowledge?**

Why do roads not go straight up and down mountains?
Which of the following examples is an inclined plane?

a. ramp   d. stairway
b. hill   e. wedge
c. gangplank   f. head of an axe

A person moved a 100-pound safe up an inclined plane 20 feet long and 2 feet high.
How much effort did the person have to use to move the safe?

▶ **What Is the Advantage of Using a Wheel and Axle? (3–8)**

**What concepts might
students construct?**

A **wheel** is a simple machine that aids in moving an object.
Every wheel has an axle. The wheel is used to turn the axle, or the axle is used to
turn the wheel.
The work obtained from a simple machine is equal to the work put into it minus
the work used in overcoming friction.
A small effort applied to a large wheel can be used to overcome a large resistance
on a small wheel.

A **wheel and axle** machine usually consists of a large wheel to which a small axle is firmly attached.

The mechanical advantage is equal to the radius of the wheel divided by the radius of the axle.

What materials will you need?

Screw hook
Block of wood
Rubber bands
Ruler
Sheets of coarse sandpaper
5 or 6 round pencils

4 thread spools
1 bicycle per class
1 of the following: pencil sharpener, meat grinder, or can opener
Balance weight

PART I   How Do Wheels Affect the Motion of Objects? (3–8)

What inquiry question could you ask?

In what way does the wheel help to move objects?

What will students do?

1. Turn the screw hook into the end of a block of wood. Attach a rubber band (or a spring scale) to the hook.
2. With the rubber band on your finger, lift the block into the air and measure the stretch with a ruler, as in (a) in the diagram. Record your measurement.
3. Position the block on a table with the rubber band extended, as in (b) in the diagram, and measure the stretch of the rubber band. Now drag the block on the table and measure the rubber band's stretch once the block begins to move. Record your measurements.
    What change is made in the stretch of the rubber band?
4. Repeat the procedure in Step 3, this time with sandpaper beneath the block, as in (c) in the diagram.
5. Now place two round pencils underneath the block and drag it across the table, as in (d) in the diagram. Measure the stretch of the rubber band just before and after the block begins to move.

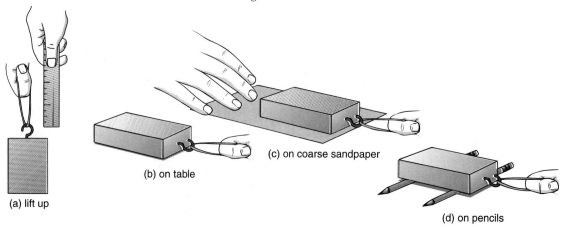

(a) lift up

(b) on table

(c) on coarse sandpaper

(d) on pencils

What happens to the stretch of the rubber band this time?
What difference do the pencils make underneath the wood as you try to move it?
How does your measurement change?
What do you suppose is the purpose of measuring the movement of the block of wood?

6. Try the experiment again, only this time use four spools for the wheels and round pencils for the axles. Place the wood on the axles.
   Observe what happens as you push the block of wood very gently.

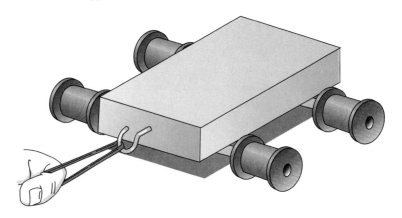

Measure the stretch of the rubber band as you pull the block of wood.
   What difference is there in the stretch of the rubber band this time compared to moving the board without wheels?

What should you know?   Older students can repeat the activity using the spring scale.

PART II   How Does a Wheel and Axle Change Force Needed to Move Weight? (3–8)

What inquiry question could you ask?   *What is a winch?*

What will students do?

1. Obtain a small winch or use a pencil sharpener, meat grinder, or can opener.
   What is the advantage of using a winch?
2. Hook a weight to the axle as shown in the diagram.

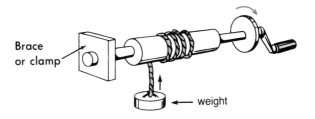

Brace or clamp

← weight

What do you think will be gained if a large wheel is turned to move a small axle?

3. Turn the large wheel.

4. Count the number of turns you make to raise the weight 2 inches.

What should you know?

A small force applied to a large wheel can be used to move a large resistance attached to the axle. This is done, however, at the expense of distance, because the large wheel has to be moved a great distance to raise the resistance a short way.

PART III   What Are Some Applications of a Wheel and Axle? (3–8)

What will students do?

Observe a bicycle.

Where on a bicycle is friction used to advantage?
How is the bicycle wheel constructed to help reduce friction?

What should you know?

The wheel produces less friction because there is less surface area coming in contact with pavement than if a weight such as a person were pulled along a surface.

Where are the wheels and axles on a bicycle?
When you ride a bicycle, where do you apply the force?
Why do you apply the force to the small wheel?

What should you know?

The effort is applied to the small wheel to gain speed. Using a great force, you move the small sprocket a short distance, and it, in turn, moves the large wheel a greater distance but with less force. Look at the diagrams of the following objects and decide whether they increase the ability to move heavier objects or increase the speed.

Wheel & axle   Pencil sharpener   Meat grinder   Winch

How could students apply their new knowledge?	Pulling an object across the table produced a force. *How can you tell which required a greater amount of force to pull: the board without pencils under it or the board that had the pencils as axles?*
What should you know?	A spring scale can be substituted for the rubber band. If you have a balance, you can determine how much force you need to pull the board across the table. If you use a rubber band, you must calculate how far the rubber band stretches. The rubber band will not stretch as much the first time. *How are roller bearings and ball bearings used?* *You want to move a heavy desk drawer across your room to another shelf.* *How can you go about doing this with the least amount of effort and the greatest amount of speed?*

▶ *What Is a Screw, and How Is It Used? (3–8)*

What concepts might students construct?	A **screw** is an inclined plane wrapped around a rod. As with an inclined plane, force is gained at the expense of distance. A large weight can be moved by a small force if the smaller force is applied over a greater distance.
What materials will you need?	Triangular pieces of paper Tape measure Colored pencil or crayon Pieces of soft wood Pencil Screwdriver Colored string C-clamp Several large screws
What inquiry questions could you ask?	Show the class several examples of screws and ask the following questions: *What are these called?* *What purpose do they serve?* *Where are they in the classroom?* *What advantage do they have over nails?* *What type of machine studied thus far resembles a screw?*
What should you know?	A screw is a circular, inclined plane.

....

PART I   What Is a Screw? (3–8)

What will students do?	1. Obtain a small piece of paper and cut it in the shape of a triangle as shown in the diagram. 2. Color the edge of the paper so you can see it and then wind the paper around the pencil.

What kind of machine did the paper represent before you rolled it around the pencil?

PART II   How Do Screws Work? (3–8)

What inquiry questions could you ask?

What is this called? (See diagram.) What is it used for?

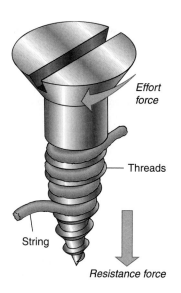

What will students do?

1. *If you wrap a piece of string around the threads of this screw, which will be longer: the length of the screw or the length of the string? Why?*
   Try it and measure and compare.
2. *How can you fasten two pieces of wood together using a screw and a screwdriver?*
   Do it.
     How far did the screw go into the wood?
     How many turns of the screw did it take?
     Why?
     In what direction did the screw turn?
     In what direction did the screw move into the wood?

What should you know?   Screw threads change screwdriver force into downward force. Less effort is needed to screw into wood, although it takes many turns.

How could students apply their new knowledge?
What are examples of screws in your daily life?
How do these work?

What should you know?   Some examples of screws used in daily life include a bolt, lightbulb, and screw top. As these objects are turned, their threads tighten into the nut, light socket, and bottle, respectively.

PART III   What Are Some Applications of Screws? (3–8)

▶ *How is a Screw Used in a Jack?*

What inquiry questions could you ask?
What kind of machine did the paper in Part I represent after you rolled it around the pencil?
How are the screw and the inclined plane related?

What will students do?   1. Obtain a C-clamp and insert a pencil as shown in the diagram.

Pencil

What do you think will happen to the pencil when you move the screw inward?
How much effort will have to be applied to break the pencil?
2. Look at the diagram of the jack.

Jack

Describe how the jack works.

> *How is the jack similar to a screw?*
> *What is the purpose of using a jack on a car?*
> *How is it possible for a person who weighs 150 pounds to lift a car weighing 3,000 pounds by using a jack?*

How could students apply their new knowledge?

> *When were jacks used in old barber shops?*
> *Where else are jacks used?*
> *How many seconds would a person have to exert a force to raise a car a small distance?*
> *What machine is involved in a spiral notebook?*
> *If you were asked to push a heavy rock to the top of a hill, how would you move it up the hill?*

What should students know?

Involve the custodian of your school to show your students examples of simple machines.

▶ ***What Is a Movable Pulley, and How Can You Use It? (3–8)***

What concepts might students construct?

Pulleys that move with the resistance are called **movable pulleys.**
Movable pulley systems have a mechanical advantage greater than 1.
The mechanical advantage of a movable pulley system is equal to the number of stands holding up the resistance.

What materials will you need?

Ring stand and clamp for attaching pulleys
2 single pulleys
String or nylon fishing line for the pulley

Spring scale
100-gram weight
50-gram weight
Yard- or meterstick

What will students do?

1. Obtain a ring stand and a clamp for attaching a pulley, a single pulley, some string or nylon fishing line, a spring scale, and a 100-gram weight. Assemble your equipment as shown in the diagram.

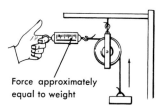

Force approximately equal to weight

How much do you think you will have to pull on the scale to raise the 100-gram weight?

2. Pull on the scale and raise the weight.
   How is the scale affected when you raise the weight?
3. Repeat this activity several times and record each measurement.
   What do you think will happen when you use two pulleys to raise the 100-gram weight?
4. In addition to the equipment you have, obtain a second pulley and a 50-gram weight. Assemble your equipment as shown in the diagram.
5. Pull the 50-gram weight and record your observations.

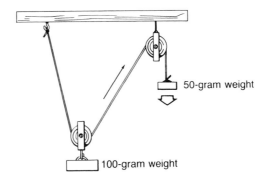

50-gram weight

100-gram weight

6. Remove the 50-gram weight and attach the spring scale to the free end of the fishing line, as shown in the following diagram.
   How will the scale be affected when you raise the 100-gram weight?
7. Raise the weight by pulling on the scale.
   What happens to the scale when you raise the weight?
8. Repeat the activity several times and record each measurement.
   Why is there an advantage in using this type of pulley system?
9. Remove the scale and once again attach the 50-gram weight.
   How far do you think the 50-gram weight will move when it raises the 100-gram weight?
   How far do you think the 100-gram weight will move when it is raised by the 50-gram weight?

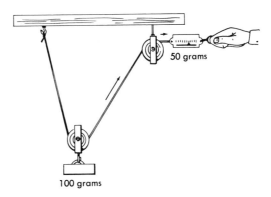

50 grams

100 grams

10. Obtain a yard- or meterstick.
11. Move the 50-gram weight and measure how far both the weights move.
12. Repeat this part of the activity several times and record your measurements.
    What can you say about pulleys from the measurements you just recorded?
13. Look at the measurements you recorded when one pulley was used and those you recorded when two pulleys were used.
    What does the information tell you about pulleys?

How could students apply their new knowledge?

What kind of pulley system would be needed to raise a piano weighing 300 pounds? Draw a sketch of that pulley system.

▶ *What Is a Lever and How Can You Use It? (3–8)*

What concepts might students construct?

A **lever** is a simple machine.
A lever cannot work alone.
A lever consists of a bar that is free to turn on a pivot called the **fulcrum.**
    By using a first-class lever, it is possible to increase a person's ability to lift heavier objects. This is called the **mechanical advantage (M.A.).** The mechanical advantage of a lever is determined by the formula

$$\text{Mechanical advantage} = \frac{\text{Effort arm}}{\text{Resistance arm}}$$

The weight times the distance on one side of the fulcrum must equal the weight times the distance on the other side if the lever is balanced.
A first-class lever has the fulcrum between the resistance and the effort.

What materials will you need?

Roll of heavy string or nylon fishing line
Meter- or yardstick
100-gram weight
20-gram weight
Platform with an arm or ring stand and clamp for suspending objects
Assorted weights of various sizes

What should you know?

Define *resistance*, *force*, and *fulcrum* before beginning the activity.

TEACHER DEMO

What will students or a teacher do?

1. Using some heavy string, a yardstick, a 100-gram weight, a 20-gram weight, and a ring stand and clamp, assemble the apparatus as shown in the diagram.

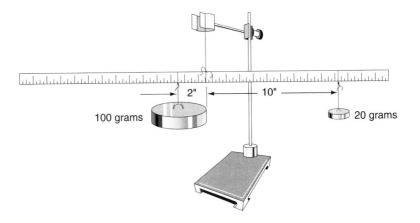

Where do you think you should attach the 100-gram weight and the 20-gram weight so the yardstick will balance?

2. Attach the weights so the yardstick is balanced.

How far is the 100-gram weight from the end of the yardstick?

How far is the 20-gram weight from the end of the yardstick?

3. Look at these three things: the string, which is suspending the yardstick; the 20-gram weight; and the 100-gram weight.

What is the relationship between the weight and distance on each side of the fulcrum?

What are the advantages of using a first-class lever of this type?

4. Use the following formula to calculate the mechanical advantage (M.A.) of the lever.

$$\text{M.A.} = \frac{\text{Effort arm}}{\text{Resistance arm}}$$

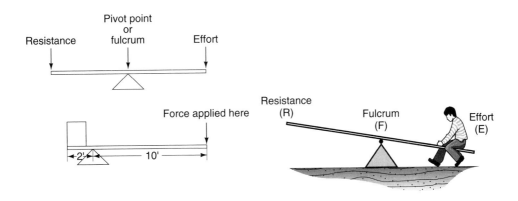

What should you know?

At the completion of the activity, explain to the class that a **first-class lever** consists of a bar that is free to turn on a pivot point called the **fulcrum.** The weight moved is called the **resistance.** The force exerted on the other end of the lever is called the **effort.** Draw the preceding diagram on the board to illustrate this point. State that in a first-class lever, the fulcrum is always between the resistance and the effort. Repeat this activity using assorted weights and calculate the M.A. using the formula given in Step 4. Use metric measurements, if possible.

How could students apply their new knowledge?

How is the M.A. affected when different weights are used?
What does an M.A. of 4 mean?
Where are first-class levers used?

MAGNETIC AND ELECTRICAL ENERGIES AND INTERACTIONS

ENGAGEMENT ACTIVITIES

▶ *What Can Magnets Do? (K–2)*

What materials will you need?

Several strong magnets, steel ball

What might happen if you bring a magnet next to a steel ball or another magnet?

What inquiry question could you ask?

What activities could students do?

Put a magnet on a table and hold a steel ball 1 inch (2–3 cm) away from the magnet's end.

What happens when you let go of the steel ball?
Try it again.
Why do you think this happens?

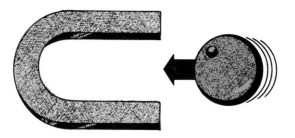

Now try the same thing using two magnets.
What happens to the magnets?

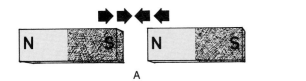

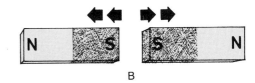

A   B

Try the same thing again, but turn one magnet around so its opposite end faces the first magnet.

What happens now? Why do you think this happens?
What other things might you be able to move with magnets?
How could you find out?

▶ **What Are the Shapes and Names of Magnets? (K–2)**

What materials will you need?

Large assortment of magnets of different sizes, shapes, colors, and materials (lodestone, bar, U-shaped, horseshoe, cylindrical, disk, doughnut-shaped); variety of items attracted to magnets (paper clips, iron or steel washers, and nails); variety of objects not attracted to magnets (rubber bands, paper, plastic chips, bits of wood); 2 shoeboxes, one labeled "Magnets Pick Up" and one labeled "Magnets Do Not Pick Up."

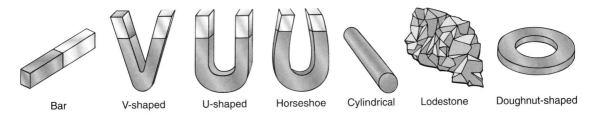

Bar   V-shaped   U-shaped   Horseshoe   Cylindrical   Lodestone   Doughnut-shaped

What inquiry questions could you ask?

How are all these things [magnets] the same?
What are they called?

What activities could students do?

Touch one magnet at a time to the piles of paper clips, iron or steel washers, and nails.

What happens to the paper clips and other things?
Try the same thing with the other objects.

What happens? Why do you think the paper clips, the iron or steel washers, and the nails were pulled to and stuck to the magnets?
Put those objects that were picked up by the magnets into the box marked "Magnets Pick Up" and those objects that were not picked up by the magnets into the box marked "Magnets Do Not Pick Up." Objects that pull and hold iron and steel things are called **magnets,** and their exact names are descriptive of their shapes, such as lodestone, bar magnet, U-shaped magnet, cylindrical magnet, and doughnut-shaped magnet.

What other shapes might magnets have?
Bring in magnets you have at home.
Where are the magnets used?

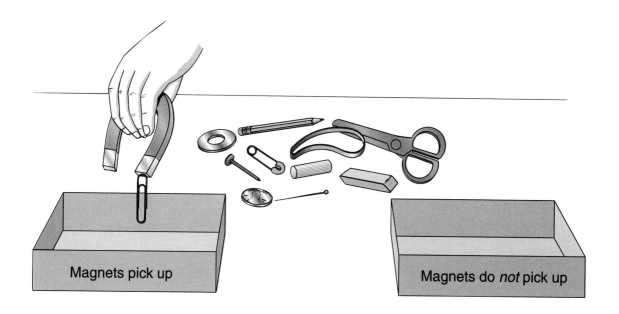

Magnets pick up

Magnets do *not* pick up

EXPLORATION ACTIVITIES

▶ What Is a Magnet? (K–5)

What concepts might students construct?

The place on the magnet where it picks up iron or steel objects is called the **pole.**
A magnet has two poles, one called the north, and the other called the south.
The same or like poles push apart, or **repel.** Different or unlike poles pull together, or **attract.**
Around every magnet is an area called the **magnetic field,** which is made up of invisible magnetic lines of force.

What materials will you need?

2 cylindrical bar magnets
2 rectangular bar magnets
String
Wooden meterstick without a metal edge
1 large and 1 small bar magnet
Paper clip
Steel washer

Steel BB
Transparent tape
Steel needle
Glass or plastic pan
Water
1/8-in. slice of cork

What inquiry questions could you ask?

The materials listed are for a group of two or three students. Set up stations and equip each group with a set of materials.

What should you know?

Display a cylindrical bar magnet for the class.
What is this called?
What is it made of?
How can it be used?
What are the properties or characteristics of a magnet?
What things can a magnet do?
What do you think would happen if two cylindrical bar magnets were placed side by side?
How could you find out?

PART I   How Can You Make Magnets Push Apart or Pull Together? (K–2)

What will students do?

1. Place one cylindrical bar magnet on the table and bring the second magnet near it. Observe what happens.
2. Reverse one of the magnets. Observe what happens.
   What happens when you put the second magnet beside the first one?
   What happens when you turn one magnet around?

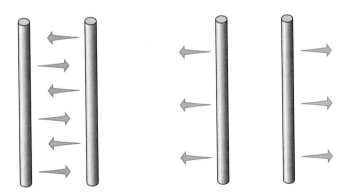

Why do you think one magnet rolls when the other comes near it?
What did you notice when the magnets pulled together?
What did you notice when the magnets pushed apart?
How do you know from this activity that both ends of the magnet are not the same?
What did you do to make the magnets push apart?
What did you do to make the magnets pull together?

PART II   How Do Magnets Affect Each Other? (K–2)

▶ What Are the Parts of a Magnet?

What will students do?

1. Using two rectangular or cylindrical bar magnets, tie a string around the middle of one of the magnets as shown.
2. By holding the string, suspend the magnet in the air.
   What do you think will happen when another magnet is brought near the suspended one?
3. Bring another magnet near the suspended one.
   Why do you think the magnet moves?
   What do you think will happen when you reverse the magnet in your hand?

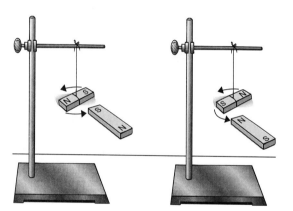

4. Reverse the magnet and bring it near the suspended one.
   Why does the suspended magnet react differently when you approach it with the other end of the magnet?
   What causes the magnet to react in different ways?
   How do you know there is a force present even though it cannot be seen?
   What is a force?

What should you know?

Point out that a **force** is a push or pull. This can be shown by pushing or pulling a child who is seated in a chair.

PART III   How Much Can Magnets Pull? (3–5)

What inquiry question could you ask?

How can you measure the force of attraction between certain objects and magnets?

What will students do?

1. Get a wooden meterstick *without a metal edge,* a large and a small bar magnet, a paper clip, a steel washer, a steel BB, and transparent tape.

2. Tape the meterstick to your desktop so it will not move. Put a paper clip at the end of the meterstick and place the large bar magnet at the 6-cm line (as shown in the diagram).

3. *Very slowly* move the magnet along the meterstick's edge toward the paper clip. Stop exactly when the paper clip starts to move toward the magnet!
   How many centimeters away was the magnet when the paper clip started to move? Record your findings on a chart like the following:

What will students do?

Object	Distance from Object to Magnet
Paper clip	

4. Repeat Step 3 two more times and then average the three findings.
   Why average three observations?
5. Do the same tests using the steel BB and the washer.
   If the distances the objects moved were different, why do you think this is so?
6. Repeat the tests using the small magnet with each object, three times each. Average the findings and record the data on your chart.

What inquiry questions could you ask?

Which of the two magnets was the stronger?
How do you know from your findings?
Why do you think the distances between the magnet and the paper clip, the BB, and the washer were different?

What do these tests tell you about the strength of magnets and how different objects are affected?

Using the data from your charts, graph the results of these tests.

PART IV   How Can You Make a Magnet? (3–5)

What will students do?

1. Obtain a steel needle, a magnet, and a pan with an inch or two of water in it. *What can you find out about the needle and the magnet?*

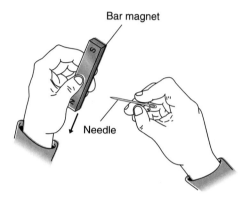

Bar magnet

Needle

2. Make a magnet of the needle (magnetize it) by holding a magnet in one hand and stroking a needle *in one direction only* 25 or more times, as in diagram (a). Lay the needle on the cork so the needle is in a horizontal position. Float the cork in the pan of water, as shown in diagram (b). (*Hint:* Adding one drop of liquid dishwashing detergent to the water will enable the floating cork to turn much more easily as the needle responds to the magnet.)

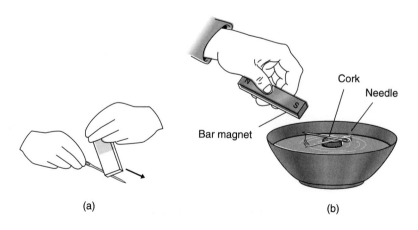

Cork

Needle

Bar magnet

(a)   (b)

3. Bring a magnet near the needle on the cork.
   Why do the cork and the needle move when you bring a magnet near them?
   What happens to the needle when it is stroked with the magnet?
   What caused the cork and needle to move?

How could students apply their new knowledge?

How does a compass work?
How could you use a magnet to make a compass?

▶ **What Is Static Electricity? (K–8)**

What concepts might students construct?

All bodies are capable of producing electrical charges.
Conductors allow electrons to move, but **insulators** do not allow electrons to
   move easily.
Like charges repel; unlike charges attract.

What materials will you need?

Carpet square	Transparent tape
Lucite or resin rod or a hard rubber comb	Balloons
	String
Wool cloth	Wire coat hanger
Flour	Glass rod
Small pieces of paper	Piece of silk about the size
Tap water	of a small handkerchief

What inquiry questions could you ask?

What is the energy that we use to produce light and to operate many machines and household appliances?
What things can produce electricity?
How can you find out if all charges of electricity are the same?

....

PART I How Can You Produce Static Electricity? (K–2)

What inquiry question could you ask?

What happens sometimes when you walk over carpet and touch a doorknob or slide across a car seat and touch a metal car door?

What will students do?

1. Stand next to a doorknob and shuffle your feet *briskly* on a carpet square at least 20 times.
   What do you think will happen if you touch the doorknob with one finger?
2. Touch the doorknob with one finger and observe what happens.
   What did you see?
   What did you feel?

How could students apply their new knowledge?

   What did you hear?

Where in nature does this happen?

What should you know?

Friction between the carpet and the student's feet causes electric charges to build up on the student. These charges, called **static electricity,** may be slowly discharged into air or rapidly discharged when the student touches a metal object such as the doorknob. Lightning is the discharge of huge amounts of electrical charges.

PART II   How Does Static Electricity Affect Objects? (K–2)

What inquiry question could you ask?

How can you produce static electricity?

What will students do?

1. Obtain the following materials: a lucite or resin rod or a hard rubber comb, wool, flour, small pieces of paper, and a source of tap water.
2. Take the resin rod (or hard rubber comb) and rub it with the wool cloth.
   What do you think will happen when the rod is touched to the flour?
3. Touch the rod to some flour.

Resin rod or hard rubber comb

Flour

What happens to the flour?
Why do you think the flour is affected by the rod?

What will students do?

4. Clean the rod, rub it again, and touch it to the small pieces of paper.
   What does the rod do to the paper?
5. Rub the rod briskly with the wool cloth.
6. Turn on a water tap so a very slow stream of water comes out.
   What do you think will happen to the stream of water when the rod is moved close to it?
7. Move the rod close to the stream.

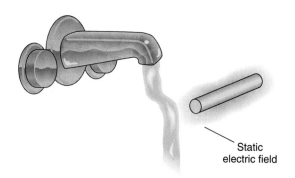

Static electric field

What happens as the rod comes near?
Why does the water react as it does?
Why do you think it reacts as it does without being touched?

What should you know?

The students should note how close they have to bring the rod before it affects the stream of water. Develop the concept that there is an invisible field of electrical force around the rod that either pushes or attracts the water. This force cannot be seen, but it must be there because it affects the stream of water. Define *force* as a push or pull. In this case, the water is pushed or pulled, without being touched, by moving the rod toward and away from the water.

How can you find out if rubbing the cloth on the rod causes the electrical force?
8. Rub the rod again with the cloth.
9. Now rub your hand over the rod.
What do you think will happen to the stream of water?
10. Repeat the procedure by approaching the slow stream of water with the rod.
What effect does the rod have on the water this time?
Why does the rod not have the same effect?
What happened to the charge that the wool cloth induced in the rod?
Why do you think the charge failed to last?

What should you know?

When the resin rod is rubbed with wool, **electrons** are rubbed off these materials onto the rod. The rod, however, is an insulator, so the electron movement is slight. The rod becomes negatively charged because each electron produces a small amount of negative charge. When a hand is rubbed over the rod, the rod becomes discharged because the electrons leave the rod and enter the hand. The rod is then neutral. Explain the difference between a conductor and an insulator.

....

PART III   What Are Conductors and Insulators? (K–2)

What inquiry questions could you ask?

After your discussion concerning conductors and insulators, would you say the rod is a conductor or an insulator?
Why do you think so?

What will students do?

1. Tear off two 12-inch strips of sticky transparent tape, making sure they don't stick to each other by keeping the sticky side on the outside.
2. Holding one strip of tape in one hand, slowly bring the second strip toward the other.
What happens?
Why?

PART IV   How Can Static Electricity Cause Objects to Attract or Repel? (3–5)

What inquiry question
could you ask?

How can you demonstrate force between like and unlike charges?

What will students do?

1. Obtain two balloons.
2. Inflate the balloons.
3. Tie a string to each balloon and suspend them from a bar or a coat hanger as shown in the diagram.

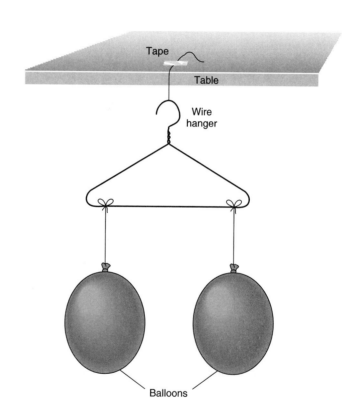

What will students do?

4. Rub each balloon with the wool cloth.
    What do the balloons do?
    Why do they repel each other?
    Do you think the balloons are conductors or insulators?
    What do you think will happen if a charged resin rod is brought near the balloons?

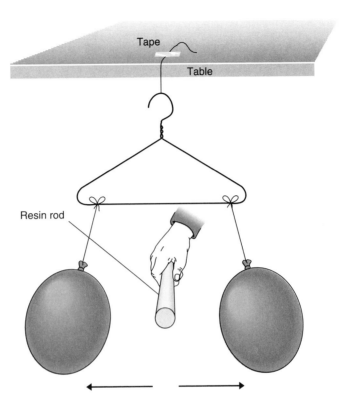

5. Rub the resin rod with wool and place it near the balloons.
   In which direction do the balloons move?
   Why do you think they were repelled by the rod?
   Do you think the balloons have a like or unlike charge? Why?
   What do you think will happen to the balloons if you touch them with a glass rod?

What should you know?   These balloons were charged in the same way; therefore, each must have the same charge. When they do have the same charge, they repel each other because like charges repel.

6. Rub the glass rod with the piece of silk.
7. Place it near the balloons.
   What happens as it comes near the balloons?
   How does the glass rod affect the balloons in comparison to the resin rod?
   What can you say about the charge on the resin rod compared to the glass rod?

What should you know?   The glass rod will have a positive charge since electrons were rubbed off the rod onto the silk. It will attract the balloons because they were negatively charged by the resin rod, and unlike charges attract.

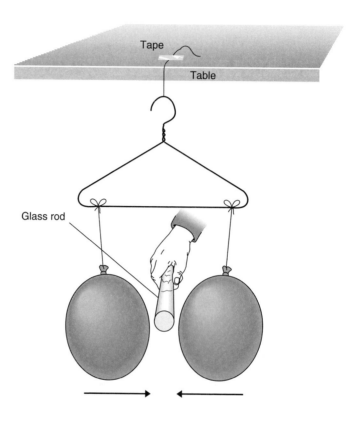

PART V How Can You Use Static Electricity to Stick a Balloon Onto a Wall? (6–8)

What will students do?

1. Vigorously rub an inflated balloon against a piece of wool.
2. Place the balloon on a wall. (See diagram.)

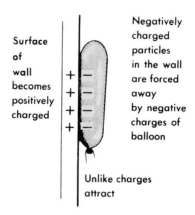

What do you think will happen to the balloon?
Why does the balloon not fall?
Is the force that pulls the balloon to the wall greater or less than the gravitational
*   force pulling the balloon down to earth?*
What happened to the negatively charged particles in the wall when the balloon
*   came near?*
After following the previous steps, what can you say about charging matter?
What is a conductor?
What is an insulator?

What should you know?

When you rub the balloon with wool, it becomes negatively charged, because it got an excess of electrons from the wool. When the balloon is placed next to the wall, the balloon's negative charge forces the electrons in the wall away from the surface, leaving the surface positively charged. The balloon sticks because the unlike charges attract. The balloon is negative and the wall surface is positive, as is indicated in the diagram.

How could students apply their new knowledge?

What is electricity?
How can you use a magnet to make electricity?
Why might you get a shock after walking across a wool carpet and then touching a
*   metal doorknob?*
Why does your hair get attracted to your comb? Why is this most noticeable on very
*   dry days?*
Why do clothes stick together after being dried in a clothes dryer?

▶ *How Can You Make Electricity By Using Magnetism? (6–8)*

What concepts might students construct?

Around a magnet there are magnetic lines of force.
If you break the magnetic lines of force, you can make electricity.
A *force* is defined as a push or a pull.

What materials will you need?

Insulated copper wire (about 3 yards)
Bar magnet
Magnetic compass

What do students know?

How is electricity used?
How does electricity get to your home for you to use?
What is the area of force around a magnet called?
What is a force?
How can you use a magnet to produce electricity?

TEACHER DEMO

What will students or a teacher do?

1. With a partner, obtain a length of insulated copper wire (about 3 yards), a bar magnet, and a magnetic compass.

2. Take the wire and wrap it 20 to 30 times around the magnetic compass as indicated in the diagram.
3. Loop the other end of the wire into a coil as shown in the diagram.

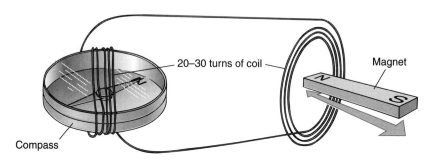

What happens when electricity goes through a wire?
What do you think the area around the wire could be called?
What has the electricity produced?
How do you think magnetism could be used to produce electricity?

4. Take the bar magnet and plunge it back and forth through the coil of wire. Instruct your partner to watch what happens to the compass.
What happens to the compass?
Why do you think the compass needle does what it does?
What attracts the compass needle?
What do you think causes the needle to be deflected?
Where do you think the magnetism was produced to cause the compass needle to move?
If there is magnetism produced in the wire around the compass, what do you think the plunging of the magnet through the coil of wire has to do with it?
When is electricity produced in the wire?
What is the force of a magnet called?
What does a magnet do to a magnetizable object?
What does a magnet do to a nonmagnetizable object?
Explain how magnetism can be used to produce an electrical current.

What should I know?

Around every magnet there is an area that can push or pull susceptible objects such as iron filings. This area can be thought to consist of lines of force. When these lines of force are broken by plunging the magnet back and forth through a coil of wire, electricity is made in the wire. **Electricity** is defined as a flow of electrons along the wire, producing an electrical current. Whenever there is an electrical current produced, there will be a magnetic field around the wire. This magnetic field causes the magnet (compass needle) in this activity to move. Using magnets to produce electricity is the principle involved in making electricity in a dynamo. Make certain that the compass is far enough away from the magnet to avoid direct magnetic influence.

How could students apply their new knowledge?

How can you use electricity to make a magnet?

▶ *How Can You Make a Temporary (Electro) Magnet? (6–8)*

What concepts might students construct?

When electricity passes along a wire, it produces a magnetic field around the wire that acts like a magnet.

A magnetic field can make iron temporarily magnetic.

The more electrical current flows through a wire in a unit of time, the more magnetism is generated around the wire.

If a circuit is broken, electricity will not flow.

What materials will you need?

Insulated copper wire
Iron nail
Dry cell battery

Teaspoon of iron filings
Paper clip

What should you know?

The supplies listed are for two to four students.

What inquiry questions could you ask?

How is magnetism made by electricity?

By using a wire that is carrying a current, how could you make a large magnetic field?

If you wanted to magnetize a nail, how would you do it?

TEACHER DEMO

What will students or a teacher do?

1. Obtain a dry cell battery, an iron nail, a piece of insulated copper wire, some iron filings, and a paper clip.
2. Wrap the wire around the nail several times as shown in the diagram.
3. Scrape the insulation off two ends of the wire. Connect only *one* end of the wire to one terminal of the dry cell.

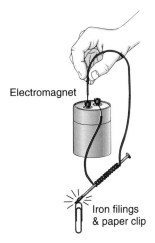

Electromagnet

Iron filings & paper clip

Safety Precaution!

CAUTION: DO NOT HOLD WIRE TO TERMINAL
FOR MORE THAN 3 SECONDS!

Safety Precaution!

4. Holding the other end of the wire along the insulated portion, touch the bare end of the wire to the other terminal of the dry cell for only a few seconds. *Caution:* Do not let the wire and terminal remain in contact for more than a few seconds because intense heat builds up, and you could get a burn through the insulation.

   What do you think will happen to some iron filings if you place them near the nail and then touch the loose end of the wire to the terminal?

5. Do this carefully, releasing one end of wire from the terminal after a few seconds.

6. Place a paper clip on the nail and repeat.

   What happens to the filings and paper clip while the loose end of the wire is touching the terminal?

   Why do the iron filings temporarily stay on the nail?

   What is temporarily produced around the wire when both ends of the wire are touching both terminals?

   What did the nail temporarily become?

   What happened to the iron filings and nail when you removed the loose wire so that it no longer touched the terminal?

   Why do they fall when you disconnect the wire?

   What must you do with the circuit to produce electricity?

   What can you say about the production of magnetism around a wire when electricity goes through it?

   What would you call the temporary magnet you made by passing electricity through a conductor? (**electromagnet**)

   How do you think you could increase the strength of the magnetism in the nail?

   What do you think would happen if you wrapped more wire around the nail?

   Will the magnetism increase or decrease? Why?

   Is the magnet you produced a temporary or a permanent magnet? Why?

   How do you know?

How could students apply their new knowledge?

Try an experiment where you test whether more turns of wire affect how many paper clips your electromagnet picks up. Collect data and set up a graph like the one shown below.

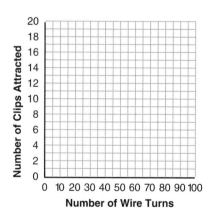

By what other means could the magnetic field around the nail be increased? What do you think might happen if you used a bigger dry cell or more dry cells connected together?

▶ How Are Parallel and Series Circuits the Same and Different? (6–8)

What concepts might students construct?

For the electrons to move in a circuit, there must be a path that is unbroken to and from the source of electrical energy.

If one lamp burns out in a **series circuit,** the circuit is broken.

In a **parallel circuit,** one lamp can burn out, but the rest of the circuit will still function.

What materials will you need?

2 dry cells	4 sockets
4 small lamps	Connecting wires
2 switches	

What inquiry questions could you ask?

In what different ways can you use a dry cell and wire to make a circuit?
How could you make a parallel or series circuit?
What would happen if one light on a string of Christmas tree lights were unscrewed? What would you do to find out?
Why is it that strings of Christmas tree lights do not all behave the same?

What will students do?

1. Connect a dry cell, two small lamps, a switch, two sockets, and connecting wires so the light works.
   What do you need to do to make the lights work?

What should you know?

The following diagram of the series circuit is for your information. It should not be shown to the students until they have completed the activity.

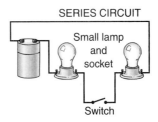

SERIES CIRCUIT

Small lamp and socket

Switch

What purpose does the switch serve?
What do you think will happen when you unscrew one of the lights?
2. Unscrew one of the lights.
   Why did the other light go out?
   What can you do to make the lights go on again?
3. Using the same equipment, rearrange the circuit so that if one light goes out, the other will still burn.

What should you know?

The following diagram of a parallel circuit is available for your information. It should not be shown to the students until after they finish this activity.

PARALLEL CIRCUIT

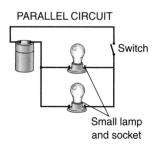

Switch

Small lamp
and socket

4. Unscrew one of the lights. If you wired it differently than the first time, one of the lights should still burn even though you unscrewed the other.
Why?
What is the difference between the two types of circuits you have constructed?

What should you know?

In a parallel circuit, there may be more than two paths for the current to take to complete its circuit. If one of the circuits is broken, the current can still use the other circuit, as indicated in the preceding diagram.

How could students apply their new knowledge?

What kind of circuits do you have in your home?
How could you find out what kind of circuit a string of Christmas tree lights is?
Examine a flashlight.
What kind of a circuit does it have?

....

LIGHT ENERGY, SHADOWS, LENSES, AND COLOR

ENGAGEMENT ACTIVITIES

▶ *How Does Light Move and Pass Through Some Things? (K–2)*

What materials will you need?

Flashlights, transparent materials (clear plastic food wrap, sandwich bags, and cups); translucent materials (wax paper, cloudy plastic); opaque materials (oaktag or construction paper, thin pieces of wood and metal); printed page of directions

What inquiry questions could you ask?

Give each student a flashlight. Darken the room and write this statement on the chalkboard, "We cannot see without light." Ask: *Can you tell what I wrote on the chalkboard? Why not? How can you use your flashlights to find out what I wrote?* Turn the lights on and discuss why light is needed for us to see things. (*Hint:* Take the flashlights away before the discussion.) Ask: *Does light move through all materials?*

What activities could students do?

Give each group of four students some samples of the transparent, translucent, and opaque materials, along with a page with print on it. Ask the students to place one kind of material at a time over the printed page you gave them. For each material, have students fill in a chart with one of these choices: (1) can see through it easily, (2) can see through it, but it is very cloudy, (3) cannot see through it.

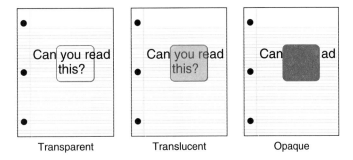

| Transparent | Translucent | Opaque |

How could students apply their new knowledge?

Make a chart like this for light sources in your apartment or house:

Room	Light source	Artificial or natural light

How could students apply their new knowledge?

Why is natural light needed?
Why is artificial light needed?

▶ *How Can You Make a Shadow Theater? (K–4)*

What materials will you need?

Flashlight or filmstrip projector, wax or rice paper, heavy cardboard or thin wood, puppets made from cardboard

What inquiry questions could you ask?

How are shadows made?
How can we use this information to make a Shadow Theater?

What activities could students do?

Have students stand in front of a source of light (e.g., a flashlight or filmstrip projector). Turn off the classroom lights and turn on the flashlight. The students will see their shadows. Explain that the students are opaque and light cannot pass through them. Shadows, then, are the result of blocked light by opaque materials. Have students make puppets from cardboard. Make a screen out of a heavy cardboard or wood frame which holds wax paper or rice paper. Shine a flashlight on the puppet that is between the flashlight and the screen, as shown in the diagram.

Flashlight

Puppet

Wax
paper screen

How could students apply their new knowledge?

How can the size of the shadows be changed?
How can you make the shadows darker or lighter?
How else can the shadows be changed?

EXPLORATION ACTIVITIES

▶ *What Does a Prism Do to White Light? (K–4)*

What concepts might students construct?

White light, when passed through a prism, disperses to form a continuous **spectrum,** or a rainbow. White light is a mixture of many colors of light. Each color in the spectrum has a different wavelength.

What materials will you need?

Prism, light source (direct sunlight, flashlight, or filmstrip projector)

What inquiry questions could you ask?	*What is a prism?* *What does a prism do?*
What should you know?	This activity should be done in groups of two or more students.

PART I   How Can You Produce a Spectrum of Colors from White Light? (K–4)

TEACHER DEMO

What will students or a teacher do?

1. Obtain a prism.
   What do you think will happen to the light rays after they pass through the prism?
2. Place the prism in the path of a strong beam of light as indicated in the diagram.

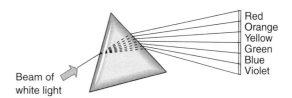

What happens to the light rays when they pass through the prism?
What colors do you see?
Which color seems to have bent the most?
Which color seems to have bent the least?
What do you know about the way the different colors of light are refracted (bent) by the prism?
What is white light made of?

What should you know?

The students should see that white light is produced by the combination of several wavelengths of light. Draw a prism on the board and have the students show how the spectrum is formed. Their drawing should be something like the previous diagram.

PART II   How Do Prisms Bend Light? (K–4)

What inquiry questions could you ask?

What do you think will happen if you look through the prism at your partner?

What will students do?

1. Look at your partner through the AB side of the prism (see diagram).

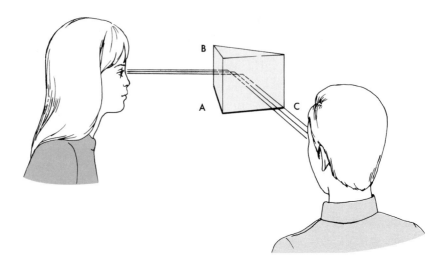

2. Record your observations.

Why is it possible to see your partner without looking directly at him?

What happens to the light entering the prism that makes it possible for you to see your partner?

What does the prism do to the light rays?

What is the difference between a prism and a mirror in the way that each affects light?

What should you know?

Prisms are used in expensive optical equipment instead of mirrors because prisms absorb less light. At the conclusion of this activity, place a diagram of a prism on the board and have the students draw how light passes through it. If they do not understand how a prism can be used in a periscope, draw and discuss the following diagram.

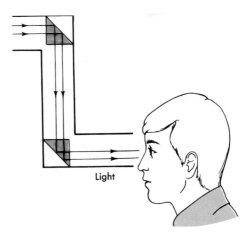

Light

How could students apply their new knowledge?	*What happens to X-rays when they pass through a prism?* *What would happen if you passed light through two prisms?* *Why are prisms used instead of mirrors in expensive optical equipment?*

▶ How Does Light Appear to Travel? (3–8)

What concepts might students construct?	To our eyes, light *appears* to travel in a straight line.
What materials will you need?	4 index cards (5 × 8 in.) Wax paper Hole puncher or pointed object (pencil) Rubber band Modeling clay Candle Flashlight Matches White paper Pie tin Comb Round (oatmeal) box
What inquiry question could you ask?	*How does light appear to your eyes to travel?*
What should you know?	You may conduct these simple activities, or students may do them by themselves, to assist them in seeing that light *appears* to our eyes to travel in a straight line. Because light appears to travel in a straight line, images appear upside down (inverted) in a camera. Focusing—moving objects back and forth—is also a result of light appearing to travel in a straight line.

PART I   Does Light Travel in Straight or Curved Lines? (3–8)

What will students do?	1. Holding all the index cards together, use a hole puncher or pointed object to punch a ¼-inch (7-mm) hole in the center of each card. Push each card into a lump of modeling clay and space the cards about 1 foot (30 cm) apart, making sure to line up the center holes as shown. *What do you think will happen if you shine the light through the first card?* 2. Shine a light using the flashlight through the first card's hole.

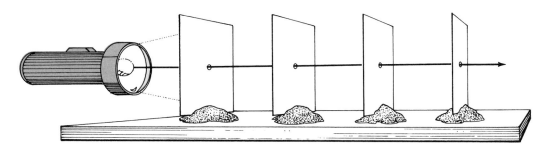

What do you notice about the path of the light?
What will happen if you move the first card 1 inch (25 mm) to one side?
3. Move the first card 1 inch to the left or right.
   What happens now?
   How is this different from what you observed in Step 2?
   What does this tell you about how light appears to travel?

PART II   What Is a Light Ray? (3–8)

What will students do?

1. Lay the flashlight flat on a piece of white paper. Stand the comb, teeth down, in front of the light.
2. Darken the room and turn on the flashlight.
   What happens to the light?
   Why?
3. Trace the light rays onto the paper.
   How would you describe the rays?

What should you know?

The rays should appear as straight lines.

PART III   How Does a Camera Work? (3–8)

What should you know?

You should demonstrate this activity for immature or unruly students. Due to the open flame, students should be carefully supervised. For older students, this activity should be done in groups of two. One student will perform the activity while the other observes, and vice versa.

What inquiry questions could you ask?

How does a camera use light?
What does it mean to focus a camera?

TEACHER DEMO

What will students or a teacher do?

1. Obtain a round oatmeal box, wax paper, rubber band, candle, and matches. Puncture a very small hole in the end of the box with your pencil. Cover the open end of the box with wax paper and secure the paper with a rubber band.
2. Place the candle (attached to the pie tin with melted wax) in front of the pin-hole end of the box and light the candle. Darken the room.
3. Move the small-holed end back and forth in front of the candle while your partner watches the wax-papered end.

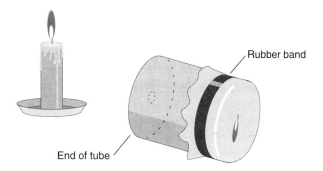

Rubber band

End of tube

What appears on the wax-papered end of the box?
What is different about the image on the wax paper?
Why do you think the image appears this way?
Why did you move the punctured end of the box back and forth?
From this activity, what would you conclude about how light appears to travel?
How do you think a picture of an object appears on the film in the back of a camera?

How could students apply their new knowledge?

What would happen to the image on the wax paper if you moved the box 3 feet (or a meter) from the candle?
What would happen to the image if you blew the candle flame out? Why?

What should you know?

After students have completed the previous activity, place the previous diagram on the board and have students draw the image of the candle. They should draw an inverted flame. Discuss how the light travels through the hole, as indicated by the second diagram, and results in an inverted image on the wax-papered end.

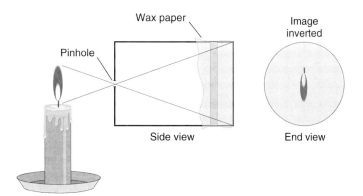

Wax paper

Image inverted

Pinhole

Side view

End view

III

Life, Ecology, and Environmental Science Activities

NSES *The National Science Education Standards state that as a result of inquiry in grades K–4, all students should develop an understanding of*

- The characteristics of organisms
- Life cycles of organisms
- Organisms and environments

As a result of inquiry in grades 5–8, all students should develop an understanding of

- Structure and function in living systems
- Reproduction and heredity
- Regulation and behavior
- Populations and ecosystems
- Diversity and adaptations of organisms

PLANT ANATOMY AND PHYSIOLOGY

ENGAGEMENT ACTIVITIES

▶ *What Kinds of Things Can We Do With Plants?*

What materials will you need?

Magazines, newspapers, colored paper, paintbrushes, poster paint

What activities could students do?

1. *Hug and feel a tree.* Have students hug a tree trunk, feel its surface, and describe how it feels. Encourage students to smell the bark. Have them draw and give a name to their favorite tree or cut pictures of trees out of magazines.
2. *Press plants.* Invite students to collect parts of plants, such as leaves and flowers. *Caution:* Stress collecting fallen plant parts only. Do not allow students to pick from

living things. Also, make sure students do not collect any parts from poisonous plants such as poison ivy. Have students press the plant parts between newspapers. Place some books or something heavy on the newspapers. After several days, remove the weights and newspapers. Discuss how drying helps to preserve the plants.

3. *Make splatter pictures of leaves.* Have students collect different types of leaves and bring them to class. Tell students to place the leaves on colored paper. Then show students how to dip brushes in poster paint and splatter paint over the leaves to make a picture outline. Have students compare the different types of leaves and what methods they had to use to make good splatter pictures. For example, ask how the thickness of the paint affected the quality of the picture.

▶ *How Can Some Plants Grow Without Seeds? (K–2)*

What materials will you need?

Small tumblers (preferably clear plastic); small sweet potatoes, white potatoes, and carrot tops (with some root); toothpicks; cuttings from coleus, philodendron, ivy, and other houseplants

What inquiry questions could you ask?

How can we get new plants to grow without planting seeds?
What is needed for new plants to grow?
How can we take good care of our new plants?

Toothpicks

Coleus and Philodendron   Sweet potato   White potato   Carrot

What activities could students do?	Put three toothpicks each in a sweet potato, white potato, and carrot, as shown in the diagram. Place the plants in small tumblers of water. Take cuttings of house-plants and place them in small tumblers of water. Put all the tumblers in a well-lit place and make sure the water levels are maintained so that the water always touches the plants. Have students observe and measure the changes in the plants, such as root development, height, number of leaves, and so on.

◖ EXPLORATION ACTIVITIES

▶ *What Is Variation? (K–2)*

What concepts might students construct?	There is tremendous variation in nature.
What materials will you need?	A variety of fallen leaves collected from home or school; ruler; large bag of pea pods; paper plates
What inquiry questions could you ask?	*How are leaves the same and different?* *How could you find out?*

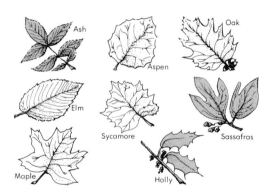

....

PART I   How Are Leaves Alike and Different? (K–2)

What will students do?	1. Collect different kinds of leaves and obtain a ruler.
	2. Place the leaves on your desk and compare them.
	     What can you say about the shapes of the leaves? How do they differ in size?
	3. Place the leaves in groups according to properties, such as color, size, kind (maple, oak, etc.), number of points, and arrangement of veins.
	     How many groups did you get?
	     Why do you think leaves vary in size, shape, color, number of points, and other characteristics?

What should you know?

Leaves may vary because of inheritance, or because of the environment in which they live. For example, the leaves of a particular species may be large if the environment in which the plant grows richly supplies the things needed by the plant.

4. Summarize how your leaves vary.

PART II How Do Seed Pods Vary? (K–2)

What will students or a teacher do?

Students: Get two pea pods, open each pod, count the number of peas in each pod, and put peas and pods on your paper plate.
Teacher: Ask who found the most peas in their pods and record this number on the chalkboard. Do the same for the least number of peas. Draw a horizontal line between the extreme numbers and divide the remaining space into equal spaces. For example, if the range is 2 to 10, mark the spaces 2, 3, 4, 5, 6, 7, 8, 9, 10.

How could students apply their knowledge?

• Have students come to the chalkboard and place an X above the number that corresponds to the number of peas in their pods. This will provide a histogram or line plot like the one shown.

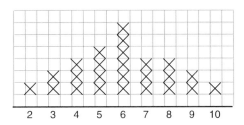

• If you open another pea pod, what might be the most likely number of peas in it? Is there a relationship between the number of peas in the pod and the pod's length?

What should you know?

You can substitute other vegetables and fruits—string beans, melons, apples—for counting and making histograms or line plots. You can guide your students to observe that seeds from plants in the same family produce identical numerical seed patterns.

How could students apply their new knowledge?

What other things in nature vary?
How do dogs vary?
How do humans vary?

▶ **What Are Seeds, and How Do They Grow? (K–5)**

What concepts might students construct?

Soaked bean seeds are different from dried beans.
A seed has different parts: the **embryo** (tiny plant), the **cotyledon(s)** (stored food), and a **seed coat** (skin). Each part is needed for the germination and growth of the plant.

PART I   What Are the Parts of a Seed? (K–2)

What materials will you
need?

1 lima bean seed soaked overnight
1 unsoaked lima bean seed
Piece of wax paper
Hand lens

What inquiry questions
could you ask?

What is a seed and what parts does it have?
How can we find out?

TEACHER DEMO

What will students or a
teacher do?

Give each student the materials listed. Ask students to respond to the following
questions, using their seeds as their sources of observation. List the responses on the
board.

How are soaked seeds different from dried seeds?
What do you think you will see when you open your seeds?
1. Open your soaked seed.
   Demonstrate for students how to open a seed.
   How does what you see compare with your hypotheses (guesses)?
2. Draw and label a picture of your open seed.

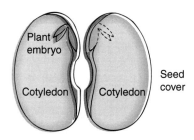

Which part of the seed do you think might grow into a plant?
What do you think might happen to the other parts of the seed?
Which parts do you think are needed for the plant to grow?
*How could you set up an experiment to test your ideas about what seed parts are
    needed for the plant to grow?*

What should you know?

This activity is an important introduction to what a seed is, what its parts are, and
the functions of those parts in producing a new plant. Activities that follow will investigate variables that affect seed germination.

PART II   Which Parts of a Seed Are Needed For It to Grow Into a Plant?[1] (K–5)

What materials will you need?

Sealable, transparent bag
Paper towel

5 soaked lima beans
Stapler

What inquiry questions could you ask?

What parts of a seed are needed for it to grow into a plant?
How can we test to see which seed parts are needed and which are not?
Which parts of a soaked bean can you remove to see if they are needed for growth?

What will students do?

1. Make a "germination bag" by lining a plastic bag with a moist paper towel and stapling the bag across its center, as shown in the diagram.
2. Prepare five soaked lima beans as follows: (1) a complete bean, (2) a bean with the seed coat removed, (3) a bean with one cotyledon removed, (4) one cotyledon only, and (5) the embryo only. Put the beans into the germination bag and number them 1–5 on the outside of the bag.

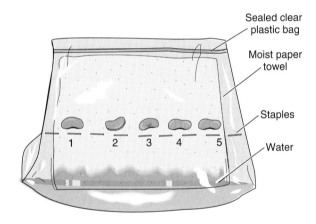

3. Put water in the germination bag as shown, close the bag, and attach it to a bulletin board, wall, or chalkboard.
4. Observe your germination bag for several days. *Note:* Open the bag daily for 15 minutes to prevent mold formation and add just enough water to keep the paper towel slightly moist.
   Which of the five seeds, if any, started to grow?
   Why do you think that is so?
   How were all seeds in your germination bag treated the same?
   Which seed or seed part grew best?

[1]For greater details and expanded directions, see "From Seed to Plant" (pp. 39–54), *Elementary Science Supplement to the Syllabus, Level 1,* 1986, Albany, NY: The State University of New York, The State Education Department.

Which parts did not grow at all?
Why do you think they did not grow?
Which seed parts are needed in order for a seed to grow?
From observing your germination bag, which seed part(s) do you think can be
    removed without stopping the seeds from growing?
Why do you think this is so?
Do all whole seeds grow? Why or why not?

How could students apply their new knowledge?

Why might seeds die after they have sprouted if they are not planted in soil?
How long might sprouts live if not planted in soil?
Why do some kinds of sprouts live longer than others?
What might happen to seeds if they remain wet for a long time?
Why do seeds not germinate if the embryos are removed?
Why will seeds die if the cotyledons are removed?

PART III   How Does Temperature Affect the Sprouting, or Germination, of Seeds? (K–5)

What materials will you need?

8 lima bean seeds
8 radish seeds
2 clear sealable plastic bags

2 paper towels
Stapler

What will students do?

1. Place four lima bean seeds and four radish seeds in two separate plastic germination bags, adding a paper towel and water to each bag, as in Part II.

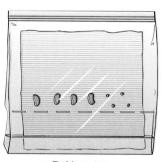

Refrigerator

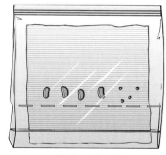

Dark cabinet

2. Put one germination bag in a cool, dark place (e.g., the refrigerator in the teachers' room or cafeteria) and one in a warm, dark place (e.g., inside a cabinet). See diagram.
    How do you think the difference in temperature will affect the germination of the
        seeds? Why were both environments kept dark?
3. Set up a chart like the example that follows. Observe your germination bags each day for 2 weeks and record your observations.
    Note: Open the bags daily for 15 minutes to prevent the formation of mold, and keep the paper towels just slightly moist.

Seed name and amount	Date planted	Germination date		Germination conditions	Number of seeds germinated
		Predicted	Actual		

4. At the end of two weeks, compare the seeds in the two germination bags.
   What differences do you notice?
   Why do you think these differences occurred?

▶ *What are Plant Growth Stages and Parts? (K–5)*

What concepts might students construct?

Plants grow from seeds to full growth in stages.
Plants have leaves, roots, stems, and flowers.
Not all plants have all four parts.
Leaves are able to make food.
The stems carry minerals and water from the roots to the leaves and flowers.
Flowers make seeds that can produce more of the same type of plant.
Some roots store food.

....

PART I   What Are the Stages of Growth in Plants? (K–5)

What materials will you need?
What inquiry questions could you ask?

Seeds germinated in germination bags from previous activities

How did our seeds grow into plants? Was there a pattern from seeds to plants?

Duplicate the following diagram. Cut and scramble the four segments for students to arrange in sequence.

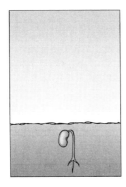   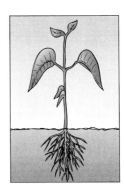

What will students do?   Review seed germination by arranging the diagrams provided by your teacher into the proper sequence. Mark "A" for the first stage, "B" for the second, and so on.

What should you know?   The progression from seed to plant *usually* follows this sequence:

A. Seed swells from moisture, coat softens and splits, and tiny root and stem emerge.
B. Upper stem breaks soil surface, and cotyledons are lifted out of seed cover.
C. Cotyledons and tiny leaves unfold. Roots deepen and spread out.
D. More extensive root system cotyledons get smaller and shrivel, and more and larger leaves develop and make food through photosynthesis.

....

PART II   How Do Roots Grow? (K–5)

What concepts might students construct?   Roots grow around objects in the soil.
Seeds need water to grow.
Roots grow downward.

What materials will you need?

4 germinated bean seeds	4 small pebbles
Paper towels	2 tongue depressors or applicator sticks
2 pieces of glass or thick, clear plastic to place seeds between	Tape

What inquiry question could you ask?   *What do you think might happen to roots if they were planted facing up instead of down, or if something were in their way?*

What should you know?   In the primary grades, this activity might have to be done as a demonstration because of the difficulty young children might have in manipulating the equipment. For older students, this activity should be done in groups of two to four students.

TEACHER DEMO

1. Place four bean seeds (that have already been germinated) between two moist paper towels. Put the paper towels with the seedlings between two pieces of glass or rigid, clear plastic. Put small pebbles under each root, place the applicator sticks or tongue depressors between the pieces of glass or clear plastic, and tape as shown in the diagram.

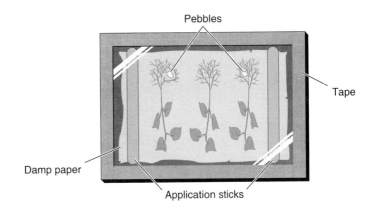

Pebbles

Tape

Damp paper

Application sticks

What is the reason for putting the tongue depressors between the pieces of glass or plastic? Why tape the sides?

What will students or a teacher do?	2. Stand the glass so the roots point up and the stems point down. *What do you think might happen to the growth of the stems and roots?*
	3. Observe the plant growth for several days and record your observations. *Was your hypothesis supported or not? Does it need to be modified?* *If you were going to do this activity again, how would you change it to make it better or more interesting?*
How could students apply their knowledge?	*How might the roots react if objects like cotton, a piece of wood, or a rock were placed in their way?* *What would happen to the roots if the glass were rotated 90° in the same direction every day? Try it and keep records of your observations.*

PART III   How Does Water Get Into a Plant? (K–5)

What concepts might students construct?	Roots absorb water through small root hairs. Root hairs are damaged when a plant is transplanted or pulled.
What materials will you need?	Radish seeds Clear, sealable plastic bags Paper towel Stapler Water Hand lens
What inquiry question could you ask?	*What could you do to determine what a root does for a plant (its function)?*
What will students do?	1. Obtain a paper towel, several radish seeds, and a sealable plastic bag. Soak the towel so it drips with water. Place the towel in the bag to make germination bag as shown on p. A-109.

2. Staple the bag across its center, insert several radish seeds, and add water. Seal and attach your germination bag upright to a bulletin board, wall, or chalkboard.
3. Observe for several days and record your observations. Use a hand lens.
    What do you notice about the roots?
    What are the small fuzzlike projections coming from each root called?

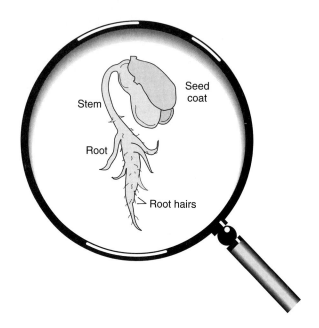

Why do you think the root has root hairs?
What could happen to the roots and root hairs of a plant when the plant is transplanted?
Why is some transplanting unsuccessful?
What would you do to determine what the function is of roots and root hairs?
What do you think might happen if you removed the root hairs from the root?
What do you think might happen if you exposed the root hairs to air and sun?

How could students apply their new knowledge?

Why are roots different shapes?
Why are some roots comparatively shallow and others deep?
How do people use the roots of plants?
What are the functions of the root, other than to absorb food materials?

....

PART IV   How Are Roots Useful? (K–5)

What materials will you need?

2 small, healthy coleus, geranium, or petunia plants
Potting soil
2 empty, clean milk cartons

What will students do?

1. Obtain two similar petunia, coleus, or geranium plants and remove all the roots from one plant. Obtain some soil and fill the bottom half of two milk cartons. Place the petunia without roots with its stem down, on top of the soil.

   What do you notice about the plant when you let go?
   How do you think roots might have helped this plant?

2. Push the bottom part of the stem to a depth of almost 2 inches into the soil. Water the plant daily. Allow it to remain undisturbed for four or five days. As a control, plant the other petunia with roots as shown.

   What do you think will happen to the plant without roots?

3. After four or five days, record what happens.

   From your observations, how do you think roots might have helped the plant?

Petunia
with
roots

Petunia
without
roots

What should you know?

Some plants might develop new roots in this situation. If they do, remove the plant and discuss the function of the newly developed roots.

··

PART V What Are the Purposes of a Stem? (K–5)

What concepts might students construct?

Water must move from the roots to the leaves if a plant is to make food and live.

One of the main purposes of the stem of a plant is to carry water from the roots to the leaves.

There are small tubes, called **capillaries,** inside the stem that carry water to the leaves.

Water moves up the stem.

What materials will you need?

Geranium, coleus, or celery stem
Red food coloring or ink
Drinking glass or clear plastic cup

Paper towel
Water

What inquiry questions could you ask?

How does water get from the roots of a plant to the leaves?
How do you think a florist produces blue carnations?
If you wanted to change a white carnation into a blue carnation, what would you do?
How could you find out if your idea was correct?

What will students do?

1. Fill a cup with water, tint with food coloring, and add a rolled paper towel, as in diagram (a).

   What do you see happening between the water and the paper towel? What is this interaction?

   Why do you think this happens?

   How does this scientific principle work in plants?

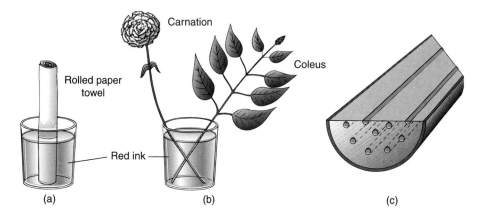

(a)   (b)   (c)

2. Obtain a geranium, celery, or coleus stem with leaves on it, some food coloring or red ink, some water, and a drinking glass. Put some water in the drinking glass and color it with the food coloring or ink.

   Important: A white flower (carnation) can be added to this activity as well. See diagram (b).

   Why do you think you added coloring to the water?

3. Cut a small slice off the bottom of the stalk of your stem and set the stem into the glass of colored water. Allow it to sit in a sunny area for two hours.

4. At the end of this period, cut open the stem. See diagram (c).

   What has happened to some of the colored water?

   What parts of the stem appear to contain the colored water? How do you know?

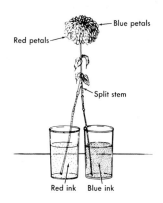

How could students apply their new knowledge?

Describe these parts.

From this activity, what can you conclude about how a stem functions?

What effects might different temperatures have on how rapidly a solution moves up a stem?

What do you think might happen if you put half of a split stem in one color of water and the other half in another color of water? (See bottom of p. A-116.)

What happens to the upward movement of water in a stem when the plant is in the dark or out of sunlight? How could you find out?

PART VI   Why Do Some Parts of Plants Grow Upward? (3–5)

What concepts might students construct?

Light and gravity play a role in determining how plants grow.

Roots respond to gravity.

Stems are affected by light.

What materials will you need?

Germinated bean seeds between glass (from Part II activity)

Sunny window or light source

Ruler

Germinated bean seeds

Potting soil

Clean milk carton

Shoebox with cover

What inquiry questions could you ask?

What do you think might happen to a plant if its light source is very limited?

What do you think might happen to the stem of a plant if it is inverted (turned upside down)?

What effect does light have on the way a plant grows?

What might happen to the way a plant grows if it were placed near a window?

What effect does gravity have on the parts of sprouting seeds?

What could you do to find out?

What should you know?

The students should suggest arranging the sprouting seeds and apparatus as shown.

Tape

Seeds on soaked paper covered by glass
or plastic wrap

What do you think might happen to the stems if you rotate the seedlings every few days?

What will students do?

1. Place the germinated bean seeds encased in taped glass or clear plastic sheets in bright light, but not in direct sunlight.
2. Keep a 1-week record of your observation of how the stems and roots grow as you rotate the glass sheets 90° each day.

What should you know?

The roots will grow down (toward the earth), and the stems will grow up (away from the earth). The plant responses that cause this are called **tropisms. Geotropism** forces roots down as auxins (plant hormones) are concentrated by gravity along the bottom cells of stems and root tips. The bottom cells in the stem are stimulated by the hormones to grow faster than cells higher up; they get longer and curl upward. Root cells are more sensitive to these hormones than are stem cells, so the root cells inhibit cell growth. Root top cells elongate faster, and root tips curve downward.

3. Graph your findings or present them in another pictorial or visual way.
   Hint: How could you use your ruler in your observations?
   What can you conclude from your data?
   What would you expect other plants and seeds to do under similar conditions?
   What results would you expect if you used different or limited light sources?
   Try this.
4. Plant four germinated bean seeds ¾-inch to 1-inch (2 cm) deep in moist soil in a clean milk carton.
5. Place the milk carton in a shoebox that has only a single, 1-inch hole cut in the middle of one end, cover the box, and turn the opening toward bright sunlight or a strong lamp, as shown in the diagram.

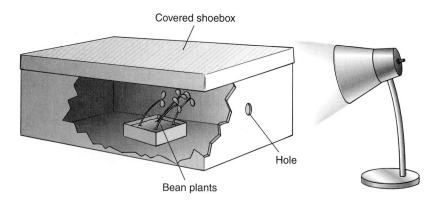

Covered shoebox

Hole

Bean plants

6. Lift the cover every 2 days and see how the beans are growing. Add water as needed.
   What is happening to the stems and leaves?
   Why do you think they are growing as they are?

What do you think might happen if you turned the milk carton with the seeds completely around?

Try it and observe what happens in 2 days. Repeat this procedure.

What should you know?	Students should see that the beans grow toward the opening in the shoebox, and when turned around, they reverse their direction of growth toward the opening again. Green plants need sunlight and are forced toward the light by **phototropism,** which causes the cells on one side of leaves to grow faster than the other. This causes the turning effect of the leaves toward the sunlight.
How could students apply their new knowledge?	*Of what value is this experiment to you?* *What other living things are affected by light and gravity?* *What are some other factors that affect the growth of plants?* *Design an experiment to test some of these factors.* *Knowing what you do about phototropism, why is it necessary to turn your plants at the windowsill every few days? What might happen if you do not turn them?*

▶ *How Is Sunlight Used By Growing Plants? (K–5)*

What concepts might students construct?	Green plants have a green substance called **chlorophyll.** Leaves produce gases and water vapor during photosynthesis. Gas will expand when heated. Because gases are lighter than water, they will go through water and escape. Water vapor from leaves condenses on plastic film. Leaves have little openings (called **stomata**) through which air enters or leaves the leaf.

What materials will you need?	Double boiler pot Water Assorted green leaves Rubbing alcohol Hot plate Rock 1″ × 4″ strip of filter paper or white coffee filter	Clear plastic cup Healthy plant growing in pot 3M Post-it® foil stars Elodea water plants 1-gal wide-mouthed jar Glass or plastic funnel Test tube	Lamp or sunlight Wooden splint Matches 2 clear plastic bags 2 small, identical geranium plants Plastic ties Hand lenses

....

PART I   What Makes Most Leaves Green? (K–2)

What inquiry questions could you ask?	*What color are most leaves? Why do you think this is so?*

TEACHER DEMO

Safety Precaution!

Caution: Because there will be boiling of water, the teacher should physically perform this activity.

What will a teacher do?

1. With water in bottom and green leaves and rubbing alcohol in top, set up double boiler pot on hot plate.
   What color are the leaves as we put them in the rubbing alcohol?
2. Heat the double boiler so that water boils for 10 minutes. Review parts of plants and discuss leaves while the water boils.
3. Remove leaves from pot and observe.
   Why are the leaves no longer green?
   What color is the rubbing alcohol now? Why?
   What do we call the "green stuff" in leaves? This is called chlorophyll.

What should you know?

Another method to find "hidden" colors in plant leaves uses the following technique, which students can perform independently or in groups.

What will students do?

1. Use a rock to rub a leaf impression about 1 inch up on a 1″ × 4″ strip of filter paper or *white* coffee filter, as in diagram (a).

Leaf   Filter paper or white coffee filter   Rock   (a)

Filter paper   Leaf rubbing   Water   (b)

2. Place enough water to cover the bottom of a clear plastic cup and fold the paper so it hangs from the cup, just touching the bottom. See diagram (b).
   What do you think will happen? Why?
3. Observe the changes.
   What happened?
   Why?
   What colors were revealed?
   Try this activity with different leaves.

What should you know?

As the water slowly rises, it hits the plant leaf "stain" and separates out some of the pigments in the leaf. This reveals the "hidden" colors of the leaf. *Note:* Using acetone (nail polish remover) in place of the water will produce better results by separating more pigments more effectively. If you use acetone, place in a closed glass jar instead of an open plastic cup.

Safety Precaution! *Warning:* Acetone fumes are potentially harmful.

PART II   How Does Light Affect Chlorophyll? (K–2)

What inquiry questions could you ask?
How do you think chlorophyll is made?
What role does light play in this process?

What will students do?

1. Select a healthy outdoor or indoor plant. Peel and stick a few foil stars on one or two leaves, while the plant is in the pot or ground and in growing conditions (has water, sun, etc.).
2. Leave stars on for 1 week.

3. Remove stars from leaves.
   What do you see?
   Why do you think this happened?
   What do you think will happen to the spots that were under the stars if the plant is put back in the sun for 1 week?
4. Do it, observe, and record your data.

Plants are green because of chlorophyll. It absorbs light energy from the sun and helps plants make food. Without sunlight, plants use up the chlorophyll, the leaf starts to turn white, and the plant eventually dies.

PART III   What Comes Out of Leaves in Sunlight? (3–5)

What inquiry questions could you ask?

What happens when your head is under water and you let some air out of your mouth? What do you see?

What do you think might happen to a leaf if it were placed under water in sunlight?

What will students do?

1. Put a water plant such as elodea in a 1-gallon wide-mouthed jar.
2. Invert a glass or plastic funnel over the elodea and place a test tube completely full of water over the stem of the funnel, as shown in the diagram.
3. Place the jar in direct sunlight for 3 days.
   What do you see coming up from the elodea plant?
   What happened to the level of water in the test tube?
   What do you think might be in the test tube?
   How might you set up an experiment to find out what is in the test tube?

Safety Precaution!

Note: The teacher or a responsible student should perform the following steps if students are too young.

4. When most of the water in the test tube has been displaced, quickly remove the test tube and insert a glowing splint or lit match into the test tube, as shown in the diagram.

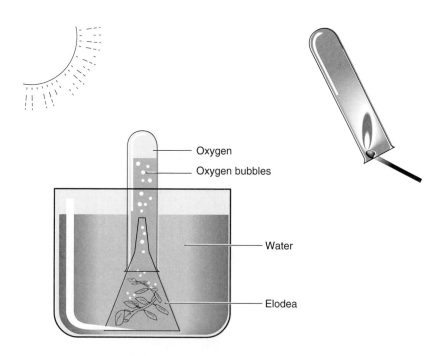

Oxygen

Oxygen bubbles

Water

Elodea

What do you see happening to the wooden splint or lit match?
Why do you think this happened?

What should you know? If students do not infer from this activity that the splint burned brightly because of oxygen given off from the elodea plant in sunlight, you can tell them. Students can be guided to see that oxygen is given off by plants during photosynthesis.

Leaves have small pores called stomata through which air enters and gases escape (see drawings).

Have students use hand lenses to view stomata.

PART IV   What Else Comes Out of Leaves in Sunlight? (3–5)

What will students do?
1. Place a clear plastic bag over one geranium and tie the bag around the stem, just above the soil level.
2. Wave a second plastic bag through the air and tie it as well, as illustrated in the diagram.
3. Put both plastic bags in direct sunlight for at least 3 hours.

   After 3 hours, what do you see forming on the top of the plant in the plastic bag?
   What do you think they are?
   Where do you think they came from?
   Why do you think the plastic was tied off above the soil line?
   How is the plastic bag without the plant different after 3 hours?
   Why do you think this happened?
   Why do you think the empty plastic bag was used in this activity?
   What is this called in an experiment? (Control)

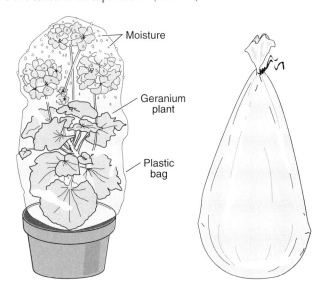

Moisture

Geranium plant

Plastic bag

What should you know?   Moisture is formed in the plastic bag with the plant as a by-product of photosynthesis in the leaves. The purpose of tying off the bag at the stem was to prevent moisture evaporating from the soil from entering the bag. The "empty" clear plastic bag is the control.

ANIMAL ANATOMY AND PHYSIOLOGY

ENGAGEMENT ACTIVITIES

▶ What Do Fish Need to Live? (K–2)

What materials will you need?   Gallon (4-liter) glass or clear plastic container (such as commercial-sized mayonnaise jar, obtainable from fast-food restaurant), seasoned water (tap water left to stand overnight to remove chlorine), gravel or sand, aquatic plants, 2 or 3 goldfish or guppies, dip net, live or dried fish food

What inquiry questions could you ask?   *What things do fish need to live?*
How can we learn to take care of our fish?
What must we do to keep the fish healthy?

What activities could students do?   Refer to the aquarium activities on pages A-174 and A-175 to find the instructions for setting up and maintaining a freshwater aquarium, using the materials listed here. Help students set up the aquarium and establish routines for feeding, cleaning, and changing the water when it becomes smelly or cloudy. Point out that guppies and goldfish can be raised at normal classroom temperatures. Discuss why the following elements are needed for the fish to live: water, plants, food, and light. Carefully remove any pregnant fish (usually identified by a swollen abdomen with a dark spot) with the dip net and place them in a separate aquarium. For older students, discuss the relationships among variables, parts of the aquarium, and the effects upon the lives of fish. For example: *How does the amount of light affect the algae in water? What is the number of fish 1 gallon of water will support, as observed by fish gulping at the top of the water? How do overfeeding and pollution of the water affect the fish? Note:* See "How does a lack of oxygen affect animals?" (page A–133).

▶ What Are the Stages That Insects Go Through? (K–5)

What materials will you need?   Jars with covers (clear plastic, if possible), mealworms (from pet shop), bran or other cereal flakes, hand lenses, spoons, pictures of people and insects at different growing stages

What inquiry questions could you ask?   *What are the stages insects, such as moths, butterflies, and mealworms, go through in their life cycles?*

What are the stages people go through as they grow?
How are the stages alike and different?

What activities could students do?

Using pictures of people and insects at different stages of growth, discuss how these living things grow. Introduce the mealworms and challenge students to hypothesize how the mealworms will grow and change in several stages. Using spoons, you or the students can transfer several mealworms and some bran or cereal flakes into a jar with a lid. Provide a jar for each student or group of two or three students. Punch several small holes in the lids for air. Have students observe the mealworms twice a week and record on a chart or log any observed changes in appearance (color, length, stage, etc.) or behavior. At the end of observations, help students make a chart comparing the stages of insects' lives with humans', like the one shown.[2]

Stages	
People	*Insects*
Child	Larva
Teenager	Pupa
Adult	Adult

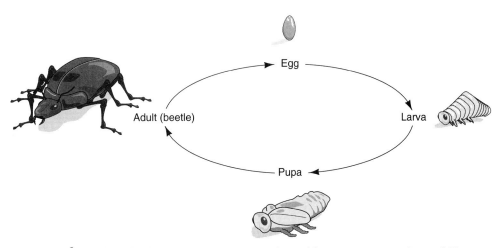

Egg

Adult (beetle)

Larva

Pupa

[2]For additional information on insect stages and record keeping, you are urged to read *Elementary Science Supplement to the Syllabus, Level I* (pp. 62–64), 1988, Albany, NY: The University of the State of New York, The State Education Department.

In addition, make a diagram with students, similar to the one shown, and include photos or drawings to visualize the stages of mealworm (and other insect) metamorphosis.

Make the same kind of diagram for stages of human life (infant, child, teenager, and adult).

EXPLORATION ACTIVITIES

▶ How Do Ants Live? (K–2)

What concepts might students construct?

Ants are social insects.
All insects have three body parts: the head, thorax, and abdomen.
All insects have six legs.
Ants are beneficial because they help keep the forests and fields clean.
There are different kinds of ants in a colony.
These different ants do different kinds of work in the colony.

What materials will you need?

Large-mouth glass jar (commercial mayonnaise or pickle jar) with screw top punctured with very small holes
Empty washed soup can
Soil to fill the jar two-thirds full
Small sponge
Pan large enough to hold the large-mouth glass jar
Sheet of black construction paper
Crumbs and bits of food: bread, cake, sugar, seeds
Colony of ants

What inquiry questions could you ask?

What do the different kinds of ants look like?
In what ways are the ants different?
How does the body of a worker ant compare with that of a queen ant?
How many pairs of legs do ants have?
What are the antennae on the head used for?
What does the egg of an ant look like?
Where do ants make their homes?
How do ants move?
How could you keep ants from leaving a jar?

What should you know?

You should become familiar with the life cycle and body parts of ants, such as shown in the diagram.

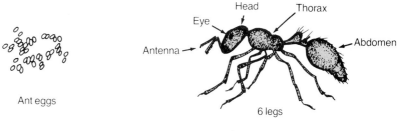

Ant eggs

Mature ant

What will students do?

1. Obtain a large-mouth glass jar with a screw cover, a clean empty soup can, soil to fill the jar two-thirds full, a sponge, a large pan, a sheet of black construction paper, crumbs and bits of food (bread, cake, sugar, and seeds), and water.

   How could you arrange these materials to make a home for ants?

   What effect will a sheet of black paper placed around the jar have on the ants? (This simulates the dark underground so ants will tunnel close to the sides of the glass jar.)

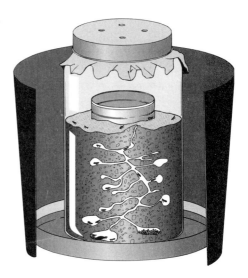

Why place the soup can in the center of the jar with soil around it to the sides of the jar? (So ants will not burrow into the center but will tunnel out to the jar's sides and be more visible)

Where might you get ants? (Pet shop or home or school grounds)

What is the purpose of placing the jar in a pan of water? (So the ants cannot escape)

2. Construct the ant home and add some ants.
3. Observe and record what the ants do.
> *How do the ants connect their homes in the jar?*
> *What might happen to the ants if they did not carry soil to the surface?*
> *What do you think might happen if there were no queen in the ant colony?*
> *What changes have been made by the ants since they were first placed in the jar?*

How could students apply their new knowledge?

In what ways are ants useful to people?
What are some other insects that live and work together?
What are some living things that are sometimes mistaken for insects?
What might happen if the ant colony were placed in a light, warm place?
How are ants different from spiders?
What would be a good description of social insects?

▶ *What Do You Know About the Birds Around You? (K–5)*[3]

What concepts might students construct?

Birds vary in color and size.
Birds sing different songs.
Birds make different kinds of nests.
Birds eat different kinds of food.
The male bird may have a more colorful plumage than the female.
Some birds migrate.
Some birds change color with the season.
Birds care for their young.
Some birds prey on other birds.
Some birds dominate the eating of food.
Birds need trees and shrubs for protection from predators.

What materials will you need?

Bird food (bread, popcorn, commercial birdseed)
Bird feeders (commercial or made in class)
Plastic cups

Small pieces of cloth
Water trays
Bird book (showing local birds)
Pictures of birds.

What inquiry questions could you ask?

Carefully record on the board the responses of students to the following questions:
> *How might we attract birds to our school grounds so we can observe them?*
> *What kinds of birds might we attract in our neighborhood?*

[3]For more specifics on bird behavior, food preferences, and relevant observational activities, see *Outdoor Biology Instructional Strategies: For the Birds Folio* 1980, Berkeley, CA: The Regents of the University of California, published by Delta Education, Inc., 80 N.W. Blvd., Nashua, NH 03063, www.delta-ed.com.

How are birds alike and different?
Where do some birds go during the winter?
What kinds of homes do birds live in?
What are some behaviors that are unique to birds?
What kinds of foods do birds eat?
Where would be the best place to set up a bird feeding/observation station on our
school grounds?
What are the names of some local birds?
What do these birds look like?

What should you know?   If the natural environment lends itself to feeding and observing birds, have students observe birds on the way to and from school, or take a class field trip to a local area, park, or zoo. In a city, you will probably see sparrows or pigeons, jays in picnic areas, ducks in ponds, geese on golf courses, and seagulls at the seashore. In addition, you may want to provide pictures of different birds, nests, and eggs for students to handle, observe, and discuss.

What will students do?   *As a result of our discussion, what would make a good bird feeding/observing area?* (Tree and shrub shelter that is free from predators and visible from the classroom) *How could we find out?*

1. Survey your school grounds and pick the best spot.
2. Find out what kinds of birds are common in your area, what their food preferences are, how they eat (on the ground or from feeders), and any other information that will make your feeding/observing most useful for birds.
3. Put up bird feeder(s) and a water tray.
4. Design an experiment or follow the suggestions provided to answer one or more of the following questions about birds. Try it.

A. What kinds of foods do different birds prefer?
Try offering small equal amounts of two kinds of food (e.g., bread and birdseed) to the birds at the same time. *Caution:* Do *not* feed birds directly from your hand; instead, place food on the ground.
   Which food do they prefer?
B. How can you get birds to come as close to you as possible?
(Offer food; be quiet and motionless)
C. Where do birds prefer their food to be put?
Put some food in such places as a birdfeeder on a tree limb or a pole, on the ground, in a plastic cup, under a piece of cloth, and so on.
   Did different birds like different places?
   What was the most popular feeding spot?

D. Does one individual bird or kind of bird get the most food?
Try to find one bird or kind of bird that seems to get most of the food.
> *How does he do it?*
> *What happens when you try to give food to the other birds?*
> *Why do you think this happens?*

E. Do loud noises or sudden movements affect birds more?
While birds are gathered, make a really loud noise, but make sure to remain perfectly still.
> *What happens to the birds?*

Now make a sudden dramatic movement, but be very quiet.
> *What happens now?*
> *Did the loud noise or the sudden movement scare the birds more? How do you*
>> *know?*
> *Why do you think this is so?*

How could students
apply their new
knowledge?

> *How can you find out more about birds?*
> *Why is it so important to continue feeding birds and supplying water once we*
>> *begin?*
> *Why is it so much fun to feed and observe birds?*
> *How are these "wild birds" the same and different from domestic (pet) birds like*
>> *parrots and canaries?*
> *How do birds help people?*
> *How might birds harm people?*
> *What are some different ways birds in our neighborhood build their nests?*

What should you know?

The following types of questions can be asked about any of the local birds. These questions may have to be modified, however, depending on the kinds of birds that are found in your region.

Redheaded Woodpecker. (1) *Where does the woodpecker build its nest?* (2) *How does it build its nest?* (3) *What kind of food does the woodpecker eat?* (4) *How does the woodpecker benefit and harm our environment?*

Hummingbird. (1) *How does the male hummingbird differ in color from the female?* (2) *Where do hummingbirds get their food?* (3) *Are hummingbirds as big as a cardinal or sparrow?* (4) *Why do you have difficulty finding their nests?* (5) *How do hummingbirds help in the pollination of plants?*

Starling. (1) *Why do many other birds prefer not to live near starlings?* (2) *What color is the starling?* (3) *How does the starling vary in color compared with the hummingbird and woodpecker?* (4) *Why do farmers dislike starlings during fruit harvesting season?*

▶ *How Do Birds Differ From Mammals? (3–8)*

What concepts might students construct?

Birds are the only animals that have feathers.
Both mammals and birds are warm-blooded.
Birds have two legs and two wings.
The female mammal has glands for nourishing her young with milk.
Mammals are more or less covered with hair.
Birds do not vary as much in structure as do mammals.
The bones of birds are somewhat hollow and light in weight.
Mammal bones are not hollow and are proportionately heavier.
Birds tend to eat approximately the amount of their weight in food each day.
Mammals do not eat as much per body weight as do birds.
Birds use considerable energy in flying and therefore need a great amount of food.
Female birds lay eggs.
Almost all female mammals give birth to live babies.
Only a few mammals, such as the platypus, lay eggs.

What materials will you need?

Live or stuffed specimens of birds and mammals or pictures of them.
Beef and chicken bones (one of each for every two students). If possible, these
    should be cut in half.
Wing bones of chickens (or any other bird).

What inquiry questions could you ask?

Give as many common characteristics of birds as you can.
Give as many common characteristics of mammals as you can.
    In what ways do birds differ from mammals?
    What could you do to compare more closely the differences between birds and
        mammals?

What should you know?

Record on the board students' responses to the previous questions. Or allow students to divide into groups and discuss the questions. Each group could report its
ideas to the class.

What will students do?

Do this activity in groups of two or more students. Encourage students to bring
specimens, alive or stuffed, to school. Perhaps a pet day or an animal show might
be arranged to make the most of this activity. Allow students to help furnish any of
the other activity materials, such as beef and chicken bones. Encourage students to
bring pictures of animals to class; place these on a bulletin board.

1. Obtain a cut chicken bone, a cut beef bone, and a wing bone of a chicken.
    How did you know which bone was from a chicken and which was from a steer?
    Examine the centers of the two bones and record how the structure of the beef
    bone differs from that of the chicken bone.
2. Look at the chicken wing bone.
    How does its structure compare with the arm of bones of a person?

3. Make a list of the characteristic ways birds and mammals differ.
4. Compare your list with those made by other members of your class. Make any corrections or additions to your list that you think should be made, perhaps including the items that follow.

Birds

Lay eggs

Have feathers

Woodpecker

Duck

Hawk

Mammals

Are warm-blooded

Have hair

Are born alive

Other mammals: man, whales, bears, deer, etc.

How could students apply their new knowledge?

What are the main structural differences between birds and mammals?
How does the structure of a feather help a bird to fly?
How does the structure of a feather help keep birds warm in winter?
What do birds do to their feathers to make themselves warmer?

▶ **How Does a Lack of Oxygen Affect Animals? (3–5)**

What concepts might students construct?

Animals need oxygen to live.
Oxygen dissolves in water. Some animals need dissolved oxygen in water.
A gas will dissolve better in a cool liquid than in a hot liquid.
Fish breathe through gills.

What materials will you need?	2 pint-sized jars with caps 2 goldfish or other small freshwater fish in a small bottle Electric hot plate on which to boil water Matches Pan large enough to boil a pint of water
What inquiry questions could you ask?	*What happens to the air dissolved in water when you boil water?* *What do you think might happen to fish if they were placed in water that had been boiled and then cooled?* *What would you do to find out?*

TEACHER DEMO

What will students or a teacher do?

The teacher may choose to boil the water ahead of time for younger students.

1. Obtain a bottle with two fish, two pint-sized jars with caps, an electric hot plate, and a large pan.
2. Heat the water to boiling and let it boil for several minutes.
3. While the water is being heated, label one jar "Boiled Water" and the other "Tap Water."
4. After the water has boiled, turn off the heat.
5. Carefully pour the boiled water into the jar labeled "Boiled Water," cap the jar, and allow the water to cool to room temperature.
    What might happen if you place a fish in tap water?
6. Fill the second jar with tap water, put in one fish, and cap the jar.
    Observe the fish's movements.
    What might happen if you place a fish in the cooled boiled water and cap the jar?
7. Place the other fish in the jar of cooled boiled water and cap the jar. Observe the fish's movements .(*Caution:* If the fish turns on its side, take it out of the jar immediately, gently shake it in the air by the tail for a second, and place it into a jar of regular tap water.)
    How did the movements of the two fish vary?
    Why did the fish in the cooled boiled water seem to vary in its movements compared with the other fish?

Tap water
A

Cooled boiled water
B

What should you know?

When water is boiled, the air molecules dissolved in it move more rapidly and escape into the air. The water lacks air as a result. Fish get the oxygen they need from air dissolved in water. When the air passes over the gills, the oxygen is absorbed by the blood passing through the gills. Fish are not able to survive in the cooled boiled water because it contains little oxygen for the gills to absorb.

> *Why did you first heat the water and then cool it?*
> *Why was the lid put quickly over the heated water?*

8. If you have not already done so, take the fish out of the jar of boiled water, gently shake it for a second or two by the tail, and place it in a jar of plain water.

> *Why is it necessary to shake the fish in the air for a few seconds?*

What should you know?

Shaking the fish causes air to pass over the gills so the fish gets oxygen from the air; the shaking also stimulates the circulation of the blood in the fish.

> *What do animals in the sea need to live?*
> *How do they get the oxygen they need?*

What should you know?

Explain to the class that air is composed of a mixture of gases and that it is the oxygen in the air that animals need to breathe.

How could students apply their new knowledge?

> *What experiment would you do to determine whether other animals require air (oxygen) to live?*
> *How could you use the gill movement of fish to show that the boiled water does not contain oxygen?*
> *Why might it be more difficult for fish to get oxygen from water containing a lot of algae than from clear water?*
> *How might water pollution, like large amounts of detergents, affect fish breathing?*

··

HUMAN ANATOMY, PHYSIOLOGY, NUTRITION, AND HEALTH

ENGAGEMENT ACTIVITIES

▶ *How Does Your Body Cool Itself? (K–5)*

What materials will you need?

2 old socks (wool or cotton are best) for each student, electric fan

What inquiry questions could you ask?

> *Why do you feel cool on a hot summer day when you come out of the water after swimming?*
> *What parts of your body are at work to cool you down when you come out of the water?*
> *Why does a fan cool us even on a hot day?*

What activities could students do?

Have students remove their shoes and socks and put a dry sock on one foot and wet sock on the other foot. Ask:

Which one feels cooler? Why?

To improve the cooling effect, use a fan to blow air over the students' feet. *Hint:* Suggest to students that they go to the bathroom before doing this activity.

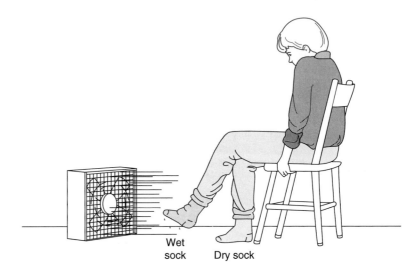

Wet sock   Dry sock

▶ *How Big Are Your Lungs? (3–5)*

What materials will you need?

Dishpan, 2 ft (60 cm) of rubber or plastic tubing, ruler, measuring cup, water, gallon jug

What inquiry questions could you ask?

How much air do your lungs hold?
Do boys have bigger lungs than do girls?
Do smokers have more lung capacity than nonsmokers?
Do joggers' lungs hold more air than the lungs of people who do not jog?

What activities could students do?

Fill the dishpan about one-quarter full of water. Fill the jug to the very top with water. Put your hand tightly over the mouth of the jug and invert it in the dishpan, making sure not to let any air get into the jug. Put one end of the tubing in your mouth and slip the other end into the mouth of the jug. With one continuous breath, keep blowing until you are completely out of air, as shown in diagram (a). *Important:* Make sure the mouth of the jug remains below water level.

When you cannot blow any more water out of the jug, slide your hand over the jug's mouth and turn it right side up. To measure how much air you exhaled, do this:

1. Pour measuring cups filled with water into the jug until you have refilled the jug, as shown in diagram (b).

2. The amount of water you use to refill the jug is the amount of air you exhaled.

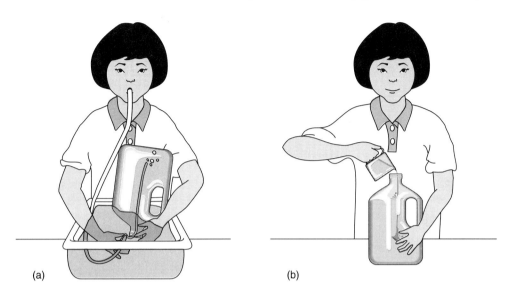

(a)   (b)

Caution: For hygienic reasons, use separate plastic tubing for each student. It is inexpensive when purchased from pet or aquarium shops.

EXPLORATION ACTIVITIES

▶ *How Do Humans Breathe? (K–8)*

What concepts might students construct?

When a person exercises, breathing rate increases.
Breathing increases because more carbon dioxide is produced.
Carbon dioxide causes the diaphragm to involuntarily work more rapidly.
When the diaphragm moves up the rib cage, it forces air out of the lungs.
When the diaphragm moves down, air is pulled into the lungs.
Lung capacity varies from person to person and can be increased by aerobic
    training.
Gases and water vapor are exhaled from the lungs.

What materials will you need?

Mirror (preferably metal)
Tape measure
3 plastic cups
Turkey baster
Plastic drinking straws
½ c or 100 cc of limewater or calcium
    hydroxide (obtain from a drugstore)

Water
Stopwatch
Plastic sandwich bag
Rubber bands
Small balloons
Scissors
Model or chart of the chest cavity

PART I   What Comes Out When You Breathe? (K–2)

What inquiry questions could you ask?	*What do you see when you breathe outside on a very cold day?* *Why do you think that happens?* *How might we find out?*

What will students do?

1. Obtain a mirror.
   When you breathe, what leaves your mouth?
   How might you find out?
2. Hold a mirror near your nose and mouth and exhale on it.

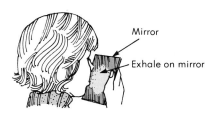

What do you see on the mirror?
Why does moisture collect on the mirror?
Where does the moisture come from?
What kinds of gases do you think you exhale?

What should you know?

Explain that exhaled air contains about 80 percent nitrogen, 17 percent oxygen, 0.03 percent carbon dioxide, and small percentages of other gases.

How could students apply their new knowledge?

What happens to the nitrogen you inhale?
What gas in the air do you need?
What gas do you exhale more of than you inhale?
How might we find out?

PART II   Does Breathing Change Your Chest Size? (K–2)

What inquiry questions could you ask?

How does the size of your chest vary when you breathe?
How might you find out?

What will students do?

1. With a tape measure, check and record these measurements.

	Top of Chest	Lower Diaphragm
Inhale		
Exhale		

2. Construct a class graph to illustrate variations in measurement among students. *Is there any observable correlation between inhale and exhale and chest measurements between boys and girls, tall and short, and so on?*

PART III   How Can We Test Our Breath? (3–5)

What will students do?

1. Obtain two clear plastic cups, a turkey baster, a straw, and 100 cc of limewater (or some calcium hydroxide). Mix half the limewater with regular water in each cup. Let the water settle.
2. Put a straw in one cup and the turkey baster in the other. *Describe how the limewater in the cups looks.*
3. One of you blow through a straw into the limewater while the other pumps the bulb of the turkey baster into the limewater.

(a) Breath in limewater

(b) Baster in limewater

What happens to the limewater as you blow (exhale) through the straw into the water?

What do you notice at the bottom of the cup after a minute or two of blowing through the straw?

Why does the water get "cloudy"?

What do you think is on the bottom of the cup?

What happens to the limewater when you squeeze the turkey baster into it?

Why do you think the limewater did not change?

Why do you think the turkey baster part of the activity is important?

What would the turkey baster part of the activity be called in an experiment?

What should you know?

When carbon dioxide is added to limewater, the water changes to a milky color because the carbon dioxide combines with calcium hydroxide to form a white precipitate. You can test the white powder that falls to the bottom by adding some vinegar; vinegar will cause calcium or carbonate to foam. The turkey baster was used to pump air into the limewater to show that air does not affect the limewater. This is our control. The variable being tested is carbon dioxide in breath.

How could students apply their new knowledge?

Why would an increase in carbon dioxide in the blood cause the heart to beat faster?

What does the following hypothesis mean: "A person needing oxygen naturally breathes faster"?

What other things would make you breathe faster? How could we find out?

....

PART IV   What Makes You Breathe Faster? (3–8)

What inquiry questions could you ask?

How many times a minute do you breathe?

How do you know?

How would you go about finding out?

What should you know?

This activity should be done in groups of three students: One does the activity, one is the timekeeper, and one is the recorder. At the completion of each activity, the students should rotate in their tasks until all have completed the activity. For exercise, students may run in place. For students unfamiliar with how to use a stopwatch, show them how it is used. Also explain that one breath is the exhale phase as a cloud forms on the mirror, and not both the exhale and inhale phases.

What will students do?

1. Do the following with two other students: Using a stopwatch, one of you counts the number of times a second student normally breathes. Do this by counting the breaths on a mirror. Let the third student record the number of times the second student breathes. Do this three times, 1 minute apart.

2. Have the student being tested run in place for 1 minute and then repeat Step 1.
3. Use this chart for recording your data.

Time	At Rest	After Exercise
1 minute		
2 minutes		
3 minutes		

4. When you finish three "At Rest" and three "After Exercise" data collections, rotate the jobs until all three of you have breathed, counted breaths, and recorded data.
   What is the average number of times per minute a person breathes at rest?
   How would you figure that?
   What is the average number of times per minute a person breathes after exercise?
5. Graph your rest and exercise record on a diagram like the one shown.

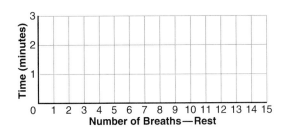

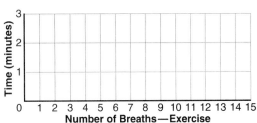

What makes a person breathe faster?
Why did you count the number of times a person breathes in three minutes rather than in just one?
What gas do you need from the air?
What do you breathe out or exhale?
How can you prove that you exhale water? (Hint: See the activity in Part I.)
What gas do you breathe from the air that your body does not use?

PART V   How Can We Make a Model of Lungs? (3–8)

What should you know?
You may wish to punch a hole in the plastic cups (see Step 3) before students begin this activity. The heated tip of an ice pick will pierce the plastic easily.

What will students do?
1. Obtain a plastic drinking straw, a small plastic bag, 2 rubber bands, a clear plastic cup, a small balloon, and scissors.
2. Cut the straw in half.
3. In the bottom of the cup, punch a hole the same width as the straw.
4. Stretch and blow up the balloon a few times.
5. Using a tightly wound rubber band, attach the balloon to the straw. Be sure the balloon does not come off when you blow into the straw.

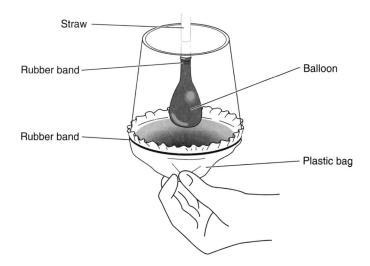

6. Push the free end of the straw through the cup's hole and pull until the balloon is in the middle of the cup.
7. Place the open end of the cup into the small plastic bag and fold the bag around the cup, securing it tightly with a rubber band or masking tape if necessary. The plastic bag should be loose, not stretched taut, across the cup's opening.
   What do you think might happen to the balloon if you pull down on the plastic bag at the bottom of the cup?
8. Pull down on the plastic bag. Record your observation.
   What do you think might happen if you push up on the plastic bag?
9. Push up on the plastic bag. Record your observation.
   Why do you see these changes?
   Where in your body do you have something that works like this?

What should you know?

Introduce the word **diaphragm.** Use a model or a chart of the chest cavity for reference. *Where do the diaphragm, lungs, and chest lie in relation to one another in the chest cavity?*

10. Diagram and label the parts of the body used in breathing, as shown in the diagram.

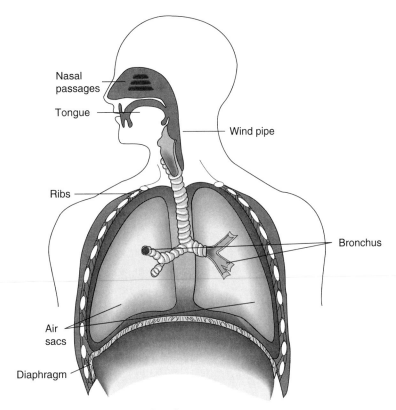

Respiratory system

▶ *How Does Our Skin Protect Us? (3–8)*

What concepts might students construct?

The skin protects us from microorganisms that cause disease.

A cut or wound in the skin can let microorganisms enter the body.

Microorganisms sometimes cause infection and disease.

A cut or wound in the skin should be properly treated immediately to prevent microorganisms from causing infection.

Antiseptics kill microorganisms; thus, they can be used for the treatment of cuts or wounds.

Heat can kill microorganisms.

What materials will you need?	4 unblemished apples 3 sewing needles Book of matches Candle on a pie tin	Rotten apple Small sample of soil 5 small pieces of cardboard for labels Rubbing alcohol

What inquiry questions could you ask?

How is the covering of an apple or an orange like your skin?
What are the advantages of the covering on apples, oranges, and other types of fruit?
How does the covering of your body, the skin, protect you?
What does it mean when a person says he or she wants to sterilize something?
In what ways might you sterilize something?

What should you know?

If open flame is not permitted in your school, or if you feel your students cannot handle it, you should sterilize the needles over open flame yourself. Otherwise, demonstrate to students how to safely do this.

TEACHER DEMO

What will students or a teacher do?

1. Obtain five pieces of cardboard for labels, a candle in a pie tin, a match, three needles, and one rotten and four unblemished apples.
2. Put the labels (a), (b), (c), and (d) on the four unblemished apples.
3. Sterilize three needles by heating them in the flame of a candle.
4. With a sterile needle, puncture apple (a) in three places. Apply rubbing alcohol over two of the punctures.
5. Push the second sterilized needle into the soil and then into three places in apple (b).
6. Puncture apple (c) with the third sterile needle, but do not apply any rubbing alcohol to the three punctures.
7. Do nothing to apple (d) or to the rotten apple.
8. Place all four labeled apples in a warm place for several days.
   Why was apple (d) not punctured?

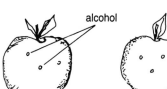

alcohol

(a) Three punctures with sterile needle; alcohol applied on two punctures

(b) Puncture with needle stuck in soil

(c) Puncture with needle but no alcohol

(d) Control (no holes)

Rotten

What should you know?

If necessary, point out that apple (d) is the control in the experiment. Be sure students understand the term *control*.

What do you think might happen if the apples stand for a few days?
In what ways do you think they will look alike?
How will they be different? Why?

9. Observe the apples daily. Every other day make a diagram or illustration of the changes taking place. Discuss these with your lab group.

What has happened to some of the apples?
How are the apples alike?
How are they different?
What do you think might have caused some of these changes?
Which spots on the apples seem to be the most prominent? Why?
Which other apple does apple (c) resemble most?
What has happened to apple (d)?
What was apple (d) in your experiment?

Safety Precaution!

10. Cut all five apples in half. *Caution:* Do not eat the apples because the rubbing alcohol is poisonous.

Which apples seem to look most like the rotten apple?
Why do you think so?
Why did you apply rubbing alcohol over only two punctures in apple (a)?
What effect did the rubbing alcohol have? What about the third puncture?

What should you know?

Rubbing alcohol is an antiseptic. The rubbing alcohol destroyed most microorganisms present in the wound.

What happened to all the microorganisms on the needles after they had been heated?
The skin of an apple is similar to what part of your body?
Why did the rotten spots seem to grow a little larger each day?

What should you know?

Microorganisms have a fantastic growth rate. As long as there is a substantial amount of food present and space enough for growth, they will continue to reproduce.

What do you think might happen if your skin were punctured?
What might a person do to a wound or puncture if he or she did not want to get an infection?

What should you know?

The wound should be cleaned, an antiseptic applied, and the wound covered with a sterile bandage.

How could students apply their new knowledge?

How might you set up the previous experiment using oranges instead of apples?
What do you think would happen?
Conduct the same experiment, but this time place the apples in a cool place.
What effect does temperature have on decay?
In what other ways does your skin protect you?

▶ Why Does Your Body Need Food For Growth and Health? (3–8)

What concepts might students construct?

Our bodies grow at different rates during different times in our lives.

Students are constantly changing in height, weight, length of hair and nails, and so on.

Food is needed for growth.

Food is needed for energy to do things in our everyday lives.

Foods contain nutrients necessary for energy, growth, and good health.

There are simple tests for identifying nutrients in foods.

What materials will you need?

Students' pictures of themselves
Pictures of malnourished children
Tape measures
Scales for weighing students
Whole shelled walnuts
Needle
Cork

Ringstand
Water
Measuring cup
Saucepan or Pyrex® flask
Celsius thermometer
Matches

....

PART I   Why Is Food Needed for Growth? (3–8)

What should you know?

Before 3 years of age, human growth is very rapid and then slows a bit. When a girl is 10 or 11, her cells begin to rapidly grow again. Boys at 13 do the same. Our bodies grow by making new cells, and these cells need food, water, and oxygen.

What inquiry questions could you ask?

Have you always been the size you are now?
Are you growing now? How do you know?
What helps you grow?
What could prevent you from growing?

What will students do?

1. Using information from your parents, fill in the chart on the next page. Attach photos of you at each year to make a timeline that shows how you have grown.
2. Look at the pictures of malnourished or starving children provided by your teacher.
   What differences do you see between these children and your pictures?
   Why do you think these children are so thin and sickly looking?
3. Keep a weekly record of your current growth. Include your height and weight and any other characteristic you want.
4. Make a list of some of the activities you engage in each day, such as running, bike riding, and so on.
   How does food help you do these things?
   How might you find out?

PART II   How Does Food Give Us Energy? (3–8)

What should you know?

Because this activity uses open flame, use your discretion as to whether you do it or allow students to do it. Guide your students to see that the unit for measuring heat is the calorie, just as the unit for measuring temperature is the degree. The **calorie** is the amount of heat needed to raise 1 gram (about half a thimbleful or 1 M&M candy) of water 1 degree Celsius. *Note:* This calorie is known as the "small" calorie. The large Calorie in food calories is equal to 1,000 small calories, and is spelled with a capital "C."

Age in Years	Height in Inches	Weight in Pounds	Photo
Birth			
1			
2			
3			
4			
5			
6			
7			
8			
9			
10			

TEACHER DEMO

What will students or a teacher do?

1. Put a whole, unshelled walnut on the point of a needle and push the other end of the needle into a cork. Put the cork and walnut on the base of a ringstand with the walnut pointing up.
2. Put 1 liter of water into the saucepan and place the pan on the ringstand so that it is 1 inch above the walnut, as shown in the diagram (p. A–148).
3. Measure and record, in degrees Celsius, the temperature of the water.
4. With the match, light the walnut until the walnut is burning well.
5. As soon as the walnut stops burning, check and then record the temperature of the water.

6. Subtract the water temperature before burning from the water temperature after the burning stopped.

   What is the difference in temperatures?

What should you know?

You can introduce the concept that the difference in temperatures indicates the amount of energy (calories) released by the walnut when burned.

How could students apply their new knowledge?

Which of the following foods, in equal quantities, do you think will give more energy?
                    bread   celery   olive oil   sugar   apple

How might you find out?

How many Calories do you think your body "burns up" each day in activities?
   How might you find out?

If you eat more food Calories than you "burn up," what might happen to you?

If you eat fewer food Calories than you "burn up," what might happen to you?

Who probably "burns up" more food Calories: a professional basketball player or a "couch potato"? Why do you think so?

What other things does food give you besides energy? How can you find out?

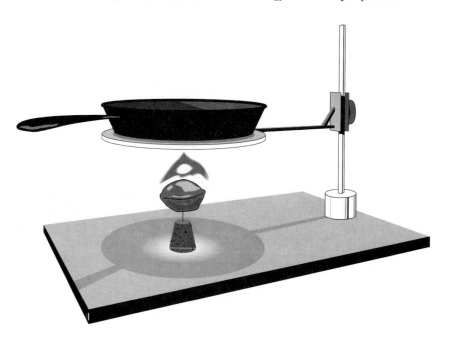

▶ *What Else Do We Need From Food, and How Can We Test For It?* (3–8)

What concepts might students construct?

Water is essential for life.

Water and these types of nutrients are needed to keep our bodies healthy and growing properly: carbohydrates (starch and sugar), fats, proteins, minerals, and vitamins.

We can test foods to see which nutrients and how much water they contain.

Because we are all different, we need different amounts of nutrients.

People who study nutrients (called **nutritionists**) suggest average amounts of nutrients. These amounts are called the Recommended Daily Allowances, or RDA.

Sometimes nutritionists recommend selecting foods from the basic food groups, such as meats, fruits, vegetables, breads and cereals, and dairy products. However, there are people (called **vegetarians**) who are very healthy and yet never eat meat or dairy products. They get their needed nutrients from other foods.

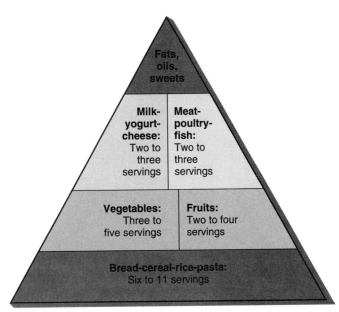

U.S.D.A Food-group pyramid

....

PART I   How Much Water Is in Our Foods? (3–8)

What should you know?

Although water is not one of the basic nutrients, you must have it every day. You could not live without it. Besides getting water from the tap, here are some common foods and the percentages of water we get when we eat them.

lettuce	95%	carrots	90%
yogurt	90%	apple	85%
pizza	50%	bread	35%

What materials will you need?

Blunt plastic knives
Weighing scale or wire hanger balance
Box of paper clips
Apples, lettuce, tomatoes
Hand juicer

Paper plates
Small paper cups
Thick white bread
Bread toaster

What inquiry question could you ask?

What will students do?

How could we find out how much water is in certain foods?

1. Using a weighing scale or the wire hanger balance shown in the diagram, weigh all foods and record their weights in the "Before" column of the chart.
2. Spread the lettuce leaves out on paper plates to dry overnight.
3. The next day, weigh and record the weight of the lettuce leaves left out overnight. Record your measurements in the "After" column of the chart.

Water Content Chart		
	Weight (in grams or paper clips)	
Food	Before	After
Lettuce		
Tomato		
Oranges		
Apples		
Bread		

Did the leaves weigh more or less than before?
Why do you think this happened?
4. Weigh a tomato and record its weight in the "Before" column.
5. Using a hand juicer, squeeze out all the tomato juice.
6. Weigh the tomato pulp (without the juice) and record this number in the "After" column.
7. Using the orange and the apple, repeat steps 4, 5, and 6.
8. Weigh the piece of thick white bread and record the weight in the "Before" column.
9. Toast the bread in the toaster, weigh it, and record the number in the "After" column.

How could students apply their new knowledge?

What foods can you think of that are eaten in both fresh and dried forms?
(Grapes/raisins, apricots, plums/prunes, etc.)
How does the shape of cut fruit pieces change when they dry out (shrink)?
How might we find out? (Cut up fruit pieces, trace their shapes with a marking pen, and compare the shapes when they dry.)

PART II What Is Starch, and How Do You Test for It? (3–8)

What concepts might students construct?

Starch forms a large proportion of the nourishing parts of wheat, oats, corn, rye, potatoes, and rice.
Starch is part of a group of substances called **carbohydrates,** which all contain the same chemical elements: carbon, hydrogen, and oxygen.
All ordinary plants are carbohydrates.
Starch turns blue-black in the presence of an iodine solution.

What materials will you need?

Paper plates
Medicine dropper
Thin slices of banana, apple, potato, white bread, cheese, egg white, butter

Cracker
Cornstarch
Iodine solution
Granulated sugar

What inquiry questions could you ask?

Which of these foods contains starch?
How might we find out?

What should you know?

Safety Precaution!

Iodine is used to test for starch. When iodine comes in contact with starch, the starch turns blue-black. *Caution:* Iodine solution is poisonous, may cause burns if it is too strong, and can stain clothing. It must not be eaten. For this reason, you may opt to dispense the iodine drops yourself if your students are too immature to safely do so themselves. In either case, point out the dangers to your students.

TEACHER DEMO

What will students or a teacher do?

1. On a paper plate, arrange and label each food sample as shown on page A–152.

2. Look at the colors of each food and record them on a chart.
3. Either the teacher or a student should place a drop of iodine solution on each sample of food.
4. Look at the color of each food where the iodine drop touched it.

How have some of the food colors changed?

Which foods have something in common after getting an iodine drop?

If starch turns blue-black in iodine, which of your sample foods would you say contain starch?

Which do not have starch?

Important reminder: Because iodine is poisonous, do *not* eat any of the tested foods or give them to pets. Dispose of them properly.

PART III   What Are Fats, and How Do We Test For Them? (3–8)

What concepts might students construct?

Some foods have a lot of fat, and others have little or no fat.

Fats that are thick (solid) at room temperature usually come from animals like cows, pigs, and sheep. These fats are called **saturated fats.**

Fats that are soft (semisolid) at room temperature usually are made from animals (e.g., lard and butter) or are manufactured (e.g., margarine).

Fats that are liquid at room temperature usually come from plants (e.g., peanut oil, olive oil, corn oil).

Fats are needed by our bodies, but too much fat can cause stomach and heart diseases.

Fats supply more than twice as much fuel and energy for the body as the same amount of starch, sugar, or protein.

Fats leave greasy spots, which is a simple test for identifying them.

What materials will you need?

Paper plates
Water
Butter
Vegetable oil
Samples of common snack foods: peanuts, bread, margarine, celery, carrots, mayonnaise, lettuce, bacon, corn and/or potato chips, pretzels, cheese, cookies, cake, apple, whole milk, yogurt, chocolate
Brown paper bags or brown paper towels cut into 2-in. squares (provide enough squares so that there is one for each food sample)
Source of light: sunlight or lamp
Medicine dropper

What inquiry questions could you ask?

Why is it important to know which foods contain fats?
How much fat should we have in a healthy diet?
How are fats alike and different?
Are some fats "better" for the body than others?
What is cholesterol and what are the latest scientific findings about it and health?
How can we test some of our foods to see whether or not they contain fats?
What are some variables that we must control in our experiments?

TEACHER DEMO

What will students or a teacher do?

Gather the class and ask:
How do you think we might test to see if foods contain fat?
List all suggestions, and then introduce this one if it was not suggested:

1. Put several drops of water on one square of brown paper, as in diagram (a). On a second square, put drops of oil (b).

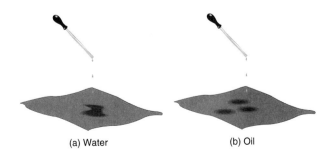

(a) Water   (b) Oil

How did the oil feel?

What should you know?

Another test for fats is that they feel "slippery" when rubbed between the fingers.
> *Describe how the stains look.*
> *What do you think will happen to the two stains after 10 minutes?*
> *Write your guesses on the chalkboard.*

2. After 10 minutes, return to the paper and check.
> *What happened to each stain?*
> *Where did the water drop go?*
> *Why are oil drops still shiny?*

What should you know?

The water evaporated, but the oil stains remained shiny. This is the spot test for fats. Have groups of two to four students conduct their own spot tests using the samples of snack foods.

3. Get a paper plate containing samples of snack foods, 17 squares of brown paper, and a copy of the Fat Spot Test Lab Sheet shown in the diagram.
4. Mark an X in the "Predicted Fat" column for foods you think contain fat.

5. Firmly rub each food sample 10 times on a separate square of brown paper, and label the paper with the food's name.
6. After 10 minutes, hold each paper square up to a source of light.
7. Mark an X in the "Contains Fat" column of your chart for each food that left a greasy spot.
> *How did your predictions compare with your findings?*
> *How would you summarize your test findings as to which foods contained the most fat?*

What should you know?

Bring the following information to students' attention: Many scientists recommend that every day we should get no more than 30% of our Calories from fat, with no more than 10% of these Calories coming from saturated (animal) fat, and no more than 300 mg of cholesterol. Discuss how students might select foods with less fat and the importance of reading food labels for ingredients.

FAT SPOT TEST LAB SHEET		
Food Samples	Predicted Fat	Contains Fat
Peanuts		
Bread		
Margarine		
Celery		
Carrots		
Mayonnaise		
Lettuce		
Bacon		
Corn/Potato chips		
Pretzels		
Cheese		
Cookies		
Cake		
Apple		
Whole milk		
Yogurt		
Chocolate		

How could students apply their new knowledge?

What might happen to people if they eat too much fat, especially saturated or animal fats?

How could we have a party, serving good-tasting foods, and still cut down on the amount of fat we eat?

Why might it be healthier to eat such foods as skim milk, lowfat cottage cheese, and nonfat ice cream?

....

PART IV   What Is Protein, and How Do We Test for It? (3–8)

What concepts might students construct?

Protein is one group of food nutrients that the body uses for building tissues and repairing broken down cells.

Proteins are very vital for children's proper physical and mental growth and development.

Proteins are made up of many **amino acids.**

Some amino acids are synthesized in the body's cells, but others, the **essential amino acids,** must be supplied through the diet.

Amino acids are found in egg whites, milk curd, wheat gluten, the muscle fiber of meat, and beans and other vegetables.

Those foods that contain all the essential amino acids are called **complete proteins;** those with only some of the essential amino acids are **incomplete proteins.**

Protein cannot be made by, or stored in, the body and must be eaten regularly to promote the repair of used body cells.

What should you know?

Tests for protein may be dangerous for some students, because they usually involve open flame or acids. Therefore, avoid the use of certain tests, do the tests as a teacher demonstration, or have more mature students (i.e., middle schoolers) do them after careful instruction and under close supervision.

What materials will you need?

Matches
Candle in pie tin
Water or fire extinguisher
Feather
Sample foods: granulated sugar or cube; 1-inch-thin slice of cooked egg white, white bread, white turkey meat, cheese, mashed soybeans; flour (for second test)

Copper sulfate
Cup with 2 tbsp water
Paper plate
Two medicine droppers
Limewater

What inquiry questions could you ask?

What is protein?
Why does our body need protein?
Which foods contain protein?
How can we test for protein?

TEACHER DEMO

What will students or a teacher do?
Safety Precaution!

1. Light the candle in the pie tin. Using a clothespin to hold a feather, put the feather in the flame. *Caution:* If students are immature, the teacher should perform this step. Check your school policy on using an open flame. Have water and/or fire extinguisher handy.

    How would you describe the smell of the burning feather?

    That smell is the same as the one produced when protein is burned.

How might we find out if burning proteins smell like burning feathers?

2. Using the clothespin as a holder, try burning bits of the sample foods.

   Which foods smell like burned feathers?

   What do you think these foods are made of?

   How else might we test for protein?

Here is another test for protein:

Safety Precaution!

1. Dissolve as much copper sulfate as you can in 2 tablespoons of water in a cup. (*Caution:* Copper sulfate is a poison, so do not taste or eat.)

2. Arrange food samples on a paper plate as shown.

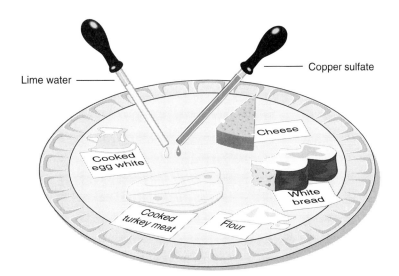

Lime water ———

——— Copper sulfate

Cheese

Cooked egg white

White bread

Cooked turkey meat

Flour

Safety Precaution!

3. Put a clean medicine dropper in the limewater and another one in the copper sulfate solution. *Caution:* After each use, make sure each medicine dropper is replaced in the proper solution. Do not mix the solutions.
4. For each food sample, do the following:
    a. Squeeze two drops of limewater on the sample.
    b. Squeeze two drops of copper sulfate solution in the same spot as the limewater on each food sample.
    What color do you see on some food samples?

What should you know?

If the mixture of the limewater and the copper sulfate solution turns violet, the food contains protein. The darker the violet color, the greater the protein content.
Why do you think some of the foods turned violet?
Why were some foods darker violet than others?
Why did some foods not turn violet?

How could students apply their new knowledge?

Make a list of high-protein foods that you and your family eat.
What do you think might happen to the quality of an incomplete protein if you mixed it with another incomplete protein, such as in dishes like macaroni and cheese, rice and beans, or bread and peanut butter? What other combinations might be tried?
Why do scientists caution us to eliminate, or drastically cut back on, animal proteins, even though they are complete proteins?

....

PART V   What Are Minerals, and How Do We Test For Them? (3–8)

What concepts might students construct?

Minerals make up a large part of our bones and teeth, which is why minerals are so important for children.
Although we need small amounts of many minerals (called *trace elements*), calcium is needed in larger quantities for bone and teeth formation.
Calcium is found in large quantities in milk and milk products and in smaller quantities in green leafy vegetables and oranges.
Vinegar (acetic acid) reacts with calcium and can be used as a test.

What materials will you need?

2 chicken leg bones stripped of all meat
2 covered jars large enough to hold the chicken bones
Soap
Water
Paper towels

What inquiry questions could you ask?

What do bones do for our bodies?
Why must bones be strong and hard?
What might make bones strong and hard?

What might cause bones to get soft and weak?
How might we test for calcium?

What should you know?

Vinegar indicates the presence of calcium or a carbonate by fizzing and bubbling. Because vinegar is a mild acid, you and your students should wash your hands with soap and water after conducting the activity. After a few days, the chicken leg bone left in vinegar will get rubbery and very soft.

TEACHER DEMO

What will students or a teacher do?

1. Pass both chicken leg bones around the classroom.
   How do the bones feel? Are they hard or soft?
2. Place a chicken bone in each jar.
3. Pour vinegar in one jar only and water in the other, cover both jars, and let stand for several days.
4. Remove the bone from the jar of vinegar, rinse it thoroughly with water, and dry it well with a paper towel. Remove the other bone from its jar of water.
5. Pass both bones around the classroom and ask:
   Do both bones feel the same?
   If not, how are they different?
   Why do you think the bone that was in vinegar is soft and rubbery?

How could students apply their new knowledge?

Why do you think it is so important for students to eat a lot of milk products?
What might happen if you did not eat enough milk products?
Why would it be healthier to eat lowfat or nonfat milk products?

....

PART VI   What Are Vitamins, and How Do We Test for Them? (3–8)

What concepts might students construct?

Scientists have discovered more than 25 vitamins our bodies need, but they believe there are many more.

The lack of one vitamin could result in a vitamin deficiency disease such as rickets, scurvy, or pellagra.

Vitamin C is probably the best-known vitamin and is found in citrus fruits, tomatoes, raw cabbage, strawberries, and cantaloupe.

We can easily test for the presence of vitamin C.

What materials will you need?

Teaspoon	Empty plastic gallon jug
Cornstarch	Iodine
Measuring cup	Ruler
Water	6 clean baby food jars
Pan	Variety of juices that are canned, frozen, or fresh:
Hot plate	orange, apple, grape, pineapple, etc.
Medicine droppers	6 wooden stirrers

What should you know?

A simple, easy-to-make vitamin C indicator liquid can be made ahead of time and will keep for several days. You will know when it is time to dispose of it, because it will lighten from its optimum color of royal blue to a very pale blue. To make 1 gallon of vitamin C indicator:

1. Boil 1½ teaspoons (6 mL) of cornstarch in 1 cup (250 mL) of water for 2 minutes.
2. Put 10 full droppers of the cornstarch mixture into a gallon jug of water, use a clean dropper to add 1 dropper full of iodine, cover the jug, and shake it until you have a uniform blue color.

When using the vitamin C indicator liquid, explain that the fewer drops of juice needed to make the blue color disappear, the more vitamin C that juice contains.

What will students do?

1. Using your ruler to measure, pour 1 centimeter (½ in.) of vitamin C indicator liquid into each of the six clean baby food jars. Label each jar with the name of the juice you will test for vitamin C.
2. Using a clean medicine dropper for each juice, add one kind of juice to each jar of indicator liquid, one drop at a time, and record the number of drops. (See the diagram.) Stir the liquid indicator with a clean wooden stirrer as you add drops.

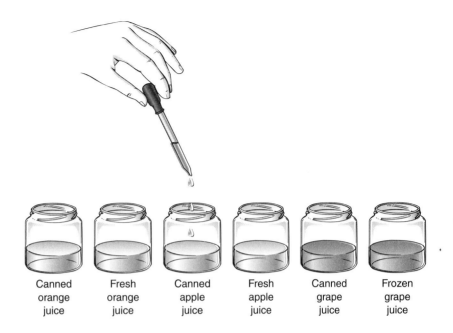

| Canned orange juice | Fresh orange juice | Canned apple juice | Fresh apple juice | Canned grape juice | Frozen grape juice |

3. When the indicator is no longer blue, the test is finished.

   Which juice(s) caused the blue color to disappear with the least number of drops?

   Which juice(s) caused the blue color to disappear with the most drops?

   From these tests, which juice(s) had the most vitamin C?

How could students apply their new knowledge?

How do you think the following conditions could affect the vitamin C content of foods: heat, sunlight, air, age of food, and so on? How could you design experiments to test these variables?

Which do you think is better for you—vitamins eaten in foods or vitamins taken in pills or supplements? How could you find out?

What might happen if you got too much of a vitamin?

PART VII   What Are Sugars, and How Do We Test for Them? (3–8)

What concepts might students construct?

Sugars are sweet substances made by green plants and are used mainly by humans for energy.

Sugars belong to a larger family of substances called saccharides or carbohydrates. These substances all contain carbon, hydrogen, and oxygen.

The chemical names of all saccharides ends in -ose. Fructose (found in ripe fruits) is called a simple sugar, or monosaccharide; mono- means it is made up of one sugar molecule. If two sugar molecules combine, they form a disaccharide; di- means two. Sucrose, or table sugar, is a disaccharide of glucose and fructose and is usually made from sugar cane or sugar beets.

An indicator for monosaccharides, or simple sugars, is TES-Tape™, used by diabetics to test for the presence of glucose in their urine.

The change in the yellow TES-Tape™ to a dark green characterizes a positive test for simple sugar.

Some common simple sugars are found in milk, honey, and ripe fruits, especially bananas. Starches broken down by chewing will also test positive for simple sugars.

What should you know?

Common table sugar will give a negative result on TES-Tape™, because sucrose is *not* a simple sugar. Other tests, such as ones using Benedict's solution or Fantastic™ cleaning solution, can test other sugars, but the teacher should demonstrate these because they require heat and the chemicals involved are poisonous. With proper instruction and careful supervision, responsible middle-school students could conduct these tests. Use your discretion.[4]

What materials will you need?

TES-Tape™ (get in drugstore)	Oranges
Bananas (fairly ripe)	Maple syrup
Milk	Honey
Different kinds of apples (MacIntosh, Delicious, Rome)	Paper plates
	Small paper cups
Table sugar, moistened with water	

What will students do?

Note: For efficiency in distribution, the teacher and/or designated students should prepare the following beforehand for each group of two to four students: paper plate containing cut samples of foods and small cups with very small samples of honey, milk, and maple syrup; 1-inch TES-Tape™ strip for each food to be tested; data collection sheet.

1. Get a paper plate that contains food samples, TES-Tape™ strips, and a data collection sheet.

---

[4]For ideas on how to perform other tests for sugars, see Robert C. Mebane and Thomas R. Rybott, *Adventures with Atoms and Molecules Book II: Chemistry Experiments for Young People and Adventures with Atoms*, 1987, Hillsdale, NJ: Enslow Publishers; Mebane and Rybott, *Molecules Book III: Chemistry Experiments for Young People*, 1991, Hillsdale, NJ: Enslow Publishers; and Jean Stangl, *The Tools of Science: Ideas and Activities for Guiding Young Scientists*, 1987, New York: Dodd, Mead and Co.

2. Assign one group member to each of the following tasks: tester, observer, and recorder.

3. *Tester:* Number each food, then write the numerals 1 through 10 on separate TES-Tape™ strips.

   Using the appropriately numbered strip that corresponds to the food being tested, touch ½ inch of the TES-Tape™ to each food separately, until the strip is wet.

   Now hand the TES-Tape™ to the observer.

4. *Observer:* Look at the wet end of the TES-Tape™. *What color is the wet end?*
   Give the following information to your recorder:
   a. the number of the sample TES-Tape™ strip,
   b. the name of the food sample, and
   c. the color of the wet end of the TES-Tape™ strip.
   Repeat the preceding procedures with all of the food samples.

5. *Recorder:* As each food is tested, record on the TES-Tape™ data collection sheet the data that the observer gives you. Attach each TES-Tape™ strip in the appropriate place on the chart.

TES-Tape™ SUGAR TEST DATA COLLECTION SHEET		
Food Samples	Tape Color After Test	Tape Strip
Orange		
Banana, ripe		
Banana, green		
Maple syrup		
Milk		
Honey		
Mac apple		
Yellow Delicious		
Rome apple		
Table sugar		

From the data collected, which foods contain simple sugar?
What evidence do you have to support this?
From the changes in the TES-Tape™ color, which foods appear to have the most simple sugar? The least?
Which foods, if any, did not change the color of the TES-Tape™?
Why do you think this happened?

How could students apply their new knowledge?

Bring in labels from food packages, read the ingredients list, and list all the forms of sugar each food contains, such as honey, brown sugar syrup, sweeteners, corn sugar, corn sweeteners, molasses, invert sugar, sucrose, fructose, dextrose, maltose, lactose, and so on.

What are some of the health problems that might develop if you eat too much sugar? Find out the amounts of sugar (both labeled and "hidden") in the common foods you eat, such as soft drinks—which can contain about 8 teaspoons per 12 ounces—or breakfast cereals—which contain about 2½ teaspoons (10 g) of sugar plus 3 teaspoons (13 g) of other carbohydrates for a total of 5½ teaspoons (23 g) per 1-ounce serving.

What do you think might happen if you tested artificial sweeteners (saccharin, Aspartame, etc.) with TES-Tape™?
Why would it be healthier to eat fresh fruit as a snack rather than cakes, candy, and soft drinks, even though all of these contain sugar?

▶ *How Can You See Which Soda Has More Sugar?* *(3–8)*

What concepts might students construct?

Diet sodas are lighter than regular sodas because of the large quantity of sugar in regular sodas (as much as 8 teaspoons or more per can!).
Sugar is heavier than water.

What materials will you need?

3 pairs of 12-oz cans of soda, unopened, assorted flavors and brands; each pair
     should contain 1 diet and 1 regular of same flavor and brand
Aquarium filled with water
Scale

What inquiry questions could you ask?

Which cans will float, and which will sink?
Are the sodas the same?
Which is heavier, sugar or water?
How do you know?
How might we test this?

What will students do?

1. Place the six unopened sodas in the aquarium filled with water.
   Do you see any difference between the cans in the water?
   Why? Do you see any pattern?
2. Weigh each can and record your data in a chart like the one shown.

Pair	Brand	Flavor	Diet Weight	Regular Weight	Weight Difference
1.					
2.					
3.					

What does your data show? What accounts for the weight differences?
How do the weights of the diet sodas compare?
How do the weights of the nondiet sodas compare?
Check the list of ingredients on soda cans to see the order of abundance.

What should you know?

The mass of a diet soda is usually about 10–15 grams less than the mass of a nondiet soda. The difference is usually sugar or corn syrup.

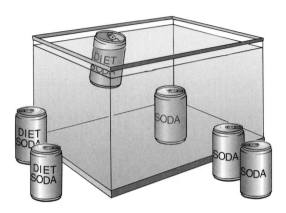

▶ *How Does Your Body Change and Use Starch in the Foods You Eat?*
(K–8)

What concepts might students construct?	Large food particles must be broken down into smaller molecules before they can be absorbed into the body.

Large food particles must be broken down into smaller molecules before they can be absorbed into the body.

The breaking down of food by chemical means is called **digestion.**

Food must be dissolved before it can be used by the body.

Starch is a nutrient.

Starch must be changed to dissolved sugar for it to pass through the lining of the small intestine.

What materials will you need?

2 jars with covers	Iodine (a small bottle with a medicine dropper)
4 cubes of sugar	Crackers
Water	Funnel
Teaspoon	Paper towels
Cornstarch	Medicine droppers
3 clear plastic cups	TES-Tape℠
Sugar	4-in. squares of wax paper
Wooden stirrers	

Safety Precaution!

Caution: Iodine is poisonous; do not allow students to handle it unsupervised. Also, iodine may stain skin, clothing, and other materials.

What inquiry questions could you ask?

How will a cracker be used by your body when you eat it?

What is going to happen to the cracker?

When will the cracker be ready to be used by your cells?

How will your body prepare this cracker for use?

If your body does not use every bit of the cracker, what is going to happen to that which is not used?

Where will your body digest this cracker?

What substances does your body contain to break down the cracker into usable substances?

PART I   How Can Large Molecules Be Broken Down? (K–2)

What will students do?

1. Pour equal amounts of cold water into two jars. Place two cubes of sugar into each jar and screw the covers on tightly. Place one jar aside and let it stand still. Shake the other jar vigorously.
2. Compare the results occurring in the two jars.

No shaking   Shaking

Why did the sugar cubes break down and dissolve faster in one jar?
What does this activity tell us about chewing food before swallowing it?

What should you know?

The more students chew their food, the more enzymes will be able to mix with the food to break it down chemically. Chewing also helps to break the food down into smaller particles so more of it comes in contact with the enzymes.

PART II   How Is a Starch Solution Different from a Sugar Solution? (3–8)

What will students do?

1. Obtain a teaspoon of cornstarch, two clear plastic cups ¾ full of water, and a teaspoon of sugar. Put the cornstarch into one cup of water and the sugar into the other. Stir each glass with a separate wooden stirrer.
    How does the starch solution appear?
    How does the sugar solution appear?

Water and sugar   Water and cornstarch

Which has dissolved? How do you know?
What do you think might happen if you let both glasses stand for a day?
How would the results of this experiment help to explain why starch has to be changed so your body can use it?

2. Stir the starch and water again until the starch is mixed with the water. Take a teaspoon of the starch and water mixture and put a drop of iodine into it to dilute the mixture to a straw color, as in diagram (a).

What should you know?

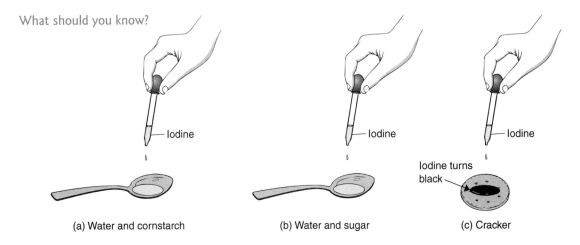

(a) Water and cornstarch   (b) Water and sugar   (c) Cracker

What should you know?

As pointed out in previous activities, iodine is used to test for starch. Starch in the presence of iodine turns blue-black.
What color does the mixture turn?

3. Rinse the spoon thoroughly and repeat Step 2, substituting sugar water for the starch and water mixture (b).
How does the result differ?

4. Put a drop of iodine on a cracker (c).
What is the result?
How does the color of the iodine on the cracker compare with the iodine in the starch and water solution?

What should you know?

The water-sugar and water-cornstarch solutions should be saved for use in Part III.

PART III   How Does Molecule Size Affect the Ability to Pass Through a Filter? (3–8)

What will students do?

1. Line a funnel with a piece of paper towel and set the funnel in an empty clear plastic cup. Stir the starch solution (from Part II) again. Slowly pour some of the

starch water into the funnel. After the water has run through the funnel, look at the inside of the paper.

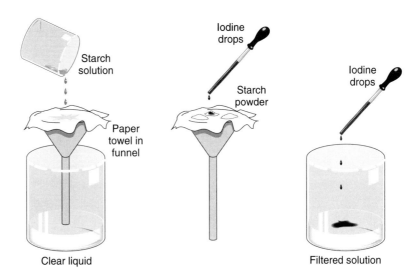

Is there any powder left inside the funnel?

How could you test to see if it is starch?

How could you test to see if there is any starch left in the water that passed through the filter?

2. Perform the test for starch in water shown in the diagram.

   What color did the mixture turn?

   Is there starch present?

   What do you think will happen if sugar water is poured through filter paper?

   How could you tell if there was sugar in the water before and after you poured it through the funnel?

   Which do you think could go through the wall of your intestine better—starch or sugar? Why?

PART IV How Does Saliva Affect the Digestion of Starch?

What inquiry question could you ask?

How can we verify that saliva begins the process of digestion by changing starch to sugar?

What will students do?

1. Test one cracker for starch by putting a few drops of iodine on it.

   What color does the spot of iodine turn?

2. Now test the same cracker for sugar by placing a few drops of water on it and then testing it with TES-Tape™.

3. Get another cracker, place it in your mouth, and chew it slowly for 1 to 2 minutes. Put a small amount of chewed cracker on a piece of wax paper in two places.

4. Test one chewed cracker sample for starch using the iodine test.
   What do you observe?

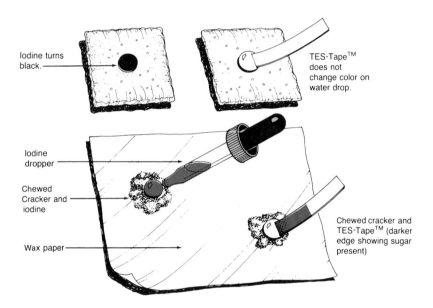

Iodine turns black.

TES-Tape™ does not change color on water drop.

Iodine dropper

Chewed Cracker and iodine

Wax paper

Chewed cracker and TES-Tape™ (darker edge showing sugar present)

5. Test the other chewed cracker sample for sugar using the TES-Tape™.
   What change do you observe?
   How has the saliva in your mouth changed the starch in the cracker?

Safety Precaution!

   Caution: Dispose of wax paper and chewed cracker samples immediately. Do not touch other chewed cracker samples.

How could students apply their new knowledge?

   How does saliva affect other foods such as poultry, fruits, and vegetables?
   Why should diabetics control the amount of starchy foods they eat?
   Test other foods for starch content.
   How might heat affect the digestion of starch?

What should you know?

   Note: At the conclusion of your study of nutrients and health, a summary chart could be made using the mnemonic Cats Wait For Mice Very Patiently, as shown here.

The Nutrient Chart

	Nutrient	Bodily Function	Food Source
CATS	Carbohydrates (starch and sugar)	Energy	Grains; fruits; vegetables
WAIT	Water	Maintenance: carries nutrients in blood; maintains temperature	All
FOR	Fats	Energy/maintenance; carry some vitamins	All
MICE	Minerals	Maintenance: regulate and maintain body functions	Fruits/vegetables, dairy products
VERY	Vitamins	Maintenance: regulate and maintain body functions	Fruits/vegetables
PATIENTLY	Protein	Growth; tissue building/repair	Meats, legumes, dairy products

ECOLOGY AND THE ENVIRONMENT

ENGAGEMENT ACTIVITIES

▶ How Clean Is the Air You Breathe?

What materials will you need?	For each group of two to four students: four 10-cm square pieces of wax paper, four 12-cm square pieces of wood, petroleum jelly, 16 thumbtacks, hand lens
What inquiry questions could you ask?	*How can we find out if air in some areas has more particles in it than air in other areas?* *Where do you think we might find these areas?* *What might account for air in some areas having more particles in it than does air in other areas?* *Where could the particles in the air have come from?* *What effect could dirty air have on your health?*
What activities could students do?	With thumbtacks, attach squares of wax paper to wood blocks and coat the wax paper with a thin coating of petroleum jelly, as shown in the diagram.

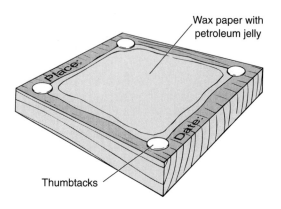

Put the wood blocks—"Particle Collectors"—outside in places where you think the air is "dirty," such as where there is a lot of bus and car travel, near airports, next to factories, and so on. Also, put some in wooded areas, such as parks, and some indoors at home or at school. Make sure no one disturbs your collectors. Write down the place you put each collector and the date.

After 4 or 5 days, bring the collectors back to class, making sure you do not touch the sticky side of each collector. Look at the wax paper with a hand lens.

Which collectors (places) had the most particles? Why?

Which collectors (places) had the fewest particles? Why?

▶ Which Materials Break Down (Decompose) Easily? (K–5)

What materials will you need?

For each group of two to four students, supply a sealable plastic storage bag that is about 10½ × 11 inches (27 cm × 28 cm), garden soil (*not* packaged fertilized potting soil), solid wastes, water, and earthworms.[5]

What inquiry questions could you ask?

What happens to our garbage after it is picked up by the garbage collectors?

Where is it taken?

Do some things break down (decompose) better than others?

What are they made of?

Do some things resist decomposing?

What are they made of?

What activities could students do?

Put about 5 inches (12 cm) of garden soil in the bottom of the plastic bag. (Do *not* use packaged, sterilized soil, because you want bacteria and insects if possible.)

---

[5]If you cannot get earthworms from local gardens or pet shops, send for *red worms* from Flowerfield Enterprises, 10332 Shaver Road, Kalamazoo, MI 49002, (616)327-7009, Email nancy@wormwoman. com. Information on composting with worms can be gotten from this activities guide: *Worms Eat Our Garbage: Classroom Activities for a Better Environment*, Flower Press, 10332 Shaver Rd, Kalamazoo, MI 49002.

Safety Precaution!

Add ½ inch (1 cm) of thin pieces of solid wastes from the garbage or from the environment, such as leafy vegetables, fruits, aluminum foil, rubber bands, wooden toothpicks, different kinds of cloth and paper, Styrofoam, and other plastic items. *Caution:* Do not put meat scraps or fats into your bag. Slightly moisten the soil, add three or four earthworms, seal the bag securely, and leave it at room temperature or near a radiator or heat source. Gently shake the bag daily.

Observe and record what you see each week for 4 to 6 weeks, then go back and answer the questions in the preceding section.

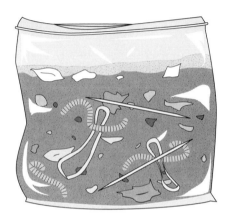

🍂 EXPLORATION ACTIVITIES

▶ *How Does the Environment Affect Living Things? (3–5)*

What concepts might students construct?

All living things have certain requirements that must be met by their environments.

A **habitat** is a place where an animal or plant naturally lives or grows.

An **environment** includes all the conditions (i.e., food, water, air, temperature, etc.) that an organism (plant or animal) needs to live.

Certain environmental factors determine community types. Different environments are needed to sustain different types of life.

A **community** is a collection of living organisms that have mutual relationships among themselves and with their environment. Some types of communities are on land and some are in water.

Land communities can be subdivided into forests, bogs, swamps, deserts, and others.

Regions with similar geography, climate, vegetation, and animal life are called **biomes.**

Ecology is a branch of science that investigates the interrelationships of organisms and their environments and looks at how all living things are connected to each other and to their environments.

Natural phenomena can change an environment, but humans are some of the most powerful change agents.

What materials will you need?	3 large, wide-mouthed, commercial-sized mayonnaise jars with lids in good condition (try fast-food restaurants) 4 cups of washed beach sand 5 small aquatic plants (approximately 3 to 4 in. or 10 cm in height) Freshwater fantailed guppy 2 water snails 5-in. or 12-cm square of fine-mesh screening material Nail Hammer Soda bottle cap 1 small cactus plant (approximately 3 or 4 in. or 10 cm in height) 2 small dried twigs (no longer than ¾ of the length of the mayonnaise jars) Chameleon, lizard, skink, horned toad, or colored lizard 4 pencils Tape Live mealworms Cup of coarse-grained gravel Several small ferns, mosses, lichens, or liverworts Small water turtle or frog Live insects or turtle food
What inquiry questions could you ask?	*What does environment mean to you?* *What are some things that live around you?* *What are some environments that you know about?* *What is ecology, and why is it important for us to know about it?* *What is an aquarium?* *What is a terrarium?*
What should you know?	All environments contain geological features, weather, climate, and living things (plants and animals), and all interrelate and affect each other. This is what the study of ecology is all about. Students should learn how to set up and closely observe an aquarium—a water home for plants and animals—and different kinds of terrariums—land homes for plants and animals. The following activities help students set up and observe closely three habitats for an extended period of time and allow them to study the ecology of each environment.

PART I   What Are the Parts of a Water Habitat (Aquarium), and How Do They Interrelate? (3–5)

What will students do?	This activity is to be done in groups of four students. Each group might be responsible for only one habitat.

1. Obtain the materials listed. *Note:* The materials listed are for all three parts of this activity.
2. Clean one mayonnaise jar thoroughly with soap and water and rinse it well.
3. Wash 2 cups of sand to be placed in the jar. Spread this over the bottom of the jar.
4. Fill the jar with water and let it stand for several days before adding plants and fish.
5. Place the five aquatic plants as suggested by the pet shop owner.
6. Place the guppy and two snails in the jar.
7. Now cover the jar with the screening material.

Food jar
aquarium

Soda bottle
aquarium

What should you know?

A simpler soda bottle aquarium can be made as an alternative. This type of aquarium is also pictured in the diagram.

How could students apply their knowledge?

Why do you think it is necessary to clean the jar before using it?

Why should the sand be washed before putting it in the jar?

What would dirty water do to the gills of the fish?

Why must the gills of the fish be kept clean?

How do fish breathe?

How could you find out?

Why do you think the water was allowed to stand for several days before the fish were placed in the aquarium?

What does our health department add to water that might be injurious to fish?

Why were the snails added to the water?

What should you know?

The snails will eat the small green algae (the slimy plants that collect on the sides of the tank).

Why were plants added to the aquarium?
What would the fish eat in nature?
Would your guppy live if it did not feed on anything? Why?
What do plants make that the fish can use?
What does the fish make that the plants can use?

What should you know?   Plants make oxygen and food, and the fish produce carbon dioxide and waste products. The aquarium is not perfectly balanced, so food must be added from time to time for the fish.

PART II   What Are the Parts of a Dryland Habitat (Desert Terrarium), and How Do They Interrelate? (3–5)

What will students do?
1. Obtain one of the large, commercial-sized mayonnaise jars.
2. Clean the mayonnaise jar and lid with soap and water and rinse them well.
3. Dry off the jar and screw the lid on.
4. With the jar on the floor, make holes in the lid by hammering the point of a nail through the lid.
5. Place the jar on its side and tape two pencils to the sides of the terrarium, as shown in the diagram, to keep the jar from rolling.
6. Spread the remaining 2 cups of sand onto the bottom of the jar.
7. Place the small bottle cap filled with water, the cactus, and one twig into the jar.
8. Place a lizard, skink, chameleon, or horned toad in the jar.
9. Cover the jar with the punctured lid.
10. Water the terrarium once every 2 to 3 weeks only if dry. Place the jar so that it receives direct sun every day. A simple terrarium can also be made from an empty soda bottle, as shown in the diagram.

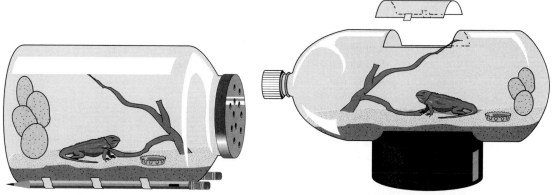

Food jar terrarium   Soda bottle desert terrarium

11. Feed the animals live mealworms (see Appendix F for feeding requirements). These can be obtained from a local pet shop.
12. Keep the bottle cap filled with water.

Why do dryland animals have such leathery skin?

Why must the terrarium be placed in direct sunlight?

Why do you think ferns or mosses would not survive in this habitat?

Would frogs or turtles be able to live in this habitat? Why or why not?

PART III What Are the Parts of a Wetland (Bog) Terrarium, and How Do They Interrelate? (3–5)

What will students do?

1. Clean one of the mayonnaise jars and its lid with soap and water and rinse them well.
2. Dry off the jar and screw the lid on.
3. With the jar on the floor, make holes in the lid by hammering the point of a nail through the lid.
4. Place the jar on its side and tape pencils or wood strips to the bottom to keep the jar from rolling.

Lid

Gravel

Tape wood strips

Bog terrarium

5. Spread the gravel out on the bottom of the jar so it will be concentrated toward the back of the jar, as shown in the diagram.
6. Place the ferns, mosses, lichens, and liverworts over the gravel.
7. Pour some water in the jar. (Do not put in so much that it covers the back portion of the arrangement.)
8. Place a dried twig in the jar.
9. Place a small water turtle or frog in the jar.

10. Cover the jar with the punctured lid.
11. Feed the turtle or frog insects or turtle food every other day (see Appendix F).
12. Place the terrarium in an area where light is weak.

How does the life found in the aquarium differ from that found in the desert and/or bog terrariums?

What kinds of conditions do the fish, turtle, frog, or lizard have to have to survive in their particular habitats?

What kinds of conditions do the bog plants require to grow well?

What kinds of food do the fish, the lizards, or the turtle eat?

What do you think would happen to the turtle if you left it in the desert habitat or to the lizard if you put it in the bog habitat?

How could students apply their knowledge?

What other kinds of environments or habitats could you make through the use of mayonnaise jars or soda bottles?[6]

What does the "environment" have to do with the kinds of organisms found in it?

What are some organisms that are able to live in many different environments?

What might happen to a fern plant if it were transplanted to a desert region?

What might happen to a penguin if it were taken to live in a desert?

What might happen to a human being if he or she were suddenly moved into an arctic region?

What statement can you make about the effect of environment on a living thing?

Complete the following chart for the aquarium or terrarium habitat you constructed, describing the food, water, shelter, and other conditions you provided for the organisms living there.

NAME OF HABITAT:	
Habitat Living Conditions	Description
Food	
Shelter	
Air	
Temperature	
Climate	
Water	
Others	

[6]For more information on building simple habitats, see: *Bottle Biology*, Kendall/Hunt, 4050 Westmark Dr., Dubuque, IA 52004-1840, 1(800)228-0810.

▶ *How Do Animals and Humans Affect Their Water Environments?*
(Water Pollution) (3–8)

What concepts might students construct?

All living things need water, and a steady supply of clean water is vital. People make their water impure or unclean (polluted) by adding such human and factory wastes as human sewage, nitrates from overuse of chemical fertilizers, pesticides and herbicides, phosphates from detergents, and so on. Because of the interrelationship of all parts of a habitat or environment, water pollution affects all living things.

What will you need?

See each individual activity for needed materials. *Note:* Some items may be used from previous activities.

....

PART I   What Are Some Effects of Water Pollution? (3–8)

What should you know?

Humans often do things, sometimes unknowingly, that result in water pollution. This water pollution can affect water environments in ways that are extremely detrimental to the organisms that inhabit the water.

You can do this activity as a teacher demonstration or group activity. For each group of four students, four jars should be set up, by you and/or by designated student helpers, 2 weeks in advance of conducting this activity.

1. Fill four containers (see "What materials will you need?") one-third full with aged tap water, ½ inch (4 cm) full of pond soil or aquarium gravel, and then fill the rest of the jar with pond water and algae.
2. Add 1 teaspoon of plant fertilizer to each jar, stir well, and loosely screw on the jar covers.
3. Put the jars near the window in good, indirect light, or under a strong artificial light.
4. Label the jars A, B, C, and D.

What materials will you need?

4 quart-sized or 2-liter clear containers (plastic soda bottles, food jars with covers, etc.)
Tap water aged for 3 to 4 days
Soil and/or gravel from an aquarium or pond
Water with algae and other aquatic microorganisms from a freshwater aquarium or a pond

Measuring cup and spoon
Plant fertilizer
Hand lens
Liquid laundry detergent (not green)
Motor oil
Vinegar

What will students do?

1. Each group has four jars that were set up 2 weeks ago. They contain pond water, algae, pond soil or aquarium gravel, and fertilizer.
   On your recording sheet, describe how each jar looks. Make sure to use your hand lens.

RECORDING OBSERVATIONS		
Date _____ Observers'/Recorders' Names _____		
Jar	Observation Before Additive	Observation After Additive
A		
B		
C		
D		

Why do you think pond water, pond soil, and fertilizer were put into the jars?
Why do you think the jars were given a lot of indirect light?

2. Add 2 tablespoons of detergent to jar A; enough motor oil to cover the surface of jar B; and ¼ to ½ cup (250 mL) of vinegar to jar C. Jar D will not have any additive and will be the control. See the diagram.

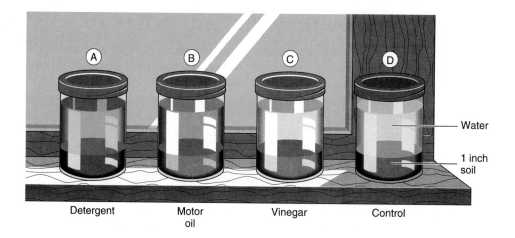

Detergent   Motor oil   Vinegar   Control

Water

1 inch soil

3. Loosely cover the jars and return them to the light as before.
   What do you think might happen in each of the jars?

4. Observe and record your observations two to three times a week. After 4 weeks, summarize your observations.
   Why do you think jars A, B, and C went through such changes?
   How could students apply their new knowledge?

How could students apply their new knowledge?	*How might you set up activities to try to reverse the effects of the pollutants used in jars A, B, and C?* *Where in everyday life do we see the effects of water pollution like that in jars A, B, and C?* *How could these effects be prevented?*

....

PART II   How Can We Try to Reverse the Effects of an Oil Spill? (3–8)

What materials will you need?	Aluminum pan Water Motor oil Feathers Paper towels	Dishwashing liquid 4 hard-boiled eggs Paper plate Very large rubber band Turkey baster

What inquiry questions could you ask?	*How difficult do you think it is to clean up an oil spill?* *How do you think it could be done?* *What is the most effective way to clean up an oil spill?* *What devastating effects does an oil spill have on the environment?*

What should you know?	Oil spills adversely affect land and water plants and animals directly by coating them with oil, often leading to their deaths. In addition, an oil spill affects future plant and animal life by destroying eggs and interfering with plant reproduction. Sometimes, the procedures used to reverse oil spills can interfere with environmental interrelationships, especially when chemicals are used.

What will students do?	Fill an aluminum pan half full of water, cover the water surface with motor oil, and use it for the following parts of the activity.

Feathers in Oil/Water

1. Leave feathers in the oil-water mix for several minutes.
2. Remove the feathers.

How do you think we might remove oil from the feathers?

Try wiping the feathers with paper towels.

Did wiping with paper towels remove all the oil?

Try cleaning the feathers with dishwashing liquid.

Which method of cleaning the oil off the feathers was better?

What other ways might we try to remove the oil from feathers? Try them.

Eggs in Oil/Water

1. Put four hard-boiled eggs (with shells on) into the oil-water mix and then remove one egg at a time after each of these intervals: 15 minutes, 30 minutes, 60 minutes, 120 minutes.

What happens to the eggs?

2. Try removing the oil from the eggs with the methods you used for the feathers.
3. After cleaning the oil off the eggs, crack and remove the shells.

Did the oil get inside the egg that was in the oil for 15 minutes? The one for 30 minutes? The one for 60 minutes? The one for 120 minutes?

Record your findings.

If oil did get into the egg, can it be removed?

Removing or Containing Oil

Using the following materials, how might you remove or keep the oil from spreading: paper towel, dishwashing liquid, turkey baster, large rubber band?

1. Lay a paper towel on the surface of the oil and let it stay for 3 minutes.
Remove the paper towel and put it on the paper plate.
What do you see happening to the paper towel and oil?

2. Add more motor oil, if needed, and spread a very large rubber band on the top of the oil.
What happens to the oil?

3. Using the turkey baster, try to suck up the oil.
What happens to the oil?

4. Squeeze the oil back into the pan of water. Add several drops of dishwashing liquid.
What happens to the oil?
Which method was best for removing the oil?
Which method was best for keeping the oil together in one place?

A Paper towel soaking up oil

B Rubber band containing oil

C Turkey baster removing oil

D Dishwasher liquid breaking up oil

How could students apply their new knowledge?

What possible problems and adverse effects might result when chemicals are used to remove oil from animals in a real oil spill?

How might an oil spill in Alaska affect people in the continental United States?

Sometimes oil spills are purposely set on fire. What adverse effects might this have on the environment?

PART III How Might We Reverse the Effects of Water Pollution by Phosphates? (3–8)

What concepts might students construct?	Phosphates, from fertilizers and certain detergents, run off the land and pollute water ecosystems.
What should you know?	Phosphates can cause an overgrowth of algae, which may kill other living things by depleting the amount of oxygen in the water and adding too much carbon dioxide. These phosphate pollutants can be cleaned using calcium.
What materials will you need?	Jar A from Part I containing pond water, algae, fertilizer, and dishwashing detergent. 2 clear jars Teaspoon Lime (from plant nursery)
How could students apply their new knowledge?	Remind students how the pond water with algae was altered by adding fertilizer and dishwashing liquid. The chemicals overstimulated algae growth. Now ask: *How do the adverse effects of too much fertilizer and detergent affect water environments?* *Can phosphate pollution of water be reversed?* *How might we do this?*

What will students do?	1. Divide the pond water from jar A equally into two jars marked 1 and 2.
	2. In jar 1, add 1 teaspoon of lime, stir well, and mark it 1—Lime Added. Mark the other jar 2—Control and do nothing to it.
	  What change do you see in either jar?
	  What do you think the white substance might be on the bottom of jar 1?

How could students apply their new knowledge?	*If overfertilization can cause phosphate pollution, how can we safely fertilize our lawns and gardens?* *How might composting food and organic scraps (like grass clippings and leaves) help with both waste and fertilizing problems?* *How might we wisely use detergents to prevent phosphate pollution?*

▶ **What Is Air Pollution, What Causes It, How Does It Affect the Environment, and How Might It Be Prevented and Reversed? (K–8)**

What concepts might students construct?	Fuels made from things that were once living (wood, coal, oil, etc.) are called **fossil fuels.** When fossil fuels burn, they give off a sooty material called carbon, as well as several invisible chemicals. Particles and chemicals in the air are called **pollutants,** and they can cause health and other environmental problems.

When smoke particles and the moisture in the air are trapped near the earth's surface, they combine to form **smog** (*smoke* + *fog*).

Statues, monuments, buildings, and other things in our outdoor environment are slowly being destroyed by pollution in our atmosphere.

We can sample our air to find air pollutants.

Cigarette and cigar smoking are dangerous for the smoker and pollute the air for others.

Gas wastes from automobiles and factories react with water in the air to form acids. These acids fall to earth in some form of precipitation (snow, rain, hail, sleet, mist, or fog) and in this form are called **acid rain.**

Acid rain is harmful to plants, animals, physical features of the environment, and people.

There are things that can be done to prevent and reverse air pollution.

What materials will you need?

See each individual activity for needed materials. *Note:* Some items may be used from previous activities.

....

PART I What Are Air Pollutants, and How Are They Formed? (K–8)

What materials will you need?

Paraffin candle
Aluminum foil pan
Matches
Clothespin
Masking tape

Safety Precaution!

If students are too young or not yet responsible enough to use open flame, you should perform this activity.

TEACHER DEMO

What will students or a teacher do?

1. Light a candle. Tell students you are going to use a clothespin to hold the pan over the candle for 20 seconds.
   What do you think might happen to the pan?
   What do you see on the underside of the pan?
2. Rub the black substance with the sticky side of a piece of masking tape.

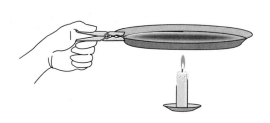
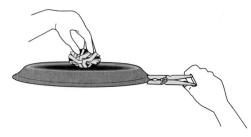

What do you think the black substance is?
Where have you seen material like this before?
Where might we find evidences of burned materials in our environment?

PART II How Might Pollutants In the Air Affect the Growth of Plants? (K–8)

What materials will you need?	Clean milk cartons 2 spray bottles

What materials will you need?

Clean milk cartons   2 spray bottles
Soil   Water
Bean seedlings   Vinegar

What should you know?

Either use bean seedlings from previous activities or plant new ones a week or two before this activity.

What will students do?

1. Get two clean milk cartons, punch small holes in the bottom, fill the cartons with potting soil, and put four to six bean seedlings in each carton.
2. Label one milk carton Water and the other one Vinegar.
3. Fill one spray bottle with water and label it Water. Fill the other bottle with vinegar and label it Vinegar.
4. Put both milk cartons in direct sunlight. Spray the Water milk carton with water and the Vinegar milk carton with vinegar, as shown in the diagram.
5. Repeat Step 4 daily for 1 week, making sure to spray each milk carton with its corresponding sprayer.
   What happened to the bean seedlings in the milk carton sprayed with water?
   What happened to the bean seedlings in the milk carton sprayed with vinegar?

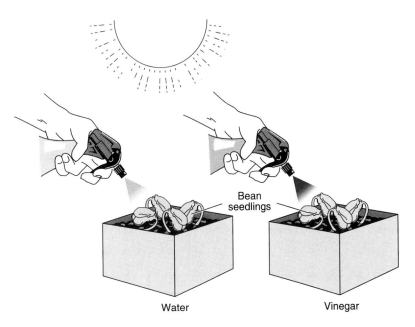

Bean seedlings

Water   Vinegar

From your experiences with previous activities, how could you find out the pH of the soils?

How is this activity related to the effects of acid rain on plants?

PART III   How Can We Find Air Pollutants in Our Environment? (3–5)

What materials will you need?

Funnels
White filter paper
Litmus or hydrion paper

Jars
Hand lens

What should you know?   This activity works best on a rainy day.

What will students do?

1. Put a funnel in a jar and line the funnel with white filter paper.
2. On a rainy day, place several jars with funnels in different spots on your school grounds.
3. When the rain stops, collect the jars and remove the filter papers.
4. Open the filter papers and allow them to dry.
5. While the filter papers dry, test the rainwater in each jar with litmus or hydrion paper.
   Why do you think we are going to test the water with litmus or hydrion paper?
       What do you think we are looking for?
   If the pH of the rainwater tested is above 7, what might that mean?
6. Make a list of all the other pH values obtained by other members of the class. Compare the findings.

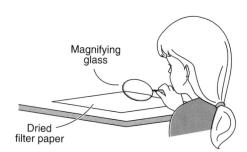

If differences are found, how might they be explained?

How might findings differ if samples were gathered from different places in your community such as bus stops, an airport, or factories?

7. Now that the filter paper has dried, use a hand lens to look at it.
   What do you see on the filter paper?
   Where do you think the residue came from?
   If you repeat this activity on a dry day, do you think you might collect more or fewer particles than on a rainy day? Why?
   Try it and compare.

PART IV   How Can We Find Out if Vehicles Pollute the Air? (3–8)

What should you know?   Safety is a prime factor in this activity. You, a parent, and/or your school custodian should work together with students to conduct this activity. When doing the actual data collection, have the driver start the vehicle with the car in park and with the hand brake on. A second adult should stay with students to make sure they are away from the vehicle at all times!

What materials will you need?

Index cards
Jar of petroleum jelly
Thumbtacks

Yard- or meterstick
Cars, school buses
Hand lens

What will students or adults do?

1. Make a chart on the back of each index card that contains the following information:

Date of testing	
Vehicle manufacturer	
Model	
Year of vehicle	
Last tune-up date	
Name of tester	

2. Fill in this information *before* testing each vehicle.
3. Then lightly smear petroleum jelly on each card to be used.
4. With thumbtacks, attach the card, petroleum jelly side up, to a yard- or meterstick.
5. Go outside, accompanied by adults, to a parking lot. While one adult starts a vehicle, you and a second adult hold the yardstick 6 inches (15 cm) from the vehicle's exhaust pipe for 1 minute. *Caution:* Stay as far away from the vehicle as possible while still holding the card 6 inches from the exhaust.

Safety Precaution!

6. Return to the classroom and use a hand lens to examine the index cards.
   What kinds of solid particles did you find?
   Do you think there might be pollutants you cannot see?
   How might a Vehicle Inspection Station give you additional information about vehicle pollutants?
   Which vehicles might give off more pollutants than others?
   Why is it important to have vehicles inspected and tuned-up regularly?

After you and your classmates have tested several buses and cars, try to answer these questions:

Does the age of the car affect the amount of pollutants it emits?
Does the size of the car and engine make any difference?
Does the kind of gasoline used (regular unleaded, high-test unleaded, diesel, etc.)
   affect the amount of pollutants?
Does the brand of gasoline make any difference?

PART V   What Is Smog and How Is It Formed? (3–8)

What should you know?

Because of the use of matches and open flame, decide if you or your students will conduct the following activity.

What materials will you need?

Warm water	Rope
Large clear glass jar or bowl	Aluminum foil
Matches	5 to 6 ice cubes

TEACHER DEMO

What will students or a teacher do?

1. Put some warm water in a jar or bowl, swish it around, and pour it out, but leave some water droplets inside to make the air moist in the bowl.
2. With a match, light a piece of rope and drop it into the jar or bowl.
3. *Quickly* cover the top of the bowl tightly with aluminum foil.
4. Place ice cubes on top of the foil as shown in the diagram.

What happens to the air inside the bowl when the temperature drops because of the ice cubes?

How do you know? (Smoke rises.)
Why is this phenomenon called smog? (smoke + fog)
In real life, what things that contribute to atmospheric smog are like the burning rope
    (vehicle and factory emissions), ice cubes (cold air inversion), and warm
    water (water vapor in the air)?

PART VI How Does Cigarette and Cigar Smoking Add to Our Pollution? (3–8)

What should you know?   This activity should be conducted by you, and preferably done *outdoors*.

                                                    Glass turkey baster
What materials will you   Cotton   Matches
need?   Cigarette

TEACHER DEMO

What will the teacher   1. Put a piece of cotton into the glass part of the turkey baster.
do?   2. Light an unfiltered cigarette and insert the unlit end into the baster's spout, as
                            shown in the diagram.
                         3. Compress and release the rubber bulb until the cigarette is completely finished
                            smoking.
                              What did you notice coming out of the cigarette?
                         4. Remove the cotton from the baster.
                              What do you see on the cotton?

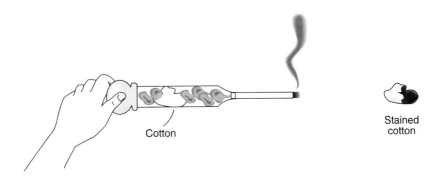

Cotton

Stained
cotton

If we did this activity with a filtered cigarette, would the results be any different?
How would you go about testing your ideas?
How would you test to see if pollutants go into the air as well as into the cotton?
Do smokers pollute the air as well as harm themselves?

PART VII   How Do Smokers Pollute the Air? (3–8)

What materials will you need?

3 index cards
Stapler
Twine

Petroleum jelly
Hand lens

What will students do?

1. Give each index card a label: *Frequent, Rare,* or *Never.*
2. Staple a long piece of twine to each card.
3. Cover each card with a thin layer of petroleum jelly.
4. Following the labels you used in Step 1, hang each card from the ceiling in a room where:
    a. people *frequently* smoke cigarettes,
    b. people *rarely* smoke cigarettes, or
    c. people *never* smoke cigarettes.
5. After 1 week, collect all the cards and bring them back to the classroom. Examine with a hand lens.
    Using a hand lens, what do you see on each card?
    What differences do you see between cards from smoking and nonsmoking rooms?
    What do you think might cause the difference?
    What does this activity tell you about how smoking cigarettes might affect others as well as smokers themselves?

PART VIII   How Does Air Pollution Affect the Physical Things in an Environment? (3–8)

What materials will you need?

Small squares of wood
Various colors and types of paint (water-based, oil-based, acrylic, etc.)
2 plastic garbage bags

What should you know?

After the garbage bags are filled full of painted squares, ask one of the school bus drivers to fill the bags with bus exhaust.

What will students or the bus driver do?

1. Paint the small wooden squares with a variety of paints and colors.
2. After the squares are dry, on the back of each square record the colors and types of paint used.
3. Place half of the squares of wood inside one large plastic garbage bag and half in a second garbage bag.
4. Have the school bus driver fill the garbage bags with bus exhaust and fasten the bags quickly and tightly to retain the fumes.
5. At the end of 1 week, check the pieces of wood in one garbage bag.
    What changes, if any, do you see?

How could students apply their new knowledge?

6. At the end of 2 weeks, check the pieces of wood in the other garbage bag.
    What changes, if any, do you see?
    How do the pieces of wood that were in the bag for 1 week compare to those that were in for 2 weeks?
    What were the changes?
    What caused this to happen?
    Based on your observations in this activity, why do you think we have to paint our buildings so often?

PART IX   What Are Some Ways to Clean Polluted Air? (3–8)

What materials will you need?

Disposable vacuum bag full of dust
Large metal bucket
Plant sprayer with water

What should you know?

Discuss how some industries have soot and dust rising from them all the time. Some industries burn garbage too. They must use pollution-control devices to clean the air in their smokestacks. One of these devices is the **scrubber,** which removes dirt particles and most of the poisonous sulfur and nitrogen oxides from the soot. A scrubber sprays a liquid on the pollutants, trapping them, then carries the pollutants away before they can go out of the smokestack. The liquid and pollutants form a thick liquid or paste known as **sludge.** This sludge is then treated with a chemical and made into nonpolluting cakes. Researchers are trying to turn these cakes into building materials to recycle them.

Do this activity yourself, outdoors, and make sure students are upwind to avoid the dust.

TEACHER DEMO

What will the teacher do?

1. Go out to a spot on the playground that is far away from the school building.
2. Slowly pour dust from the vacuum bag into the bucket. As the dust falls, squirt it gently with water from the plant sprayer. Do not use a hard, fast water jet.
    What happens to the dust?
    How is the wet dust, called sludge, now less polluting than when it was dry?
    How do you think this process is used to keep soot and dust from escaping from factory smokestacks?
    What do you think can be done with the dried sludge?

PART X   What Can We Do to Control Air Pollution in Our Environment? (3–8)

What materials will you need?

Low-level-light houseplants: spider plants, golden pothos, azaleas, mums, Dracaenas, bamboo, ficus

What should you know?   NASA and other scientific groups have found that houseplants are excellent filters of indoor pollution because they take in pollutants and trap them in the soil. The plants listed above are especially suited for this purpose and are ideal for school. They tolerate low light conditions, dryness, and periods of neglect, such as vacation periods. For a free fact sheet about plants that have proved to be effective air cleaners, send a self-addressed, stamped envelope to the Foliage for Clean Air Council, 4405 N. Washington St., Falls Church, VA 22046.

What inquiry questions could you ask?   *What are some ways we could clean the air in our classroom?*
Discuss ways of cutting indoor air pollution and recommend growing plants if students do not suggest it.
How can we find out which plants are best for cleaning indoor air and how to care for these plants?

What will students do?   1. Make a list of the most desirable air-cleaning plants and collect as many as you can by buying them, bringing in plants from home, asking local plant nurseries to donate plants and/or cuttings, and so on.
2. Find the best places in the classroom for each particular plant.

How could students apply their new knowledge?   *If a minimum of one 12-inch-tall plant is recommended for every 100 square feet of floor surface, how many air-cleaning plants should we have in our classroom?*
What other kinds of air-cleaning plants might we consider for our classroom?
Why would mixing fish-tank-filter charcoal with the soil in our air-cleaning plants help filter out air pollutants?
Why is NASA so interested in researching plants that filter air pollutants?

Earth and Space Science Activities

NSES *The National Science Education Standards state that as a result of their activities in grades K–4, all students should develop an understanding of*

- Properties of earth materials
- Objects in the sky
- Changes in earth and sky

As a result of their activities in grades 5–8, all students should develop an understanding of

- Structure of the earth system
- Earth's history
- Earth in the solar system

....

ASTRONOMY (EARTH IN SPACE)

🌊 ENGAGEMENT ACTIVITIES

▶ **What Causes Shadows, and How Can They Be Changed? (K–2)**

What materials will you need?

Flashlight, 2 pieces of white paper, scissors, paste, funnel, pencil or crayon

What inquiry questions could you ask?

What are shadows, and how are they formed?
How can you make shadows larger or smaller?
What are some of the things (variables) that affect the size of shadows?
Why do shadows change shape and size during the day?

What activities could students do?

Work with a partner. Put a funnel on a large sheet of white paper. One of you should shine the flashlight on the funnel while the other one traces and cuts the shadow out with scissors, in this sequence.

1. First, while holding the flashlight low, trace and cut out the shadow of the funnel.
2. Next, put a new piece of white paper under the funnel, hold the flashlight high, and then trace and cut out the shadow of the funnel.
3. Compare the size and shape of the two cut-out shadows.

Why do you think the shadow was longer when the flashlight was held low? During what part(s) of the day do shadows look this way outdoors?

▶ *How Can Shadows Help You Tell Time? (K–2)*

What materials will you need?

For each student or group of 2 to 4 students: Long nail, hammer, 8½″ × 11″ pieces of white paper, square board big enough to hold the paper, pencil

What inquiry questions could you ask?

Do you think that shadows outdoors change during the day? How might we find out? If shadows change, at what time will they be the shortest? The longest? Why do you think so?

What activities could students do?

Put a piece of paper in the middle of the board and drive the nail into the board and paper as shown, making sure the nail will not easily come out of the board.

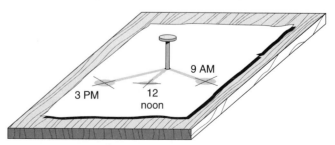

Place the board where it will get sunlight all day. Every hour, draw an X at the tip of the shadow cast by the nail. Write down the time you marked the X as well. Repeat this activity with a new piece of paper every school day for 1 week, keeping the board in exactly the same spot. At the end of the week, assist students in answering these questions:

At what times during the day were the shadows the longest? The shortest? Were these times the same each day?

EXPLORATION ACTIVITIES

▶ Why Is There Day and Night? (K–2)

What concepts might students construct?

The earth **rotates,** or turns around.

The earth rotates from west to east.

It takes 24 hours for the earth to make one complete turn or rotation. The rotation of the earth explains why part of the 24-hour period is night and part is day.

The sun is always shining, even when it is night and you cannot see the sun.

What materials will you need?

Clay or Styrofoam ball   Strong flashlight or filmstrip projector
Knitting needle   Pin

What inquiry questions could you ask?

When it is daytime here, where is it night?
When it is night here, where is it day?
What could you do to find out about daytime and nighttime on the earth?

What will students do?

1. Make a clay ball as large as a baseball; use it as a model of the earth. A Styrofoam ball may be used instead.
   In what way do you think the ball is like the earth?
2. Push the knitting needle through the clay or Styrofoam globe. Darken the room. Let the flashlight or filmstrip projector, which represents the sun, shine on the ball.
   What side of the earth (ball) do you think is having night?
   What side of the globe do you think is having day?
   What tells you that the sun is always shining somewhere on the earth?

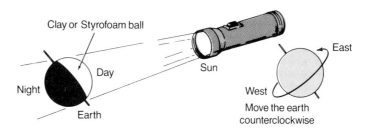

3. Stick a pin in the ball to represent the place where you live. Turn the ball slowly in a counterclockwise motion.

Using the clay or Styrofoam ball, how could you make night come to the place where you live?

What should you know?

The ball, representing the earth, is turned slowly counterclockwise to show where night would begin to fall and where it would be midnight and sunrise.

What time of day is it when your pin is on the same side as the sun?
When your pin is away from the sun, what time of day would it be?

How could students apply their new knowledge?

What would happen if the earth did not turn?
If the earth did not turn, which side would you rather be on? Why?
Why is it inaccurate to say the sun "rises" in the east and "sets" in the west?
If it is 9 A.M. in New York City, what time will it be in San Francisco?

▶ Why Does the Moon Shine? (3–5)

What concepts might students construct?

Objects are seen when they give off their own light or when they reflect light from another source.
The moon does not give off its own light. Its light is reflected light from the sun.

What materials will you need?

Large ball
1-in. diameter ball of foil, with attached string
Masking tape
Box with tight-fitting lid (shoebox) lined with dull black paper
Flashlight
2-in. diameter Styrofoam ball, with attached string

What inquiry questions could you ask?

Darken the room, place a ball on the table, and ask:
What is on the table?
What do you need to be able to see the object?
Turn on the lights.
Why do you see the ball now?
Do you see it because it is giving off its own light or because it is reflecting light from some other source?
Look at the ceiling lights.
Why is it possible for you to see the lights? How is this light different from the light you see when you look at the ball?
Darken the room.
What are two reasons why you may not see any lights in the room?
How do you think the moon shines?
What is reflected light?

What will students do?

1. Suspend the foil ball on a 1-inch string from inside the box lid lined with dull black paper, as shown in the diagram. Insert the flashlight in the end of the box and seal any space around it with masking tape. Make a small eyehole under the flashlight.

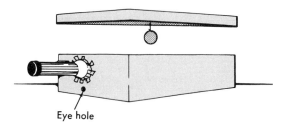

Eye hole

2. Put on the lid and seal the edges around the lid with tape.
   What do you see when you look through the eyehole? Why?
3. Turn on the flashlight.
   What do you see when you look through the eyehole? Why?
   Do you see the ball because it reflects light or because it gives off its own light?
   What two kinds of light do you see?
   What is the source of each kind of light?
4. Look out the window.
   Why are you able to see some objects?
   What is the source of light?
   Do the objects seen outside the window give off reflected light or light of their own?
   What does the sun give off?
   Why does the moon shine?
5. Obtain a Styrofoam ball that has an attached string. Use your box, flashlight, and suspended foil ball but add the larger Styrofoam ball, suspending it 2 inches from the top, as shown in the diagram. Seal the edges of the box again. Then seal the old eyehole and make a new eyehole in the side of the box, as indicated in the drawing.

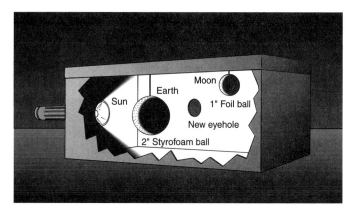

If the small ball is the moon, what does the flashlight represent?

6. Turn on the flashlight and look through the new eyehole in the side of the box. *What does the large ball represent?*

7. Look at the ball representing the earth and tell which side is day and which side is night.

On which side would you be if you could see the moon?

How is it possible for you to see the moon if you are on the dark side of the earth?

Why does the moon shine?

How could students apply their new knowledge?

If you lived on another planet, would you be able to see earth?

What are the positions of the sun, moon, and earth (a) when it is night for you and (b) when it is day for you, as shown in the diagram?

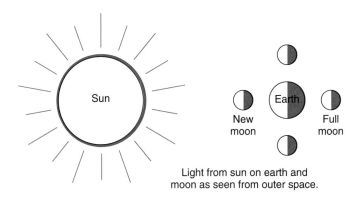

Light from sun on earth and moon as seen from outer space.

▶ **Why Does It Appear That There Are Phases of the Moon? (3–5)**

What concepts might students construct?

Sometimes the moon appears fully round, appears to our eyes to change shape, or may appear to get smaller and smaller, or even larger and larger.

What materials will you need?

Black construction paper
Globe
Basketball
Soft white chalk

Small ball
Flashlight or filmstrip projector
Straight pin

What should you know?

Before the activity, consult the local newspaper to see when the moon's quarter will be visible.

What will students do?

1. Take home a large sheet of black construction paper and some white chalk and observe the moon for the next 5 days. Draw the shape of the moon as you see it each night. *Note:* Should the skies be overcast, making it impossible to observe the moon, use the local newspaper to get the information.

In what ways does the moon's shape seem to change?

2. Arrange a globe, small ball, and a flashlight or filmstrip projector as shown in the diagram.

3. Place a pin on the night side of the earth as indicated in the diagram. The pin represents you.

Draw how much of a moon you would see if you were where the pin is.

4. Move the moon around the earth to the day side.

On which side of the earth is the moon when you cannot see it?
Where is the moon when it is full?

What will students do?

5. Make diagrams to help you explain your answers to these questions.

6. Look at the following diagram, which shows some positions of the moon in relation to the earth and the sun.

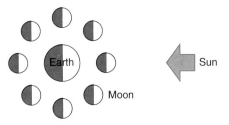

7. Choose two partners to help you. Using a basketball and flashlight, have one partner hold the flashlight and shine it on the basketball being held by your second partner, as he or she walks in a circle around you. See the diagram for how to do this.

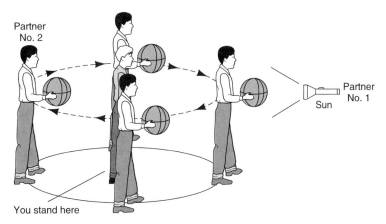

8. As you observe the light on the ball in various positions, match the following moon phases with the appropriate eight moon positions shown in the diagram accompanying Step 6. What you see is what would be observed from the earth.

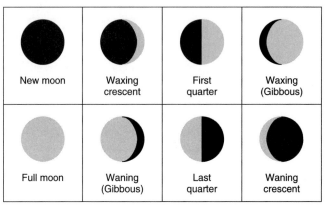

Phases of the Moon as Seen from the Earth

In what position is the basketball when it is covered by the shadow?
Where would the moon have to be when it is covered by a shadow?
When the basketball shows no shadow, what phase of the moon would this represent?
9. Draw how the full moon looks from earth.
What causes the phases of the moon?

How could students apply their new knowledge?

If the moon is not out at night, on what side of the earth must it be located?
If the moon could remain motionless in the sky, how would it look every night?

An additional activity for the whole class is to set up a Moonwatch Bulletin Board,[1] as follows:
a. Each night, have three students draw the shape of the moon on Moon Watch Cards (see diagram) by filling in the "lighted" part of the circle. (Look up phase of the moon in the newspaper if clouds prevent actual viewing.)

[1]For additional details on moon watches, see: G. Robert Moore, "Revisiting Science Concepts," *Science and Children* 32(3), November/December 1994, 31–32, 60.

b. Have the three students compare their drawings and arrive at one drawing.

3" x 5" index card

Date:

Moon Watch Card

c. Post the drawing on a bulletin board like this:
d. As a pattern develops, have the class try to predict the next day's moon shape.

	1	2	3	4	5	6	7	8	9	10	11	12	13	14	15	16	17	18	19	20	21	22
February	☽	☽	☽	●	●	●																
March																						
April																						
May																						
June																						

METEOROLOGY (WEATHER)

ENGAGEMENT ACTIVITIES

▶ How Are Clouds and Fog Formed?

What materials will you need?

Ice cubes; 2 clear, narrow-mouthed bottles; hot and cold water

What inquiry questions could you ask?

What is a cloud and how is it formed?
What is fog and how is it formed?

What activities could students do?

Fill a bottle with very hot water and let it sit for a few minutes. Now pour out most of the water, leaving about 2 centimeters (¾ to 1 inch) of water in the bottom of the bottle. For a control, set up an identical bottle with an equal amount of cold water. Place an ice cube in each bottle as shown in the diagram on p. 202. As your students observe the two bottles, ask:

What do you see happening in each bottle?
What do we call what you see in the hot-water bottle?

Why do you think clouds or fog formed in the bottle with hot water and not in the bottle with cold water?

How do clouds and fog form in nature?

▶ What Is the Greenhouse Effect? (K–2)

What materials will you need?

Large-mouthed jar with cover, 2 identical thermometers, 2 large cards, 2 rubber bands

What inquiry questions could you ask?

How does a greenhouse (where plants are grown) get so warm, even on a cold winter day?

During the summer, why is it hotter in an automobile when all the windows are shut tight rather than open?

What is meant by "solar heating"?

What activities could students do?

Get two thermometers that have identical readings and use rubber bands to attach them to large cards. Place one thermometer and card in a large-mouthed jar and screw on the cover. Set up a "heat trap" in a sunny window, as shown, to illustrate the principle of the greenhouse, cold frame, or solar house. Make sure each thermometer is shaded from the direct sunlight by the cards.

Take readings every half hour.

What differences do you observe on the two thermometers?

Why do you think the temperature in the jar is higher?

How is this knowledge used by architects and builders to make solar-heated houses?

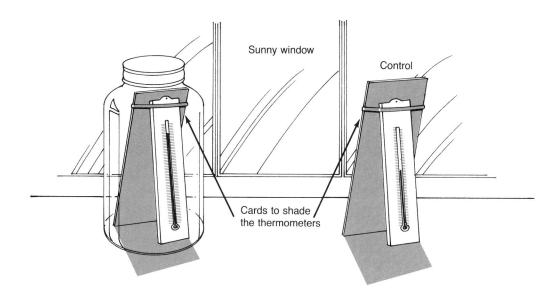

Sunny window

Control

Cards to shade
the thermometers

◆ EXPLORATION ACTIVITIES

▶ *How Can You Measure Temperature Changes? What Is a*
Thermometer? (K–2)

What concepts might
students construct?

Thermal energy (heat) gives increased energy to molecules, causing them to exert
more pressure or expand.

Warm temperatures make things expand more than do cold temperatures.

An instrument that measures changes in temperature is called a **thermometer**
(*thermo*—heat, and *meter*—to measure).

What materials will you
need?

Clear, narrow plastic drinking straw

Scissors

Cold water or rubbing alcohol

Red food coloring

Small vial or medicine bottle

Modeling clay

$3'' \times 5''$ index card

Tape

What inquiry questions
could you ask?

Where in this classroom might be the warmest places?

Where in this classroom might be the coolest places?

How could we find out the answers to these two questions?
What instrument(s) might we use in our investigation?

What should you know?

This activity can be done individually or in groups of two to four students. Thermometers measure the temperature of matter, or how hot or cold something is. Mercury or colored alcohol is usually the liquid used in thermometers. When heated, the liquid expands and moves up the tube. We say the temperature goes up. Conversely, when cooled, the liquid contracts and moves down the tube. We say the temperature goes down. Thermometers are used in many scientific, as well as personal aspects of life, such as in taking body temperatures, in measuring air or water temperatures, in cooking, and so on.

What will students do?

1. Put 2.5 centimeters (1 inch) of cold water into the small vial or medicine bottle and add several drops of red food coloring. (*Note:* Rubbing alcohol responds more quickly to temperature changes and can be used instead of water, depending on the ages and maturity of your students.)
2. With scissors, cut the end of the drinking straw at a slight angle. (*Note:* Your results will be best if you use the narrowest straw you can. Also, changes in air pressure and evaporation may affect your thermometer. To prevent this, after setting up the thermometers, put a few drops of oil into the top of the drinking straw, or seal the straw with modeling clay.)
3. Put the straw into the vial and completely seal the top of the vial with modeling clay, making sure it is airtight.
4. Tape a 3 × 5-inch index card to the drinking straw. As shown in the diagram, mark the level of the colored water in the straw.
   What do you think might happen to the colored water in the drinking straw if you put your thermometer in a warmer spot?
5. Put your thermometer in a warmer spot or in a pan of warm water and observe what happens. On the card, mark the new height of the liquid in your drinking straw.

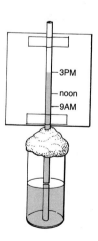

Draw a picture of what happened to the colored water in the drinking straw.
Why do you think the colored water moved up the drinking straw?
What do you think might happen now if you put your thermometer in a cooler spot?
6. Put your thermometer in a cooler spot or in a pan of cold water. Draw a picture of what happened to the colored water in the drinking straw.
Why do you think the colored water moved down the drinking straw?

What should you know?

Check each student's drawing to see if he or she observed that as the temperature went up, so did the colored water in the straw. The colored-water level went down when the temperature went down. Discuss the interrelationship between expansion and contraction of molecules and temperature, or the amount of molecular motion.

How could students apply their new knowledge?

- Each day for a week, have students observe and record where the level of the liquid is in their thermometers at the opening, lunch, and closing time of school. Then have students answer these questions:

  Of your three thermometer readings each day, which one was the highest and which one was the lowest?
  During a week, which was the warmest morning, lunch, and afternoon?
  Where do you predict tomorrow's levels will be for your three thermometer readings?

- Take thermometer readings and compare where the level of the colored water is in the coolest and warmest spots in your classroom.
- Using a commercial thermometer, measure the air temperature. Have students use this temperature to mark their drinking-straw cards with actual numerical readings. Have students take their daily readings on their thermometers for a week, with you giving them the actual numerical reading each time.
- After 1 week, ask your students to predict what the actual numerical temperature will be for the three daily readings.
- Make a list of various jobs where people use thermometers. Describe how thermometers are used in each job.

▶ *How Can Solar Energy Be Used?* (3–5)

What concepts might students construct?

Water in a saline solution absorbs the sun's energy and evaporates, leaving the salt behind. When cooled, water vapor condenses and changes into water droplets.

What materials will you need?

Salt	Large clear plastic bowl
Water	Plastic wrap
Tablespoon	Large rubber band
Small weight (rock)	Small glass custard cup
Large sheet of black construction paper	

What inquiry question could you ask?

In what ways can you make the sun do work for you?

What should you know?

This activity may be done individually or in groups of two to four.

PART I How Can You Make a Solar Still? (3–5)

What will students do?

1. Pour 3 tablespoons of salt into the larger clear plastic bowl, add 1 inch (2.5 cm) of water, and stir until all the salt is dissolved.
2. Place the small glass custard cup in the water in the center of the bowl.
3. Cover the large bowl with plastic wrap and fasten the wrap with a large rubber band.
4. Place a weight (small pebble) on top of the plastic wrap directly above the custard dish, as shown in the diagram.
   Caution: Make certain that the plastic wrap sticks tightly to the sides of the bowl and that the large rubber band keeps it sealed when the pebble is placed on the wrap.

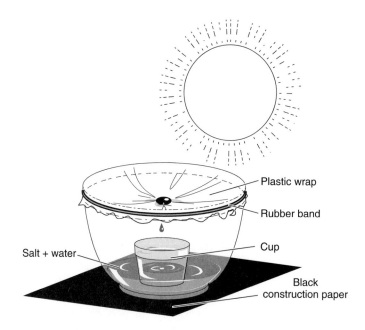

5. Carefully place the bowls in direct sunlight on a sheet of black construction paper, making sure the custard cup is directly under the weight pushing down on the plastic wrap.
   What do you think might happen to the salt water?
   Why do you think you were told to cover the salt water with plastic wrap?
   Why do you think you were told to put the bowl on black construction paper?
6. Record your observations every day.

What should you know? When there is only salt remaining in the large bowl and all the water is in the custard cup, Part II should be done by the group.

PART II What Is Desalinated Water? (3–5)

What will students do?

1. Take off the plastic wrap and taste the water in the custard cup.
    How does the water taste?
    Where did the water in this dish come from?
    What happened to your salt solution?
    Where did the water go?
    Why did the water "disappear"?
    What is left in the bottom of the large bowl?
2. Pour the contents of the large bowl onto a piece of black construction paper.
    What is this substance?

How could students apply their new knowledge?

How does the sun's energy (solar energy) benefit people?
How could this procedure be helpful to people who live near the ocean but do not have enough drinking water?
What are some other uses for this method of obtaining drinking water?
What are some other ways in which the sun's energy (solar energy) can be used to help people?
How does the pictured solar water heater work?

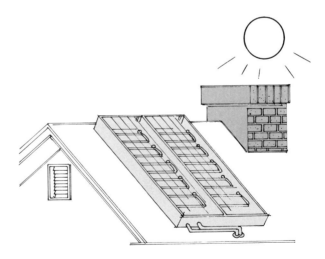

▶ *How Can You Measure Wind Direction and Speed? (3–8)*

What concepts might students construct?

Wind, or moving air, brings about changing weather conditions.
A **wind vane** is an instrument that shows the direction from which the wind is blowing.

Winds are named for the direction from which they blow. For example, a north wind is blowing from the north to the south.

An **anemometer** is an instrument that shows wind speed.

What materials will you need?

Scissors
Construction paper
Drinking straw
Glue
Pencil with eraser
Straight pin
Glass bead
Empty thread spool
Two 1-sq-ft (1000-sq-cm) pieces of corrugated cardboard

Magnetic compass
Small mirror
Long sewing needle
12″ (30 cm) monofilament nylon line
Ping-Pong ball
Protractor
Bubble level (hardware store)
Red marking pen
Tongue depressor

What inquiry questions could you ask?

How can you tell the direction the wind is blowing?
How does knowing wind direction help us understand weather and weather prediction?
What instruments can be used to find wind direction and speed?
How can we make and use these instruments?

PART I   What Is a Wind Vane, and How Do We Make One? (3–5)

What will students do?

1. Cut, from construction paper, an arrow-shaped point and tail fin, as shown in the diagram.
2. Attach the point and tail fin to the straw by cutting notches in both ends of the straw and gluing the cut-outs in place.
3. Attach the straw to a pencil by sticking the straight pin through the middle of the straw, through a glass bead, and into the pencil eraser. Make sure the straw can swing easily in all directions and is balanced. *Note:* Move pin in straw until it balances with arrow and tail attached.
4. Glue the empty thread spool to the center of the corrugated cardboard and mark North, South, East, and West on the cardboard as shown in the diagram.

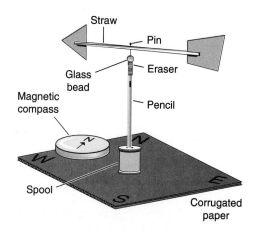

5. When the glue has dried, push the pencil into the hole of the spool and check to see that the straw moves easily. You now have a wind vane.

6. Carefully take your wind vane outdoors and line up the north label on your wind vane with the north on a magnetic compass. If wind is strong, tape the cardboard to concrete.

   What do you see happening to the arrow?

   From which direction is the wind blowing? How do you know?

   How would you name this wind?

What should you know?

The arrow will swing around until the point faces the direction from which the wind is blowing. This direction then becomes the wind's name.

How could students apply their new knowledge?

Does the wind always blow from the same direction? How could we find out?

  • Keep a record of wind observations three times a day for 1 week. Make sure to record the data on a chart:

	Monday			Wednesday			Friday		
Date	10/7								
Location	playground								
Observation time	9:30	11:30	1:30						
Wind direction	E	E	SE						
Any changes	yes; leaves blew to side of building								

  • After 1 week, do you see
    a. *any pattern of winds during the day?*
    b. *any pattern of winds from day to day?*
    c. *any prevailing or consistent direction from which the wind blows?*
    d. *any correlation between wind direction and weather conditions, such as temperatures, humidity, clouds, and so on?*
  • Check local TV weather and newspapers for wind direction.

....

PART II How Can You Detect Winds in the Sky? (3–5)

What inquiry questions could you ask?

Are winds in the sky always the same as down here on the earth's surface?

How do you know?

How might we find out?

Why is it important for pilots to know the speed and direction of winds up high?

What should you know?   You may have noticed that high clouds sometimes move in different directions from middle or low clouds. High cloud movement may also differ from surface winds. Students may work with a partner for this activity.

What will students do?   1. Set up a small mirror in the center of a cardboard square and mark North, South, East, and West, as in the diagram.

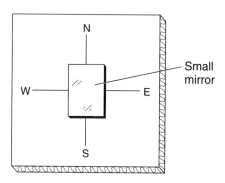

2. Place this cardboard and the wind vane from Part I next to each other in the same outdoor area. Make sure the points marked North line up with North on the magnetic compass.
3. Look into the mirror to see the clouds' reflection.
   In which direction are the clouds moving?
   This indicates wind direction at cloud level.
   In what direction is the wind on the ground moving?
4. Use the wind vane to determine the direction of the wind on the ground.
   How do cloud movement direction and ground wind direction compare?
5. Keep a log of cloud movement directions three times a day for 1 week as you did with wind vane observations.
   Notice any changes during the day and any patterns over the week. Compare the data with your weather vane data.

....

PART III   How Can You Measure How Fast the Wind Blows? (3–8)[2]

What will students do?   1. Thread a sewing needle with a 12-inch monofilament line, push the needle through the Ping-Pong ball, and knot and glue the end of the line to the Ping-Pong ball. Glue the other end of the line to the center of a protractor. With the marking pen, color the line red.

[2]The author highly recommends the following packet of activities for making and using weather instruments: *Science Activities in Energy, DOE/CA–0006* (P.O. Box 117, Oak Ridge, TN 37830: American Museum of Science and Energy/Oak Ridge Associated Universities).

2. Glue a bubble level to the protractor as shown in the diagram.
3. Glue a tongue depressor to the protractor as a handle. You now have an anemometer to measure wind speed.
4. When the glue is dry, carefully take your anemometer outside to test it in the wind.

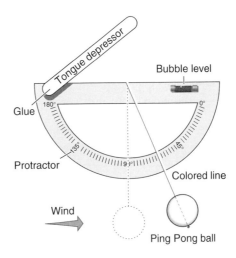

5. To take readings of the wind's speed, follow these directions:
   a. In the wind, hold the protractor level using the tongue depressor handle.
   b. Keep the protractor level by making sure the bubble is centered in the bubble level.
   c. Observe any swing of the Ping-Pong ball and string and see what angle the string makes on the protractor. For instance, in the diagram the string moved to approximately 65 degrees.

How could students apply their new knowledge?

• Use your anemometer in various spots on your school grounds, and then refer to the following chart to find the wind speed.

Protractor Anemometer Wind Speeds

String Angle	Wind Speed (Miles Per Hour)	String Angle	Wind Speed (Miles Per Hour)
90	0	50	18.0
85	5.8	45	19.6
80	8.2	40	21.9
75	10.1	35	23.4
70	11.8	30	25.8
65	13.4	25	28.7
60	14.9	20	32.5
55	16.4		

• After you have tested the wind speed in different places on your school grounds, record the data on a chart like this one:

Date								
Time								
Protractor angle								
Wind speed								
Wind direction								

Where does the wind blow the fastest on your school grounds?
Does wind blow faster at ground level or at higher levels?
Is there a place where wind blows faster, such as between two buildings or at a corner of two wings of a building? Why?

▶ *How Can You Measure Air Pressure Changes? (3–8)*

What concepts might students construct?

Air exerts pressure.
Air pressure changes.
Air pressure may indicate the type of weather.
Low air pressure usually indicates rainy or cloudy weather.
High air pressure usually indicates fair weather.

What materials will you need?

Balloons
Can with plastic snap top (e.g., coffee can) or top made of large balloon and rubber band
Straw
Glue
Straight pin
Index card

What inquiry questions could you ask?

Have each student blow up a balloon. Ask:
What is in the balloon?
How do you know there is pressure exerted in the balloon?
How can you discover whether or not air has the same pressure at all times and in all places?
What is a barometer?
What is it used for?
How might location affect the readings of a barometer?

What should you know?

Room temperature will affect the barometer students make in this activity. This barometer does not, therefore, measure only air pressure differences. You may want to have some students keep their barometers outside class and then compare the readings from the different locations.

PART I   What Is a Barometer? (3–8)

What will students do?

1. Obtain a can that has a plastic snap top, a straw, glue, a straight pin, and a card.
2. Cover the can with the plastic snap top, making certain the can is sealed completely. *Caution:* Often the plastic snap top will not sufficiently seal the can. Using a piece of a large balloon and a tight rubber band to seal the can is a good alternative.
3. Place a small amount of glue in the center of the lid and attach a straw, as shown in the diagram. Place another drop of glue on the other end of the straw and attach the pin.
4. Mark an index card with lines that are the same distance apart. Tape the card on the wall as shown in the diagram.

   What might happen to the plastic snap top or balloon if the air pressure on it increases?

   What might happen to the plastic snap top or balloon if the air pressure decreases?

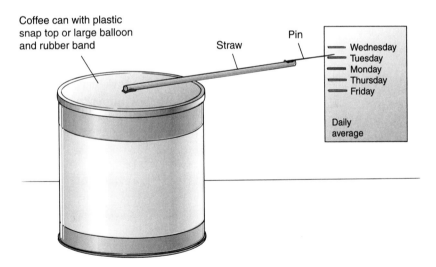

Coffee can with plastic snap top or large balloon and rubber band

Straw

Pin

— Wednesday
— Tuesday
— Monday
— Thursday
— Friday

Daily average

What should you know?

When air pressure increases, it pushes down on the plastic lid or balloon, causing the straw to give a high reading. When the air pressure is low, the opposite will happen. A falling barometer may indicate that a storm is approaching.

5. Record the readings of the barometer three times a day for a week.

   How do the readings of the barometer differ during the day?

   How do the readings differ from day to day?

   What might cause the readings to vary?

6. Record the type of weather that exists at the time of each barometer reading.
   What kind of air pressure generally existed during your fair-weather readings?
   What kind of air pressure generally existed during your stormy-weather readings?
7. Compare the readings of barometers in different locations.
   What reasons can you give for your barometer readings?

How could students apply their new knowledge?

By using the readings of your barometer, predict what the weather will be.
   Does air travel from an area of high pressure to an area of lower pressure, or from an area of lower pressure to an area of higher pressure? Why?
   What could you do to improve your barometer?
   What other materials could you use to make a barometer?

PART II   How Can We Make Another Barometer? (3–8)

What materials will you need?

Empty 2-liter soda bottle   Food coloring
Glass measuring cup   Marking pen
Water   Transparent sticky tape

What inquiry questions could you ask?

How can we make another barometer?
Which barometer do you think will show air pressure changes better?

What will students do?

1. On a *stormy or rainy day*, invert an empty 2-liter soda bottle into a glass measuring cup that has just enough colored water to go into the neck of the bottle (see diagram).
2. While holding the glass measuring cup, push down carefully on the bottle until it is very snug inside the cup.
3. While holding the cup and pushing the bottle down firmly, have your partner seal the bottle where it sits in the cup with transparent sticky tape.

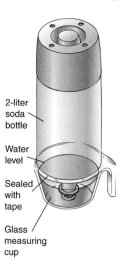

2-liter
soda
bottle

Water
level

Sealed
with
tape

Glass
measuring
cup

4. Mark a line on the measuring cup to show where the water level is inside the bottle.
5. Check the water level each day, especially on sunny days.
   Why do you think a glass, not plastic, cup was used?
   When is the water level the highest? Lowest? Why?
   How does this barometer compare with the one made in Part I?

What should you know?

The amount of air *inside* the bottle remains constant (at the atmospheric pressure on the rainy day when you sealed the bottle). The air pressure outside the bottle varies and pushes on the plastic bottle. On drier days, air pressure increases, forcing the water to rise.

▶ *How Can You Measure Humidity Changes? What Is a Hygrometer? (3–8)*

What concepts might students construct?

Air contains moisture.
Pressure and temperature affect the amount of moisture air can hold at any given time.
Relative humidity is the amount of water vapor actually contained in the atmosphere divided by the amount that could be contained in the same atmosphere.
Relative humidity can be measured.

What materials will you need?

2 thermometers
Small bottle or dish of water
Thread

Wide cotton shoelace
Empty milk carton
Piece of cardboard

What inquiry questions could you ask?

What instrument is used to measure the amount of water, or humidity, in the atmosphere?
How can this instrument be made, and how does it work?

What will students do?

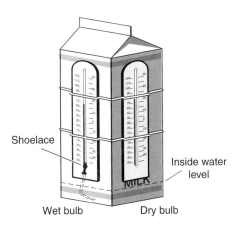
Shoelace
Inside water level
Wet bulb   Dry bulb

1. Obtain an empty milk carton, two identical thermometers, a cotton shoelace, and some thread.
2. Cut a 4-inch section from the cotton shoelace and slip the section over the bulb of one of the thermometers. Tie the shoelace section with thread above and below the bulb to hold the shoelace in place. Thread the other end of the 4-inch section through a hole in the milk carton and allow it to rest in a small bottle or dish of water inside the milk carton.

What will students do?

3. Attach both thermometers to the milk carton as shown in the diagram. You now have a **hygrometer**—an instrument that measures the relative humidity in the atmosphere. *Caution:* The two thermometers should register the same temperature before the shoelace is placed over one of them; otherwise, the difference in readings must be considered a constant that is part of all computations.

4. When the shoelace is wet, fan it with a piece of cardboard for 1 minute.
   What do you think might happen to the thermometer with the wet shoelace? Why do you think so?

5. Check the temperature readings of the two thermometers.
   How do you account for the difference in readings between the thermometer with the shoelace (called the "wet bulb") and the one without the shoelace (called the "dry bulb")?

FINDING RELATIVE HUMIDITY IN PERCENT

Difference in Degrees between Wet-Bulb and Dry-Bulb Thermometers

Air Temp	1	2	3	4	5	6	7	8	9	10	11	12	13	14	15	16	17	18	19	20	21	22	23	24	25	26	27	28	29	30
30°	89	78	68	57	47	37	27	17	8																					
32°	90	79	69	60	50	41	31	22	13	4																				
34°	90	81	72	62	53	44	35	27	18	9	1																			
36°	91	82	73	65	56	48	39	31	23	14	6																			
38°	91	83	75	67	59	51	43	35	27	19	12	4																		
40°	92	84	76	68	61	53	46	38	31	23	16	9	2																	
42°	92	85	77	70	62	55	48	41	34	28	21	14	7																	
44°	93	85	78	71	64	57	51	44	37	31	24	18	12	5																
46°	93	86	79	72	65	59	53	46	40	34	28	22	16	10	4															
48°	93	87	80	73	67	60	54	48	42	36	31	25	19	14	8	3														
50°	93	87	81	74	68	62	56	50	44	39	33	28	22	17	12	7	2													
52°	94	88	81	75	69	63	58	52	46	41	36	30	25	20	15	10	6													
54°	94	88	82	76	70	65	59	54	48	43	38	33	28	23	18	14	9	5												
56°	94	88	82	77	71	66	61	55	50	45	40	35	31	26	21	17	12	8	4											
58°	94	89	83	77	72	67	62	57	52	47	42	38	33	28	24	20	15	11	7	3										
60°	94	89	84	78	73	68	63	58	53	49	44	40	35	31	27	22	18	14	10	6	2									
62°	94	89	84	79	74	69	64	60	55	50	46	41	37	33	29	25	21	17	13	9	6	2								
64°	95	90	85	79	75	70	66	61	56	52	48	43	39	35	31	27	23	20	16	12	9	5	2							
66°	95	90	85	80	76	71	66	62	58	53	49	45	41	37	33	29	26	22	18	15	11	8	5	1						
68°	95	90	85	81	76	72	67	63	59	55	51	47	43	39	35	31	28	24	21	17	14	11	8	4	1					
70°	95	90	86	81	77	72	68	64	60	56	52	48	44	40	37	33	30	26	23	20	17	13	10	7	4	1				
72°	95	91	86	82	78	73	69	65	61	57	53	49	46	42	39	35	32	28	25	22	19	16	13	10	7	4	1			
74°	95	91	86	82	78	74	70	66	62	58	54	51	47	44	40	37	34	30	27	24	21	18	15	12	9	7	4	1		
76°	96	91	87	83	78	74	70	67	63	59	55	52	48	45	42	38	35	32	29	26	23	20	17	14	12	9	6	4	1	
78°	96	91	87	83	79	75	71	67	64	60	57	53	50	46	43	40	37	34	31	28	25	22	19	16	14	11	9	6	4	1
80°	96	91	87	83	79	76	72	68	64	61	57	54	51	47	44	41	38	35	32	29	27	24	21	18	16	13	11	8	6	4
82°	96	91	87	83	79	76	72	69	65	62	58	55	52	49	46	43	40	37	34	31	28	25	23	20	18	15	13	10	8	6
84°	96	92	88	84	80	77	73	70	66	63	59	56	53	50	47	44	41	38	35	32	30	27	25	22	20	17	15	12	10	8
86°	96	92	88	84	80	77	73	70	66	63	60	57	54	51	48	45	42	39	37	34	31	29	26	24	21	19	17	14	12	10
88°	96	92	88	85	81	78	74	71	67	64	61	58	55	52	49	46	43	41	38	35	33	30	28	25	23	21	18	16	14	12
90°	96	92	88	85	81	78	74	71	68	64	61	58	56	53	50	47	44	42	39	37	34	32	29	27	24	22	20	18	16	14

Air Temperature (Reading of Dry-Bulb Thermometer) in Degrees Fahrenheit

Example:
Temperature of dry-bulb thermometer 76°
Temperature of wet-bulb thermometer 68°
The difference is 8°

Find 76° in the dry-bulb column and 8° in the difference column. Where these two columns meet, you read the relative humidity. In this case, it is 67 percent.

| What should you know? | When the shoelace is wet, the evaporation of the water results in a cooling of the wet-bulb thermometer, whereas the dry-bulb thermometer will continue to read the temperature of the air around it. *Note:* This is the same phenomenon that occurred in a previous activity in Section 4, where students wore one dry wool or cotton sock and one wet wool or cotton sock to show the cooling effect of evaporation. |

6. Look at the relative humidity table provided. To locate the relative humidity on the table, find the temperature of the dry-bulb thermometer on the y-axis (vertical axis) and the difference between the readings of the two thermometers on the x-axis (horizontal axis). The example below the table shows a dry-bulb temperature of 76°F, a difference of 8°F (wet-bulb, 68°F), and a relative humidity of 67 percent.

7. Take readings on your hygrometer every day for 2 weeks and record your findings. Also try readings in different places.
   What reasons can you give for different readings?

| How could students apply their new knowledge? | • *Using your hygrometer, can you predict which days are better for drying clothes outside?*
• *What other instruments can you find that will indicate or measure relative humidity?*
• *How is relative humidity used by weather forecasters to predict weather?*
• *Why were you asked to fan the wet-bulb thermometer?*
• *How does relative humidity explain why you feel more uncomfortable on a humid 90-degree day than on a dry 90-degree day?*
• *Why might you feel more comfortable in winter in a room that is 70 degrees with 65 percent relative humidity, than in a room that is 70 degrees but with only 30 percent relative humidity?* |

GEOLOGY (EARTH'S CHANGING SURFACE)

 ENGAGEMENT ACTIVITIES

▶ *How Are Rocks Broken Up? (K–2)*

What materials will you need?	2 plastic vials or medicine bottles with snap lids, dry bean seeds, water
What inquiry questions could you ask?	*How can seeds break up rocks and soil?* *How can we set up an experiment to test if seeds can break up rocks and soil?*
What activities could students do?	Fill both vials or medicine bottles with as many dry beans as will fit. Add as much water as you can to one vial of beans. Snap the lids on both vials.

A Water   **B** No water

Ask students what they think might happen to the two vials. Observe both vials the next day. In the one with the water, the beans will have expanded and lifted the lid off. In the vial without water (called the control), there will be no observable change. Help students infer that swelling and growing plants change the land by breaking up rocks and soil just as the swelling beans lifted the vial's lid off. Ask students to find places on your playground or on concrete walks where plants grow through and crack rocks like this:

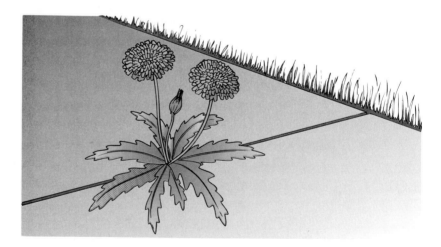

▶ *How Can You Build Stalactites and Stalagmites?*

What materials will you need?

Paper towel, Epsom salts, water, spoon, 30 cm (1 ft) of thick string, large tin can, 2 small jars or clear plastic cups, 2 heavy washers

What inquiry questions could you ask?

How are some rocks formed in caves?
What is a stalactite, and how is it formed?

What is a stalagmite, and how is it formed?
Where else are stalactites and stalagmites formed?

What activities could students do?

Fill the large tin can about three-quarters full of water. Add Epsom salts, one spoonful at a time, stirring vigorously after each addition, until no more Epsom salts will dissolve. (*Note:* Epsom salt crystals will fall to the bottom of the can when no more will dissolve.) Fill the two small jars or plastic cups with the Epsom salt solution and place the containers 5 centimeters (2 inches) apart on the paper towel. Tie a heavy washer to each end of the string. Place one washer in each of the small jars or paper cups. *Note:* Arrange the string in the cups so that you have at least 5 centimeters (2 inches) between the string and the paper towel.

After several days, mineral deposits will form on the paper towel and string as shown.

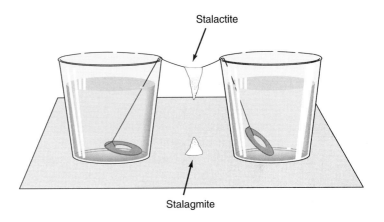

Note: Help students learn the difference between stalactites and stalagmites. Point out that the deposits that hang down are called **stalactites** (C for ceiling), while those that point up are called **stalagmites** (G for ground).

🪶 EXPLORATION ACTIVITIES

▶ *How Are Rocks Alike and Different, and How Do We Use Rocks? (K–5)*

What concepts might students construct?

Rocks exhibit eight major properties or characteristics that are used to identify and classify them: hardness, texture, color, streak, cleavage, density, chemical, and luster. Simple tests can help us identify and classify rocks by their properties. Rocks are used in many forms in our everyday lives.

What materials will you need?

Large steel nail
Glass baby food jar
Hammer

Magnifying glass
Safety goggles
Penny

Newspaper
Cloth sack
Rock samples

What inquiry questions could you ask?

Where could you find different kinds of rocks on our school grounds, at home, or on the way to school?
How are rocks the same and different?
When you feel rocks, how might they differ?
How might we test rocks to see if they are hard or soft, heavy or light, dark or light, and so on?

What should you know?

Safety Precaution!

This activity should be done in groups of two to four students. *Cautions:* (1) In hardness tests, the use of a knife is recommended, but a steel nail is substituted here for safety reasons. (2) *Always* put rocks in a cloth sack and use safety goggles when hammering rocks.

You and designated students should assemble the following items in a cloth sack before the activity begins: a large steel nail, a penny, a glass baby food jar, a newspaper, a hammer, a magnifying glass, and six samples of different rocks.

What will students do?

1. Open your cloth sack and place your materials on the newspaper.
2. Observe the rocks closely.
   In what ways are the rocks alike?
   In what ways do to the rocks look different?
   When you feel the rocks, how do they differ?
   Compare two rocks of the same size.
   How does their weight compare? Is one heavier than the other?
   Why do you think some rocks are rough and jagged?
   What do you think has happened to the rocks that are smooth and rounded?
3. Place your rocks in groups (classifying them by properties).
   How did you group your rocks? In what other ways might you group your rocks?
   How do you think you could tell the hardness or softness of a rock?
   (Scratch with steel nail, penny, fingernail, and so on.)

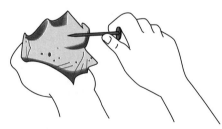

What should you know?

The Mohs hardness scale ranks rocks from 1 to 10, with talc being softest at 1 and diamond hardest at 10. Here are some common materials that students can test and approximate their hardness.[3]

[3]For an expanded Scale of Hardness chart and excellent color samples of each type of rock, see *Science Interactions–Course 2*, 1995, Westerville, OH: Glencoe Division of Macmillan-McGraw-Hill Publishing Co., 1995, 310–311.

Hardness Number	Common Materials	How to Test Hardness
1	Soft lead pencil	Greasy flakes on fingers
2	Chalk	Scratched by fingernail
3	Marble	Scratched by copper penny
4	Yellow brass	Scratched by nail
5	Glass bottle	Scratched by nail
6	Window glass	Scratched by file
7	Sandpaper	Scratches glass easily

Note: Materials above 8 are extremely hard and are not easy to test.

4. Try some of your ideas for testing other properties of rocks.
   If two rocks were the same size, how could you find out which rock was heavier (denser)?
   How could you tell whether a rock looked the same on the inside as it did on the outside? (Place a rock in a cloth sack and cover the sack with newspaper. Wear safety goggles and hit the rock with a hammer.)
   How would you find out how rocks become smooth and rounded?
   (Place rocks in a plastic jar of water and shake the jar vigorously.)
   Why are some rocks made of many smaller rocks or pieces?
   Are the pieces of the rock rounded or jagged?
   Are the pieces dull or shiny in the rock?
   Why do you think they are like that?

What should you know?   The following is a simple test to find density.

1. Weigh the rock in air and record its weight in grams.
2. Immerse the rock in water. Determine the volume of the rock by noting how much the water level changes (in cm^3).

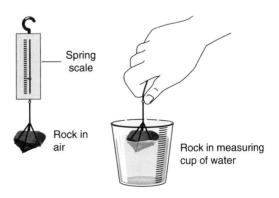

Spring scale

Rock in air

Rock in measuring cup of water

3. Divide the weight by the volume to find the density of the rock in grams/cm^3.

Do the following activity to show students that two objects with the same volume can be different weights due to their different densities.

1. Put a can of diet cola in a bowl of water and a same-size can of regular cola in another bowl of water.
2. The can of diet cola will float (because it is lighter in weight for its volume), while the regular cola will sink (because the sugar in it makes it heavier for the same volume). (See pgs. A–165 and A–166 for an explanation of why the diet cola is lighter.)

Diet cola floats

Regular cola sinks

What should you know?

Densities *under* 1.00 gm/cm^3 will *float* because water density is 1.00 gm/cm^3 (examples: cork = 0.24 gm/cm^3, fish = 1.00 gm/cm^3). Densities *over* 1.00 gm/cm^3 will sink (example: clay = 1.63 gm/cm^3).

How could students apply their new knowledge?

- *In what ways are soft rocks used?*
- *In what ways are hard rocks used?*
- Survey your school, home, and community and make a chart of where rocks or rock materials are used daily. Use the following chart as an example.[4]

Everyday Object	Product Made from Rock	Rock or Mineral
Window	Glass	Sand
Wire or old penny	Copper	Copper ore
Fishing weights	Lead	Galena
Toothpaste	Fluoride	Fluoride crystal
Pretzel	Table salt	Salt crystal
Tooth filling	Gold	Gold nugget
Food can or foil	Aluminum	Bauxite ore

- *What is concrete, how is it made, and how is it used?*

[4]For an expanded chart, see Richard David Barnes, *Popcorn Rock—An Experiment in Crystal Science*, 1989, Bountiful, UT: PR NEWS, 15.

▶ What Is a Fault, and How Does It Change the Earth's Surface? (K–5)

What concepts might students construct?	Some land has been formed by sedimentation, causing layering. When too much force is applied to the earth's layers, they crack. The line where the earth's crust cracks and moves is called a **fault.** A normal fault is where the earth's crust drops. A thrust fault is where the earth's crust rises over an adjacent part of the earth. Earthquakes may be caused by the earth's crust sliding along a fault.

What materials will you need?

1 quart jar
Sand
Humus or peat moss
Several types of soil—loamy, sandy, and clay
2 cigar-box molds filled with layers of colored plaster of paris
2 clear plastic cups
Soda straw
Straight pin
Staples
Tape
Paper clips
Water
2 × 4 × 6-inch piece of wood cut in half along a sloping line
1 *layered* cupcake per student (see instructions in Part IV)
Small paper plates
Clear plastic straws cut slightly larger than cupcake's height (5 per student)
Plastic knives
Drawing paper
Colored pencils or markers

What inquiry questions could you ask?

If great force is applied to a rock or parts of the earth's structure, what will happen to the rock or the structure?
What is an earthquake?
What causes an earthquake?

What should you know?

This activity should be done in groups of two to or four students. The molds should be made ahead of time, by you and/or designated students, by mixing two or three *separate* pints of plaster of paris with different colors of food coloring. The wet plaster of paris should be layered in the cigar boxes and allowed to partially dry before cutting it as indicated in the following steps. *Caution:* Do not let the plaster of paris become too dry or it will be too hard to cut.

PART I   How Does the Earth's Surface Form Layers? (K–2)

What will students do?

1. Obtain a quart jar, some sand, humus or peat moss, and several types of soil. Half fill the quart jar with water. Add sand to the jar until the sand is 1 inch thick in the bottom of the jar.
   What happens to the sand?
   What will happen if you pour soil and humus or peat moss onto part of the sand?
2. Try it. Add several other types of soil and humus or peat moss to the jar and observe.
   How do the materials in the jar resemble parts of our earth?
   Explain how you think parts of our earth have become layered.
   What do you think might happen if you shake the jar of water, sand, humus, and soils?
   What might happen if you let the jar stand for several days?
   Try it and record what you see in a few days.

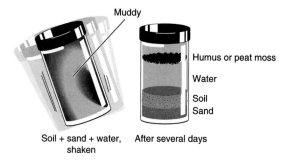

Muddy

Humus or peat moss

Water

Soil
Sand

Soil + sand + water,   After several days
shaken

PART II   How Is a Fault Caused By Water Evaporating? (K–5)

What will students do?

1. Set up a simple balance as shown in the diagram. Fill one cup with water.
   In what ways can you balance the sand and water?
   Add enough sand to balance the water cup.

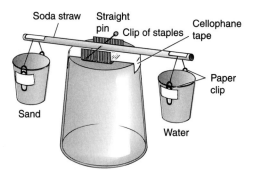

Soda straw   Straight
              pin   Clip of staples   Cellophane
                                       tape

                                       Paper
                                       clip

Sand

                                       Water

2. Use one of your methods to balance the sand and water.
   Now that these are balanced, what might happen if you take some sand from one side of the balance and place it on the other side?

3. Do this and observe.
   How is what you did with the balance similar to some of the things that happen in the earth's crust? (Materials shift on the surface of the earth.)

What should you know?   The land surface of the continents is always being worn away. The particles formed from this wearing away (**erosion**) often flow into streams and are carried to the sea. When the material gets to the ocean floor, it causes that part of the floor to become heavier and may cause the crust of the earth and the layers to bend. If they bend far enough, faults may appear. This is an explanation for one type of fault, although it is a rare type.

4. Rebalance the sand and water and let it stand undisturbed for several days.
   Why does the sand side go down?

PART III   How Do Normal and Thrust Faults Change the Earth's Surface? (3–5)

What will students do?   1. Obtain a cigar-box mold from your teacher and remove the plaster block. Your teacher has cut the block in two. Raise one of these blocks above the other as indicated in the diagram.
   A **fault** is a place where the earth's crust and layers have broken similar to the layers in your model.
   How is the appearance of the block similar to the appearance of the earth in some places you have seen?
   Explain how you think a rock structure could reach a condition similar to the one you have arranged in your model.

What should you know?   The rock structure could have formed a fault owing to stresses within the earth that drew the sections of rock apart. This stress could have caused one section to fall. This kind of fault is called a **normal fault** and is represented in the diagram.

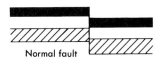
Normal fault

2. Obtain a 2 × 4 × 6-inch piece of wood that has been cut in two along a sloping line.
   How is this model fault different from the normal fault? What would you call this type of fault?

What should you know?

Explain that this type of fault is called a thrust fault. The **thrust fault** occurs when compression pushes sections of rock closer together, forcing one section of rock to move or slide up, as shown in the diagram.

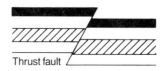

Thrust fault

How could this structure have been formed in nature?
How would you define a thrust fault and explain how it works?

What should you know?

Other faults, such as the one that caused the San Francisco earthquake of 1989, may be caused mainly by horizontal movement of the earth. The San Andreas fault in California is of this type.
What connection is there between an earthquake and a fault?

PART IV   How Can We See Layers in the Earth? (K–5)

What should you know?

Geologists study the earth and use many devices to discover what is under the surface.

Core sampling is done by putting hollow drilling tubes into the ground and extracting a sample of what the tubes went through.

What should you know?

Layered cupcakes may be made by teacher or parent volunteer as follows:

1. Use either different flavors and/or white batter mixed with food coloring.
2. Put batter in four layers in foil or paper cups.
3. Bake and frost cupcakes.

What inquiry questions could you ask?

What do you think is inside the cupcake?
How do scientists learn what's underground?

What will students do?

1. Obtain one cupcake on a paper plate, five cut clear straws, plastic knife, drawing paper, and markers.
2. Do *not* remove foil or paper cup from cupcake.
3. Draw what you think is inside the cupcake.

Point out that the cupcake represents the earth and explain how geologists use core sampling. Explain how to take side "core samples" (see next step).

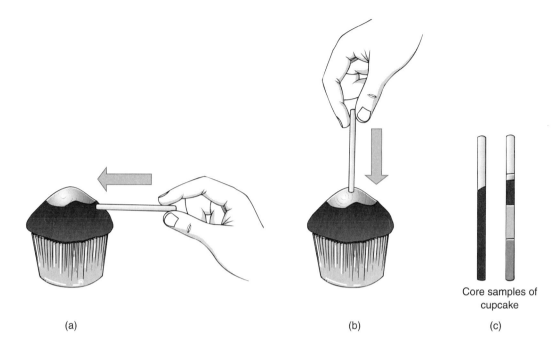

Core samples of
cupcake

(a)   (b)   (c)

4. Take two side "core samples" of your cupcake:
   a. Carefully insert a straw into the side of the cupcake [diagram (a)], rotate slightly, remove, and place sample on paper plate.
   b. Repeat with another straw.
      Can you determine what the entire cupcake looks like with these two core samples? If not, what must you do?
5. Take three samples by inserting the straw straight *down* into the cupcake, as in diagram (b).
6. Compare these samples with those taken from the side (c).
   How are they different?
7. Make a drawing of what you now think the inside of the cupcake looks like.
8. Use your knife to cut down and separate the cupcake into halves.
   How does this compare to your drawings?

What should you know?

For more information on this type of activity, see the Cupcake Geology activity in the Mesa Public Schools Curriculum Unit "Earthquakes" by JoAnne Vasquez Wolf.

▶ *How Are Crystals Formed? (3–5)*

What concepts might students construct?

Crystals are nonliving substances that form into rocklike bodies of various shapes. Crystals grow in size when more layers of the same substance are added on; the basic crystal shape, however, remains the same.

Crystal size is determined by differences in the rate of crystallization.

If crystals are disturbed in the forming process, they will break apart into hundreds of microscopic pieces.

True solids are crystalline in form.

Crystalline form is important in determining some of the properties of substances.

What materials will you need?

Tablespoon	Pyrex beaker or heatproof baby bottle
Salt	Alum
3 jar lids	Insulated cooking mitt
2 small glasses	Washer
Water	Pencil
2 pieces of string	Popcorn Rock®[5]
Magnifying glass or hand lens	Clear glass bowl
Sugar	White distilled vinegar
Hot plate	Food coloring

What inquiry questions could you ask?

What are crystals?

How could you "grow" a crystal?

What happens when a crystal is "growing"?

Why is a study of crystals important?

What should you know?   These activities can be done by individual students or by groups of two to four people.

....

PART I   Growing Salt Crystals by Evaporation (3–5)

What will students do?

1. Obtain a tablespoon of salt, a jar lid, and a small glass of water. Mix the salt into the glass of water. Stir the water well. Let the solution stand for a few minutes until it becomes clear.

   What happens to the salt?

2. Very gently pour some of the salt solution into the jar lid. Put a piece of string in the solution, letting one end hang out, as in diagram (a). Let the solution stand for several days where the lid will not be disturbed.

   What do you think might happen to the salt solution?

3. After several days have passed, use your magnifying glass to look at the materials in the lid and lift the string out of the jar lid.

4. Describe what you see with the hand lens (b).

[5]Inexpensive materials and directions for growing "Popcorn Rock" can be obtained from your local Popcorn Rock dealer or from R. D. Barnes, 389 West 100 South, Bountiful, UT 84010, (801)295-5762.

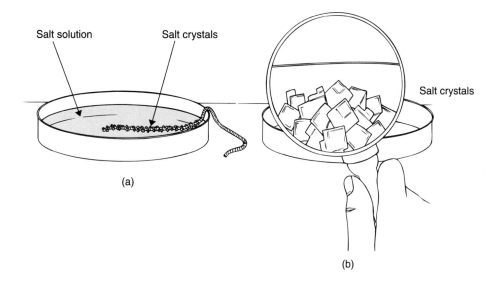

Salt solution   Salt crystals

Salt crystals

(a)

(b)

How are the materials in the lid different from your original salt solution?
Why do you now have a solid when you started out with a liquid?
What name could you give to the formations in the lid?

What should you know?   The salt dissolved in the water. When the salt water stood for several days, the water evaporated, leaving behind salt crystals. Crystals are nonliving substances that are found in various geometrical shapes.

PART II Growing Sugar Crystals by Evaporation (3–5)

What will students do?   1. Obtain a tablespoon of sugar, a jar lid, and a small glass of water. Be sure the tablespoon is clean. Mix a tablespoon of sugar into the glass of water. Stir the water well. Let the solution stand for a few minutes until it becomes clear.
   What happens to the sugar?
   How is the sugar solution similar in appearance to the salt solution?
2. Very gently pour some of the sugar solution into the lid and let the solution stand undisturbed for several days.
   What do you think might happen to the sugar solution?
3. After several days have passed, use your magnifying glass to look at the materials in your lid.

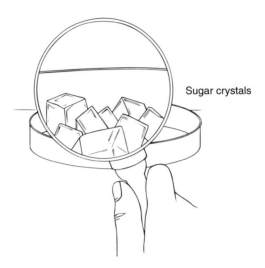

Sugar crystals

4. Describe what you see.
   How are the materials in this lid different from the salt crystals? How are they alike?
   What happened to the sugar solution?

What should you know?   When the sugar water stood for several days, the water evaporated, leaving behind sugar crystals.

....

PART III   How Does the Rate of Evaporation Affect Crystal Size Formation? (3–5)

What inquiry questions could you ask?   *Where are crystals found in nature?*
   How do crystals form?

What should you know?   The teacher or a very responsible student should set up materials for younger or less mature students.

TEACHER DEMO

What will students or a teacher do?
1. Heat 200 mL of water in a Pyrex beaker or baby bottle. Add 3 tablespoons of alum. Heat and stir the mixture until the alum fully dissolves, as in diagram (a).
2. Using an insulated cooking mitt, remove the bottle and put it on a solid surface where it cannot be moved or struck.
3. Carefully pour a small amount of the alum solution into a clean jar lid (b). Place the lid in a secure, dry place *away from* radiators or direct sunshine.

4. Tie a sanded washer to one end of a piece of string. Wind and tie the other end to a pencil so that when the pencil is suspended across the bottle top, the washer hangs down about ½ inch from the bottom of the bottle (c). Place bottle in the secure, dry place next to the jar.

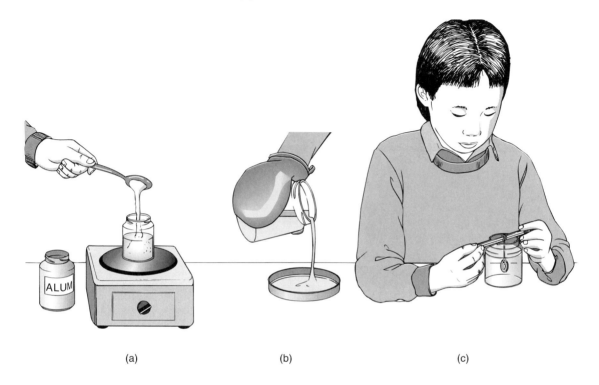

(a)   (b)   (c)

5. Observe the bottle and lid every day, but do not shake or move the containers.
6. Record your observations and use your data to answer these questions:
   Where did the first crystals form: bottom of bottle, sides of bottle, or string?
   How does the size of crystals in the bottle compare with that in the jar lid?
   Why is crystalline form important in determining the properties of a substance?
   Why do some rocks have large crystals and some have small crystals?

What should you know?

True solids are crystalline in form. Crystalline form is important in determining some of the properties of substances. Differences in the rate of crystallization determine differences in crystal size. Crystals in the jar lid are smaller than those in the bottle due to the differences in cooling times. Slower cooling (bottle) produces larger crystals, whereas faster cooling (lid) produces smaller crystals.

How could students apply their new knowledge?

How are crystals used in industry?
If there were no crystals on earth, how would people's way of living be affected?
How might you "grow" very large crystals?

PART IV   How Can You Make "Popcorn Rock" Stalagmites? (3–5)

What should you know?

Popcorn Rock is the trade name for a naturally occurring mineral found in the western United States. It is called Popcorn Rock because popcornlike aragonite crystals (calcium carbonate) can form on the rock, in the same way that limestone formations are occurring in Carlsbad Caverns National Park, New Mexico.[6]

It is recommended that the Popcorn Rock experiment begin on Thursday, as early in the morning as possible. Then allow seven days for the Popcorn Rock crystals to form, be observed, and discussed.

What will students do?

Day 1 (Thursday).   Place the Popcorn Rock in a clear glass bowl and add just enough white distilled vinegar to cover the rock completely. Place the bowl in a place where it will not be disturbed.

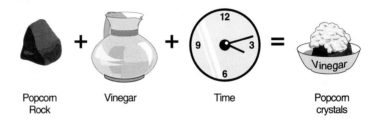

| Popcorn Rock | Vinegar | Time | Popcorn crystals |

What might happen to the rock in the vinegar?
Observe your rock three times a day and record any changes you see.
    Day 2 (Friday).   What do you see forming on the highest ridges of the rock late in the afternoon?
Let the Popcorn Rock remain undisturbed over the weekend.
    Day 5 (Monday).   What do you see about ¼ inch above the evaporating white vinegar?
    What do the crystals look like?
    What do you think those crystals are?
    Day 6 (Tuesday).   Do you think the Popcorn Rock "grows" from the bottom (like hair) or does it "grow" from the tips of the crystals (like tree branches)?

What should you know?

Bleached-blonde hair has new, dark-colored hair below the older, light-colored hair. Names carved in tree bark remain at the same level, even as the tree grows taller.
    How might we devise experiments to resolve this?

[6]The author is indebted to the following publication for excellent lessons using Popcorn Rock. The publication is available from its author: Richard David Barnes, *Popcorn Rock—An Experiment in Crystal Science*, 1989, Bountiful, UT: PR NEWS.

Day 7 (Wednesday).   How might putting a very small amount of food coloring in the vinegar help us resolve whether Popcorn Rock "grows" from the bottom or from the tips of the crystals?

Try it.

What should you know?

Capillary action, similar to osmosis in trees, pulls the vinegar, calcium carbonate, and food coloring up from the bottom. If the aragonite crystals are "growing" from the bottom, the food coloring will remain in the lower crystals, formed after the vinegar was added. Popcorn Rock "grows" from the bottom, making it a stalagmite. Let the Popcorn Rock crystals form until all the vinegar has evaporated. If crystals get broken, put the rock back in the vinegar and start over.

How could students apply their new knowledge?

Some students may have noticed that bubbles formed in the vinegar.

- *What caused the bubbles, and how might we find out what the bubbles are?*
- *What might happen if you allowed your Popcorn Rock crystals to form in a sealed plastic bag?*
- *Why do you think vinegar was used to form the Popcorn Rock crystals? Would the same thing happen if a different liquid were used? Which liquid(s) would you suggest?*
- *How might we test your hypotheses?*

V

Inquiry Science Activities for Students with Special Needs

NSES *Given the diversity of student needs, experiences, and backgrounds, and the goal that all students will achieve a common set of standards, schools must support high-quality, diverse, and varied opportunities.*[1]

The activities in this section are designed for students with special needs. You either have, or soon will have, such students in your classroom. There are over 8 million youngsters in schools today (1 in 10) with some form of special need. Public Law 94–142, now called the Individuals with Disabilities Education Act **(IDEA),** directs that all students have a right to a full free public education within the *least restrictive environment*. Further, the Americans With Disabilities Act (ADA), a civil rights law, prohibits discrimination because of disability. The current trend influenced by these two laws is the integration of students with special needs into the regular classroom for most or all of the school day. This is called **inclusion.** Therefore, whether the special need is a sensory, mental, emotional, or social one, it is important for you to educate yourself about the disability and to find ways to adapt your teaching for the students who have special needs in your classroom.

Inquiry science activities can provide a sense of achievement to students with special needs who may seldom enjoy such success in school. It is not easy to accomplish the task of providing individualized science activities; however, by becoming aware of your students' individual strengths and interests and the possible ways of adapting instruction to create a barrier-free environment, you will be able to individualize your science program.

---

[1]*From National Science Education Standards* (p. 221), National Research Council, 1996, Washington, D.C.: National Academy Press.

In the following pages, inquiry activities are presented for students with the following special needs:

1. Blindness or vision impairments
2. Developmental delays
3. Visual perception problems (as may be present in students with specific learning disabilities)
4. Emotional disorders
5. Deafness or hearing impairments

These activities are not meant to be exhaustive but are suggestions of ways to meet the special needs of some students in your science classroom. As you practice using the activities, you will get to know your students better and will be able to find additional ways to adapt science activities for them. Learning to be more sensitive to students with special needs will help you respond more sensitively to all of your students. The unexpected gain to you—focusing upon "special needs" students—will be to see all your students as individuals.

The format used in this section is the Engagement Activities format used in Sections 2 through 4. This format allows teachers more flexibility in modifying activities for individual students. As you become more confident with science activities for students with special needs, you will be able to modify some of the Exploration Activities in Sections 2 through 4, as well.

STUDENTS WITH BLINDNESS OR VISION IMPAIRMENTS

▶ *Learning About Magnets (K–8)*

What materials will you need?

Assorted magnets, common objects attracted and not attracted by magnets (paper clips, rubber bands, plastic and metal zippers, pencils, paper, wire, etc.), 2 shallow boxes, sandpaper
(*Note:* Avoid using sharp or pointed objects.)

What inquiry questions could you ask?

What are magnets?
What objects do they pick up?

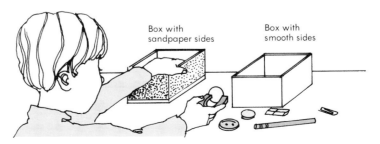

Box with sandpaper sides

Box with smooth sides

What activities could
students do?

Have students handle the magnets and describe their shapes (bar, disc-shaped, horseshoe, U-shaped, cylindrical, etc.). Ask:

How will you know if a magnet picks up (attracts) an object?

Students will readily discern by touching the magnet that something was attracted to it if an object "sticks" to the magnet. Ask students to name the objects on the table and then test to find out which objects are attracted by the magnet. They can sort objects tested by the magnet into two shallow boxes. One box with smooth sides can be for objects attracted by magnets. Sandpaper glued to another box for objects not attracted by magnets can facilitate tactile sorting. Once students understand the sorting system, they can verify the contents of both boxes by themselves and even test new objects.

▶ *Identifying Objects in the Environment (K–8)*

What materials will you
need?

Masks to cover eyes, pairs of noisemakers (rattles, party horns, "clickers," etc.)

What inquiry questions
could you ask?

Can you find your partner if you cannot see him or her? How?

What activities could
students do?

Take a group of sighted and blind or students with low vision outside your classroom to a relatively open (free of trees, shrubs, or other obstacles) lawn area. Have other students or adults keep students from moving outside the area as they engage in this activity. Play a game in which students assume the roles of limited-vision animals. Have students pair up. Instruct sighted students to wear masks over their eyes. Have one student in each pair be a predator; the other, prey. Give each prey one of a variety of noisemakers (clickers, party horns, and so on). At a signal from you, prey try to find the other prey who have the same noisemakers. Predators, in the meantime, try to capture the noisy prey.

After the game, have students all sit quietly and listen to the environmental sounds. Sighted students should still be wearing masks. Ask:

Which sounds can you identify?
Which sounds are made by the same source?
In which direction do you hear the various sounds?
Which sound do you like the best? Why?
Which sound do you like the least? Why?
How do you think a particular sound was made?

For more information about this and other life science activities for students who are visually impaired, see Jane E. Cappiello, "Hands-on Science for Blind Students," *Science Scope* 15(4), January 1992, 44–45; and Larry Malone and Linda DeLucchi, "Life Science for Visually Impaired Students," *Science and Children* 16 (5), February 1979, 29–31.

▶ *Finding Out About Body Position and Heart Rate (K–8)*

What materials will you
need?

Stethoscopes, braille-faced clocks

What inquiry question could you ask?	*Does your heart beat faster when you lie down, stand up, or run?*
What activities could students do?	After raising the question with students who are blind or visually impaired, give simple instructions on how to use the equipment and carry out the activity. Introduce the term **variable** and explain that the variable they will investigate is body position and how it affects their heart rate. Have students learn to use the stethoscope to listen to their heartbeats while counting the beats per minute on the braille-faced clock. An adult or older student can help younger students with the numbers. After students have taken and recorded their heart rates in lying, standing, and running situations, discuss the results. Help them to see the effect of body position on heart rate. You can extend the activity by asking additional questions. Ask:

> *What other variables could be investigated in this activity?*
> *What effect would the following have on heart rate: age, amount of movement, time of day, drinking soda pop, smoking, and so on?*

Encourage students to explore the variables without giving them specific directions on how to do it.

▶ *"Seeing" and Comparing Polluted Water Samples (3–8)*

What materials will you need?	4 jars of water containing different pollutants, light sensor (available on Federal Quota from the American Printing House for the Blind, P.O. Box 6085, Louisville, KY 40206), light source (sunlight or filmstrip projector)
What inquiry question could you ask?	*How can you use your sense of hearing to find out which jars contain the most polluted water?*
What activities could students do?	Prepare four jars of water with varying amounts of pollutants (soil, debris, egg shells, etc.). Introduce and demonstrate to the students the light sensor device. This device produces an auditory signal of varying pitch and volume as a result of its exposure to different intensities of light. Set up the four jars of various pollutants with a light source behind them, as shown in the diagram.

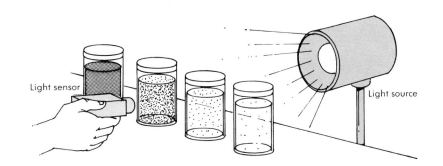

Light sensor

Light source

At close range, have students point the light sensor directly at each jar, as shown in the diagram. A beeping sound will be emitted; the greater the amount of light coming into the sensor, the higher and more frequent the beeping. Students will discover that the fewer pollutants there are in each a jar, the greater the amount of light coming through the jar, and, therefore, the more shrill and rapid the beep from the sensor. More pollutants result in much less light coming through the jar to the sensor, and thus a slower and lower pitched beep occurs. *Note:* For an excellent expanded description of using the light sensor with students who are blind, see Frank L. Franks and LaRhea Sanford, "Using the Light Sensor to Introduce Laboratory Science," *Science and Children* 13(6), March 1976, 48–49.

STUDENTS WITH DEVELOPMENTAL DELAYS

▶ *Developing a Sense of Temperature (K–8)*

What materials will you need?

Several metal bowls, water of varying temperatures

What inquiry questions could you ask?

How do hot things feel?
How do cold things feel?

What activities could students do?
Safety Precaution!

Fill several metal bowls with varying temperatures of water, from ice cold to very warm. *Caution:* Do not use water hot enough to scald or injure any student. Let the water sit in the bowls for a few minutes, then have the students feel the *outside* of the bowls. Ask:
Which bowl feels cold?
Which one feels warm?
Which one feels hot?
If a student does not know the difference, try the following procedure. Say:
This bowl feels *cold.*
Does it make your hand cold?
This bowl is *hot.*
Is your hand hot?
Where else have you felt hot and cold things?

Hot
Cold

Relate this activity to everyday experiences by comparing it to holding a glass of iced drink, a cup of hot soup, and so on.

Point out the dangers of hot and cold. Ask:

Why should we use a potholder if we are holding something hot from the oven or stove?

Why should you wear a coat and gloves when it is very cold outside?

How do coats and gloves keep you warm?

Where are very hot things in our homes and school?

Have pictures of ovens, stoves, radiators, and so on. Ask:

What materials could items be made of that might be unsafe to handle if heated? (glass, metals, etc.)

▶ Learning the Concept of Weight (K–8)

What materials will you need?

Small blocks of wood of the same size, but made of different kinds of woods, such as balsa (model airplane wood), oak, pine, or mahogany

What inquiry questions could you ask?

Which of these blocks do you think would be the heaviest? Lightest?

What activities could students do?

Ask students to explain what it means when people say something is heavy. Have them use whatever words will help them to develop the concept, as long as the words do not connote misconceptions. They might say, "It's harder to lift." If they have difficulty with the concept of heavy and light, help them to develop it. Now give them the blocks. Ask:

Do you think they all weigh the same?

Which one seems the heaviest? Lightest?

Have students feel the blocks and place them in order from heaviest to lightest. Label the heaviest block with an H and use an L for the lightest one. Ask students what things in the classroom are heavy and light. Place an H or L on the objects selected. (Some examples of heavy might be: desks, cabinets, people; examples of light: paper, pencils, paper clips; and so on.) Explain why it is dangerous to lift very heavy things.

▶ *Discriminating Among Tastes (K–8)*

What materials will you need?

Box of cotton swabs; bottles of solutions of common liquids that are salty, sweet, sour, bitter, acidic, and neutral

What inquiry questions could you ask?

How many of you would like to play a game?
Are you a good detective?

What activities could students do?

Tell students they are going to play a detective game to try to find out what is in the bottles you have. *Caution:* Tell them *never* to taste anything they are not sure about. Ask why they should be cautious about tasting unknown substances and explain the dangers of poisons. Tell students that none of the substances in the bottles is poisonous and that they are familiar tastes they experience every day.

Give each student his or her own swab and explain why this is necessary (to prevent spreading germs, colds, other diseases, etc.). Give all students a sample of something sweet, such as syrup. Ask:

What kind of taste is this?

Have them agree that it is sweet and, if possible, have them identify the source. Throw the cotton swabs away and give each student a second one. This time use a sour solution. Repeat the identification procedure and orally introduce the word *sour,* if appropriate for the group, write the word on the chalkboard. Repeat this procedure for all of the solutions.

Ask students what kinds of foods they eat that are salty, sweet, sour, bitter, acid, or neutral. Have them cut out pictures from magazines for each category. Discuss their lunch in school and visit the cafeteria to observe some foods. Have students note which category each food is in.

Note: For older or less developmentally delayed students, you can show them that different places on the tongue react more strongly to certain tastes. Touch solutions to these four sensation areas of the tongue.

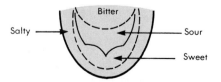

▶ *Recognizing Common Odors (K–8)*

What materials will you need?

Common strong-smelling substances in jars, such as onion, perfume, rubbing alcohol, pepper, cinnamon, peppermint, and so on

What inquiry question could you ask?

Who can tell us what this odor (smell) is?

What activities could students do?

Have students smell a familiar substance (peppermint) by holding the appropriate jar at least 1 foot from their noses and fanning the odor toward them. (This avoids overwhelming the student with the odor and teaches him or her a safe way to smell unknown substances that might otherwise injure the student's sensitive nose.) *Note:* At first, to help students learn to otherwise recognize various odors, present the smell in the appropriately labeled jar, allowing students to see the material. Then ask students to discriminate among various odors while blindfolded.

For students who are more advanced, wait to label the jars until after students identify the odors. Use both oral and written words for the names of odors, as appropriate. Have students identify odors in their homes, school, and outdoors. Have them cut pictures from magazines of common strong-smelling substances and label them, such as gasoline, flowers, paint, smoke, and so on. Have students identify odors they like and dislike. Stress that some odors are dangerous, such as gas and smoke.

STUDENTS WITH VISUAL PERCEPTION PROBLEMS[2]

▶ *Observing Properties of Leaves (K–2)*

What materials will you need?

Variety of leaves (maple, oak, elm, birch, etc.)

[2]The authors are indebted to the following article and others in the *Science and Children* issue devoted to Science for the Handicapped: Marlene Thier, "Utilizing Science Experiences for Developing Perception Skills," *Science and Children* 13(6), March 1996, 39–40.

What inquiry question could you ask?

What do you notice about the shape of this leaf?

What activities could students do?

Have each student look at a maple leaf. Ask:
What is this?
Where do you think it came from?
How many points does it have?
What color is it?
How many large lines (veins) are there coming from the stem?

Let the student experience the leaf through sensory activities, that is, feeling it with the hand, rubbing it against the cheek, smelling it, and crushing it.
What does the smell make you think of?
How else would you describe the leaf?

Ask students to think of other properties. Introduce the word *property* for students to use when referring to the leaf's attributes. Introduce other species of leaves. Ask:
How are the leaves alike? Different?
What properties are the same?
What properties are different?

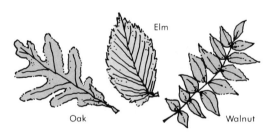

▶ **Comparing Properties of Shells or Buttons and Classifying Them (K–2)**

What materials will you need?

Assortment of shells or buttons (Similar activity could be done with various kinds of beans or seeds.)

What activities could students do?

Give each student a handful of shells or buttons. Ask:
How are these things alike?
How are they different?

Group them together by the same property.
Which properties might you use?

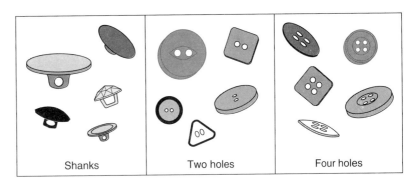

| Shanks | Two holes | Four holes |

Allow students to group the objects. Ask:
How can you group the buttons according to a different property?
Note: In this activity, students are to not only make visual discriminations but should also categorize the items based on similarities and differences they see.

▶ *Using Plants to Teach Visual Sequencing (K–2)*

What materials will you need?

What activities could students do?

Milk cartons, soil, pea seeds, chart paper, strips of paper, string, scissors

Have each student plant a pea seed in a milk carton. Make certain students keep the soil moist and that they have a certain time each day for observing the plant and recording their observations. As soon as germination takes place and plants break through the soil, set up a chart for students to use to record the growth of each plant. Have them mark on the chart each day any changes that take place. They can measure plant height with string and then cut strips of paper to match the length of the cut string. The strips of paper can then be pasted on a chart to record progressive growth over a 6-week period, as shown in the diagram.

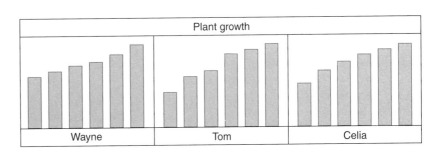

| Plant growth |
| Wayne | Tom | Celia |

When working with younger children, plant an additional seed each week so students can see plants ranging in growth from 1 to 6 weeks. This will help them with visual sequencing. They begin by observing a natural phenomenon, then learn to record small changes over a period of time and in a sequenced progression—a concept important for them to know.

▶ Learning Relative Position and Motion (K–5)

What materials will you need?

Mr. O[3] for each student, white chenille wires, gummed white dots, blocks

What activities could students do?

Students with perceptual problems usually have poor directionality concepts. "Mr. O," from the SCIS Relative Position and Motion unit, can help these students learn position in space, relative position in the environment, directionality, and figure-ground relationships.

Show students Mr. O. Tell them that he sees things only from his point of view. Cut out a Mr. O for each student. For younger children, after introducing Mr. O, play a game to familiarize them with his parts and to introduce words for directions in relation to him, as shown in the diagram.

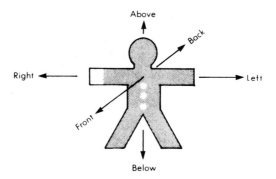

Younger children can also hang Mr. O around their necks while you point out the following things:

Mr. O's right hand is white.
Put a white chenille wire around your right hand.
Mr. O has three white buttons on the front of him.
Put three white gummed paper dots on the front of you.
Now ask the students to place a block to the right of Mr. O. Ask:

Where is the block in relation to Mr. O?
Where is the block in relation to you?
Is it near or far?

Do the same with the left side, in front of, in back of, above, and below, using only one variable at a time. Gradually build to more than one variable.

---

[3]For a detailed description of Mr. O, see Robert Karplus et al., *Relative Position and Motion* (Level 4), Teacher's Guide SCIS, 3 (Hudson, NH: Delta Education, 1992), pp. 29–39.

Once the student begins to understand this use of Mr. O, take Mr. O from around the child's neck and turn Mr. O to face him or her. Ask:

Where is Mr. O's right hand now in relation to yours?

Place the block to the right, left, front, and back of Mr. O and ask the student to report the position, relative first to Mr. O, and them to himself or herself.

Note: Students become aware of needed changes in describing directionality from a non-ego-centered frame. They begin to develop direction-giving capabilities through awareness of relative position in space and figure-ground relationships. Students with visual perception problems have great difficulty with this task and need the systematic help shown here.

▶ *Developing Visual Scrutiny and Analysis in an Outside-the-Classroom Walk (K–5)*

What materials will you need?

Small envelopes or plastic bags, paper, pencils

What activities could students do?

Select a site outside your classroom where you and your students can take a walk. Before going, instruct students to observe, record, or collect the following:

- Task cards (3″ × 5″ index cards can be used to write down what the students will look for)
- Samples of five different-colored natural objects that have fallen to the ground (caution students not to pick anything from living organisms)
- Places (to be listed on their recording sheets) where they saw
  a. three different colors on the same plant,
  b. five different shades of any one color (green, for instance) along the path,
  c. six different textures on living organisms, and
  d. as many different colors as they can find
- Samples of evidence that animals have inhabited the environment
- Samples of dead insects
- Samples of evidence that people have been in the area
- Samples of different kinds of seeds in the area
- Other samples that are applicable to your outdoor site

Have the students place their samples in small envelopes, plastic bags, or other suitable containers. With younger children or children who have severe visual perception problems, it is best to use one of the activities at a time, so they focus on one variable in their environment and filter out distractions. The activities are also progressive, moving from observing many different plants (looking at plants and finding colors) to finding the same variable on only one plant (how many different colors on one plant). Later, in the classroom discussions, help students describe their samples and share them with their classmates. Further activities in pasting samples on paper, writing descriptive words for each object, and talking about their findings aid students who have visual perception problems in developing needed skills for further exploration of their environment and for reading, writing, and spelling.

STUDENTS WITH EMOTIONAL DISORDERS

▶ *Learning About the Environment by Touching (K–5)*

What materials will you need?

Paper, crayons, chalk, soft pencils, aluminum foil

What inquiry question could you ask?

How can our fingertips give us different kinds of information than our eyes can?

What activities could students do?

Direct contact with and the understanding and mastery of everyday living experiences under a sensitive teacher's guidance can produce an extensive and exciting learning environment for the child with an emotional disorder. One such activity can be a tactile experience. Take your students (with assistance from parents) on a walk around the school. Have students select surfaces and use the suggested materials to do rubbings of those surfaces. In urban areas, they can do rubbings of sidewalks, sewer covers, grates, signs, and fences. The rubbings can be used to create texture panels and are also effective when they are individually matted and mounted. You might also attempt to get your students to talk about how the objects felt, whether they were rough, smooth, soft, hard, wet, or dry.

You can find many more activities for children with emotional disorders in the following practical book: *An Outdoor Education Guide for Urban Teachers of the Emotionally Handicapped*, proceedings presented by the State University of New York State Education Department Division for Handicapped Children, and the Division of Health, Physical Education and Recreation, in cosponsorship with State University College of Arts and Science at Plattsburgh and Clinton, Essex, Warren, and Washington Counties BOCES, Special Study Institute, funded through PL 91–230 (June 1991).

▶ *Learning About the Environment by Listening and Moving (K–5)*

What materials will you need?

A walking trip in the community

What inquiry questions could you ask?

What people-made sights and sounds can you identify?
How can you use your body to reproduce these sights and sounds?

What activities could students do?

Sitting or working in a confined space (a desk and chair, for instance) for long periods of time creates static learning experiences. This is especially true for children who have emotional disorders. They need to stretch and expand their bodies and minds, probably more than other children. These students can also begin to feel the same freedom of movement outside as they would experience in a gymnasium. Take students into the community and ask them to identify the following people-made sights and sounds.

Taxi cabs	Construction machines	Helicopters
Fire alarms	Motorcycles	Fire engines
Airplanes	Cars	Trucks
Ambulances	Buses	Air hammers

Ask:
What are the sounds of each vehicle?
How can you use your body to show the intensity and rhythm of each vehicle?
How is the sound of a fire engine different from the sound of an ambulance?
Show the differences with your movements.
Would you move in a fast, slow, or jerky way if you sounded like an airplane?
A dump truck?

How are car horn sounds different? Make the sounds.
How do various sounds make you feel? Happy? Sad?
Show how you feel by your movements.
Imitate with your body a vehicle starting and stopping.

STUDENTS WITH DEAFNESS OR HEARING IMPAIRMENTS

Students with hearing impairments can gain valuable experience in the regular classroom; however, there must be an attempt to individualize instruction.

All of the inquiry science activities described for other students with special needs are applicable for those who are deaf or hearing impaired, as are the inquiry activities in Sections 2 through 4, when you use the following minimal adaptations of your regular classroom procedure.[4]

1. Seat students where they can see your lip movements easily. Avoid having them face bright lights or windows.
2. Speak naturally, in complete, grammatical sentences. Do not overemphasize lip movements or slow your rate of speech. Do not speak too loudly, especially if the student is wearing a hearing aid.
3. Avoid visual distractions such as excessive make-up, jewelry, or clothes that might draw attention away from your lips.
4. Do not stand with your back to a window or bright light source. This shadows your face and makes speech reading difficult.
5. Try not to move around the room while speaking, or to talk while writing on the board. If possible, use an overhead projector, which allows you to speak and write while still maintaining eye contact with students.
6. During class discussions, encourage students with hearing impairments to face the speaker. Allow them to move around the room, if necessary, to get a better view.
7. In some cases, a sign-language interpreter might be assigned to a student. Allow the interpreter and student to select the most favorable seating arrangement. The interpreter should interpret everything said in the classroom as precisely as possible. The interpreter may also be asked to interpret the student's oral or signed responses to the teacher and class. Interpreters are not tutors or classroom aides but rather professional personnel who facilitate classroom communication.
8. When possible, write assignments and directions on the chalkboard or distribute photocopied directions to the class. If assignments are given orally, you might ask a hearing student to take notes for a deaf or hearing impaired student.

[4]Adapted from Norris G. Haring and Linda McCormick, eds. *Exceptional Children and Youth*, 6th ed., 1994, Englewood Cliffs, NJ: Merrill/Prentice Hall, 1.

9. Ask students who are deaf or hearing impaired to repeat or explain class material to make sure they have understood it. If embarrassed by their special needs, these students might learn to nod affirmatively when asked if they understood, even though they may not have understood the instructions at all.

10. If a student has a hearing aid, familiarize yourself with its operation and ask the student or the student's special class teacher to demonstrate it to the class. The student should assume responsibility for the care of the aid.

11. Maintain close contact with the other professional personnel who have responsibility for the student's education. If possible, regularly exchange visits with the special class teacher or therapist to observe the student in other educational settings.

Appendixes

Sixty Years of Elementary-School Science:
A Guided Tour

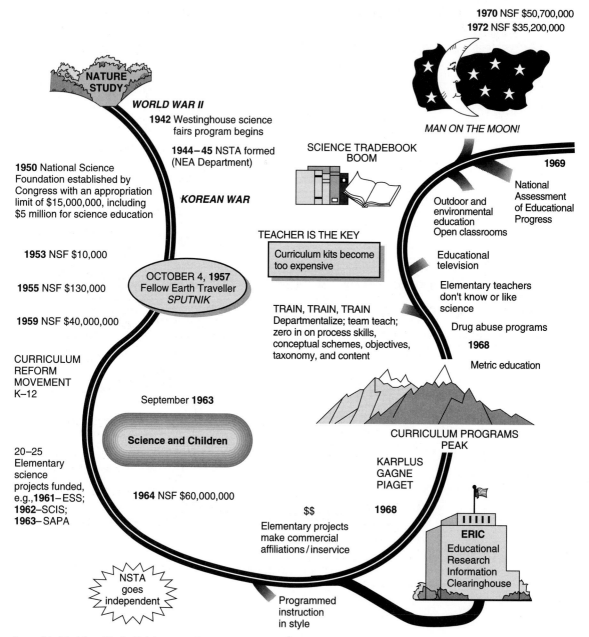

1970 NSF $50,700,000
1972 NSF $35,200,000

NATURE STUDY

WORLD WAR II

1942 Westinghouse science fairs program begins

1944–45 NSTA formed (NEA Department)

KOREAN WAR

1950 National Science Foundation established by Congress with an appropriation limit of $15,000,000, including $5 million for science education

1953 NSF $10,000

1955 NSF $130,000

1959 NSF $40,000,000

CURRICULUM REFORM MOVEMENT K–12

20–25 Elementary science projects funded, e.g.,**1961**–ESS; **1962**–SCIS; **1963**–SAPA

OCTOBER 4, **1957** Fellow Earth Traveller *SPUTNIK*

September **1963**

Science and Children

1964 NSF $60,000,000

NSTA goes independent

SCIENCE TRADEBOOK BOOM

TEACHER IS THE KEY

Curriculum kits become too expensive

TRAIN, TRAIN, TRAIN Departmentalize; team teach; zero in on process skills, conceptual schemes, objectives, taxonomy, and content

$$ Elementary projects make commercial affiliations/inservice

Programmed instruction in style

MAN ON THE MOON!

1969

National Assessment of Educational Progress

Outdoor and environmental education Open classrooms

Educational television

Elementary teachers don't know or like science

Drug abuse programs

1968

Metric education

CURRICULUM PROGRAMS PEAK

KARPLUS GAGNE PIAGET

1968

ERIC
Educational Research Information Clearinghouse

*Source:*Modified from Phyllis R. Marcuccio "Forty-Five Years of Elementary School Science: A Guided Tour" as it appeared in *Science and Children* 24, no. 4 (January 1987): 12–14. Copyright 1987 by the National Science Teachers Association. Reproduced with permission.

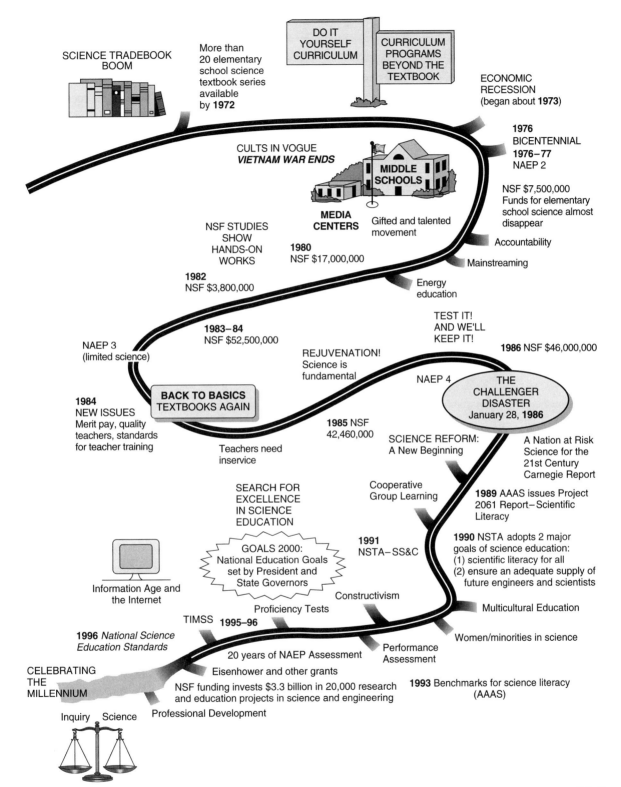

SCIENCE TRADEBOOK BOOM

More than 20 elementary school science textbook series available by **1972**

DO IT YOURSELF CURRICULUM

CURRICULUM PROGRAMS BEYOND THE TEXTBOOK

ECONOMIC RECESSION (began about **1973**)

1976 BICENTENNIAL
1976–77 NAEP 2

CULTS IN VOGUE
VIETNAM WAR ENDS

MIDDLE SCHOOLS

NSF $7,500,000 Funds for elementary school science almost disappear

MEDIA CENTERS

Gifted and talented movement

Accountability

NSF STUDIES SHOW HANDS-ON WORKS

1980 NSF $17,000,000

Mainstreaming

Energy education

1982 NSF $3,800,000

TEST IT! AND WE'LL KEEP IT!

1983–84 NSF $52,500,000

1986 NSF $46,000,000

NAEP 3 (limited science)

REJUVENATION! Science is fundamental

NAEP 4

THE CHALLENGER DISASTER January 28, **1986**

1984 NEW ISSUES Merit pay, quality teachers, standards for teacher training

BACK TO BASICS TEXTBOOKS AGAIN

1985 NSF 42,460,000

A Nation at Risk Science for the 21st Century Carnegie Report

Teachers need inservice

SCIENCE REFORM: A New Beginning

SEARCH FOR EXCELLENCE IN SCIENCE EDUCATION

Cooperative Group Learning

1989 AAAS issues Project 2061 Report–Scientific Literacy

GOALS 2000: National Education Goals set by President and State Governors

1991 NSTA–SS&C

1990 NSTA adopts 2 major goals of science education:
(1) scientific literacy for all
(2) ensure an adequate supply of future engineers and scientists

Information Age and the Internet

Proficiency Tests

Constructivism

Multicultural Education

TIMSS **1995–96**

Women/minorities in science

1996 *National Science Education Standards*

20 years of NAEP Assessment

Performance Assessment

CELEBRATING THE MILLENNIUM

Eisenhower and other grants

NSF funding invests $3.3 billion in 20,000 research and education projects in science and engineering

1993 Benchmarks for science literacy (AAAS)

Inquiry   Science

Professional Development

Notes on the Guided Tour

Notable Achievements

- Elementary school science now has a niche in elementary schools: It is accepted as important for all students, it is integrated with other subjects in the curriculum, and it is supported by principals and other administrators led by a government that expects all of its citizens to be scientifically literate.
- There is a new breed of elementary science specialists.
- Hands-on teaching is giving rise to inquiry and technology to foster creativity, intuition, and problem-solving skills. (Hands-on teachers are "guides" rather than "tellers.") The popularity of hands-on teaching is also creating a need for more inservice training and for more science centers and labs.
- Nonschool settings, such as outdoor education centers and museums, have increased their support, often introducing subject matter that includes issues of social concern like pollution, ecology, and energy education.
- Teaching tools—books, software, videos, and other multimedia products drive the changing curricula.
- Up-to-date research in science education is readily available through the Eisenhower Clearinghouse.
- Recent and projected certification programs subject teachers to more rigorous standards.
- Studies and testing, forums and conferences exist to deal specifically with the concerns of elementary science.
- The business and industry communities, concerned about the interrelationships of science, technology, and society, have sought a role in science education. Organizations like the American Chemical Society, the National Academy of Science, and the American Association for the Advancement of Science have also cooperated to forward the cause of science education.
- SI metric measure has been generally adopted to promote through science education.
- A teamwork approach to curriculum building now exists among teachers, scientists, administrators, community, and government.
- There are established pockets of commitment to science, and programs have been developed to point out excellent science teaching throughout the country.

Familiar Road Signs

- Surges in National Science Foundation funding
- Efforts following crisis situations
- The continuing presence of textbooks
- National Assessment of Educational Progress reports
- Calls for new curricula
- Calls for inservice programs

Some Remaining Problems

- Teachers continue to be educated in the same way.
- No comprehensive, agreed-upon scope and sequence has been established.

- Progress depends on funds from the National Science Foundation.
- The pool of students interested in science is shrinking—nearly half the current ninth grade class in urban high schools will not even graduate, let alone seek science-related careers.
- Despite millions of dollars spent on curriculum studies, teachers still depend on textbooks.
- The United States continues to lag behind other countries in the amount of science being taught to children.
- The best science students are not attracted to science teaching careers.
- Average Americans care more for pseudoscience than science.
- Teachers do not apply educational research.

Science Supplies, Equipment, and Materials Obtainable from Community Sources

This is only a partial list of possible community sources for science program materials in elementary and middle schools. Other sources that should not be overlooked include parents, the janitor or custodian of the school, the school cafeteria, radio and television repair shops, florists' shops, other teachers in the school, junior and senior high school science teachers, and so on. The materials are there; it just takes a little looking.

There are times, though, when in spite of the most careful searching, certain pieces of equipment or supplies are not obtainable from local sources; there are also many things that schools should buy from scientific supply houses. A partial list of some selected, reliable scientific supply houses is provided in Appendix C.

Dollar Store or Department Store

balloons
balls
compasses (magnetic)
cotton (absorbent)
flashlights
food coloring
glues and paste
inks
magnifying glasses
marbles
mechanical toys
mirrors
mousetraps
paper towels
scissors
sponges
staples
thermometers

Drugstore

adhesive tape
alcohol (rubbing)
bottles
cigar boxes
cold cream
corks
cotton
dilute acids, preferably 1–5%
dilute H_2O_2 (1 1/2%)
forceps or tweezers
limewater
medicine droppers
pipe cleaners
rubber stoppers
soda bicarbonate
spatulas
straws
sulfur
TES-Tape™
tincture of iodine, diluted to straw
  color

Electrical Appliance Shop

bell wire
dry cells
electric fans
flashlight bulbs
flashlights
friction tape
magnets (from old
  appliances)
soldering iron

Fabric Shop

cardboard tubes
cheesecloth
flannel
knitting needles
leather
needles
netting
scraps of different kinds of fabrics
silk thread
spools

Farm or Dairy

birds' nests
bottles
clay
containers
gravel
hay or straw
humus
insects
leaves
loam
lodestone
rocks
sand
seeds

Fire Department

samples of materials used to extinguish
  various types of fires
water pumping equipment

Plant Nursery or Garden Supply Store

bulbs (tulips, etc.)
fertilizers
flowerpots
garden hose
garden twine
growing plants
labels
lime
peat pots
seed catalogs
seeds
spray guns
sprinkling cans
trowels and other garden tools

Service Station

ball bearings
cans
copper tubing
gears
gear transmissions
grease
inner tubes
jacks
maps
pulleys
tools
valves from tires
wheels

Grocery Store

aluminum foil
aluminum pie tins
ammonia
baking soda
borax
cellophane
clothespins
cornstarch
corrugated cardboard boxes
food storage bags
fruits
paper bags

paper towels
paraffin
plastic wrap
salt
sandwich bags
sealable plastic bags
sponges
sugar
vegetables
vinegar
wax
wax paper

Hardware Store

brace and bits
cement
chisels
clocks
corks
dry-cell batteries
electric push buttons, lamps, and
    sockets
extension cords
files
flashlights
fruit jars
glass cutters
glass friction rods
glass funnels
glass tubing
hammers
hard rubber rods
insulated copper wire
lamp chimneys
metal and metal scraps
nails
nuts and bolts
paints and varnishes
plaster of paris
pulleys
sandpaper
saws
scales
scrap lumber
screening
screwdrivers

screws
steel wool
thermometers (indoor and outdoor)
3–6 volt toy electric motors
tin snips
turpentine
wheelbarrow
window glass (broken pieces will do)
wire
yardsticks

Machine Shop

ball bearings
iron filings
iron rods
magnets
nuts and bolts
scrap metals
screws
wire

Medical Centers Dental Offices, or Hospitals

corks
flasks
funnels
glass tubing
lenses
litmus paper
microscopes
models, such as teeth
rubber sheeting
rubber stoppers
rubber tubing
test tube holders
test tubes
thermometers
tongue depressors

Music Shop

broken string and drum heads
musical instruments
pitch pipes
tuning forks

Pet Shop

air pumps
animal cages
ant houses
aquariums
cages
fish
insects
nets (butterfly, fish, etc.)
plastic tubing

strainers
terrariums

Restaurant or Fast-Food Outlet

beverage stirrers
bones (chicken, etc.)
bottles
cans (coffee, 5-gallon size)
drums (ice cream)
five-gallon cans (oil)

food coloring
gallon jars (wide-mouthed, pickles, mayonnaise, etc.)
gallon jugs (vinegar)
pie tins
plastic spoons
plastic trays
soda straws

For additional sources of common, easily obtained supplies and apparatus suitable for your elementary- or middle-school science program, see *The NSTA Guide: Science Education Suppliers* (Arlington, VA: National Science Teachers Association, published annually).

Selected Sources of Scientific Supplies, Models, Living Things, Kits, and Software

Arbor Scientific

Demonstration equipment for physical science
P. O. Box 2750
Ann Arbor, MI 48106-2750
Toll Free: 800-367-6695
Phone: 734-913-6200
Fax: 734-913-6201
Email: mail@arborsci.com
Web site: www.aborsci.com

Brock Optical, Inc.

Microscopes—rugged enough for small children
414 Lake Howell Road
Maitland, FL 32751
Toll Free: 800-780-9111
Phone: 407-647-6611
Web site: www.magiscope@aol.com

Carolina Science and Math(Carolina Biological Supply Co.)

Instructional materials for all sciences; Science and Technology for Children (STC) guides and materials
2700 York Road
Burlington, NC 27215-3398
Toll Free: 800-334-5551
Phone: 901-584-0381
Fax: 800-222-7112

Cuisenaire/Dale Seymour Publications (A Division of Pearson Learning)

Hands-on science materials
Pearson Learning
4350 Equity Drive
P. O. Box 2649
Columbus, OH 43216
Toll Free: 800-321-3106
Web site: www.pearsonlearning.com/cuisenaire-dsp

Delta Education Incorporated

Materials, kits, and activities for hands-on science programs, including FOSS, SCIS 3+, and DSMII (Delta Science Modules)
80 Northwest Boulevard
P. O. Box 3000
Nashua, NH 03063
Toll Free: 800-258-1302
Email: mbacon@delta-edu.com
Web site: www.delta-ed.com

Discovery Scope, Inc.

Small hand-held microscopes
3202 Echo Mountain Drive
Kingwood, TX 77345
Phone: 281-360-3834
Web site: discoveryscope.net

Educational Innovations, Inc.

Heat-sensitive paper, UV-detecting beads, Cartesian diver, super-absorbent polymers, and other science supplies
151 River Road
Cos Cob, CT 06807
Toll Free:888-912-7474
Phone:203-629-6049
Fax:203-629-2739
Email:info@teachersource.com

Educational Products, Inc.

Science fair display boards and materials
1342 North I-35 East
Carrollton, TX 75006
Phone:972-245-9512

Estes Industries

Model rockets
1295 H Street
Penrose, CO 81240
Phone: 719-372-6565

Fisher Science Education

Instructional materials for all sciences
485 S. Frontage Road
Burr Ridge, IL 60521
Toll Free: 800-955-1177
Email: info@fisheredu.com
Web site: www.fisheredu.com

Forestry Suppliers, Inc.

Orienteering compasses, water, soil, and biological test kits, tree borers, soil sieves, rock picks, weather instruments, and other materials for interdisciplinary science teaching
P. O. Box 8397
205 W. Rankin Street
Jackson, MS 39201-6126
Toll Free:800-647-5368
Fax: 800-543-4203
Email: fsi@forestry-suppliers.com

Ken-A-Vision Manufacturing Co., Inc. (A Division of Quantum Internet Svc. Inc.)

Microprojectors
Quantum Internet Services, Inc.
4080 Water Tank Road
Manchester, MD 21102
Phone: 410-239-6920

Lab-Aids, Inc.

Single-concept hands-on kits for chemistry, biology, environmental science, and earth science
17 Colt Court
Ronkonkoma, NY 11779-6949
Phone: 516-737-1133
Web site: www.lab-aids.com

Learning Technologies, Inc.

Portable planetariums and other materials for astronomy teaching
40 Cameron Avenue
Somerville, MA 02144
Phone: 617-547-7724

Mountain Home Biological

Living materials, barn owl pellets, skull sets
P. O. Box 1142
White Salmon, WA 98672
Phone: 509-493-2669
Web site: mntnhome@gorge.net

NASCO

Equipment and materials supplies for all sciences
4825 Stoddard Road
P. O. Box 3837
Modesto, CA 95352-3837
Toll Free: 800-558-9595
Fax: 209-545-1669

National Geographic Society

Software, CD-ROMS, laserdiscs, videos, Geokits, learning kits for science and social studies
1145 17th Street NW
Washington, DC 20036-4688
Phone: 202-851-7000
Email: Home@nationalgeographic.com
Web site:
  nationalgeographic.com

NSTA Science Store

Books, posters, software, CD-ROMS
1740 Wilson Boulevard
Arlington, VA 22201-3000
Toll Free: 800-722-NSTA
Email: pubsales@nsta.org
Web site: www.nsta.org

Ohaus Corporation

Balances and measurement aids
29 Hanover Road
Florham Park, NJ 07932
Phone: 973-377-9000
Fax: 973-593-0359

Pitsco-Lego-Dacta

Lego construction kits, model hot air balloons, educational technology products
107 Amherst Aisle
P. O. Box 1707
Pittsburg, KS 66762

Toll Free: 800-362-4308
Email: legohelp@pitsco.com
Web site: www.pitsco-legodacta.com

Rainbow Symphony, Inc.

Lesson kits for the study of light and color, specialty optics materials, diffraction gratings, 3-D lenses, solar/eclipse safe viewing glasses
6860 Canby Avenue
Suite 120
Reseda, CA 91335
Phone: 818-708-8400
Fax: 818-708-8470
Web site: www.rainboxsymphony.com

Sargent Welch

GEMS materials, materials for all sciences
911 Commerce Ct.
P. O. Box 5229
Buffalo Grove, IL 60089-5229
Toll Free: 800-727-4368
Fax: 800-676-2540
Email: sarwel@sargentwelch.com

TOPS Learning Systems

Science lessons using simple available materials
10970 S. Mulino Road
Canby, OR 97013
Phone: 503-266-8550
Web site: www.topscience.org

Source: Compiled from the NSTA Western Area Convention Program Guide, Reno, NV, Dec. 2–4, 1999. Updated via Internet resources.

Noncommercial Sources and Containers for Living Things

Organisms	Noncommercial Source	Culture Containers
POND SNAILS	Freshwater ponds, creeks	Aquaria, large battery jars, gallon glass jars
LAND SNAILS	Mature hardwood forests: on rocks, fallen logs, damp foliage	Terraria, large battery jars
DAPHNIA	Freshwater ponds: at water's edge, and associated with algae	Gallon glass or plastic jars
ISOPODS AND CRICKETS	Under rocks, bricks, and boards that have lain on the ground for some time; between grass and base of brick buildings	Glass or plastic terraria, plastic sweater boxes (Provide vents in cover.)
MEALWORM BEETLES	Corn cribs, around granaries	Gallon glass jars with cheese cloth
FRUIT FLIES	Trap with bananas or apple slices. (Place fruit in a jar with a funnel for a top.)	Tall baby food jars, plastic vials (Punch hole in jar lids, cover with masking tape, and then prick tiny holes in tape with a pin.)
WINGLESS PEA APHIDS*	Search on garden vegetables (e.g., English peas)	On pea plants potted in plastic pots, milk cartons (Keep aphids in a large terrarium so they cannot wander to other plants in the school.)
GUPPIES	Obtain free from persons who raise guppies as a hobby. (They are usually glad to reduce the population when they clean tanks.)	Aquaria, large battery jars
CHAMELEONS*	Dense foliage along river banks or railroad tracks. (Catch with net or large tea strainer.)	Prepare a cage using a broken aquarium. (Broken glass can be replaced by taping cloth screening along sides.)

Source: Carolyn H. Hampton and Carol D. Hampton, "The Establishment of a Life Science Center." Reproduced with permission by *Science and Children* 15 (7), (April 1978), 9. Copyright 1978 by The National Science Teachers Association, 1840 Wilson Blvd., Arlington, VA 22201-3000.

*These species are difficult to obtain from their natural habitats. Unless you have a convenient source, it is better to buy them commercially. Try a local aquarium, pet shop, or science supply house.

Note: For additional excellent articles on raising and using living things in elementary-school classrooms, see Carol Hampton, Carolyn H. Hampton, and David Kramer, *Classroom Creature Culture: Algae to Anoles*, rev. ed., 1994, Arlington, VA: National Science Teachers Association.

Organisms	Noncommercial Source	Culture Containers
FROGS*	Along edges of ponds, ditches, creeks (Catch with large scoop net.)	Large plastic ice chest (Set near a sink so a constant water supply can be provided.)
CHLAMYDOMONAS AND EUGLENA	Freshwater pond	Gallon glass jars, aquaria, battery jars
ELODEA (ANARCHARIS)*	Ponds, creeks: usually along edge or in shallows	Aquaria, large battery jars
EELGRASS*	Wading zone or brackish water	Aquaria, large battery jars
DUCKWEED	Edge of ponds or freshwater swamps	Aquaria, large battery jars
COLEUS AND GERANIUM	Persons who raise them (Start by rooting cuttings in 1 part sand, 1 part vermiculite, in plastic bags.	Clay pots, milk cartons, tin cans

*These species are difficult to obtain from their natural habitats. Unless you have a convenient source, it is better to buy them commercially. Try a local aquarium, pet shop, or science supply house.

Constructing Storage Areas for Supplies and Houses for Living Things

Your classroom has unused space that can be used for storage, such as spaces below window ledges, countertops, sinks, above and around heating units (radiators), and even under student desks.

You can purchase excellent commercially made cabinets that fit any of these spaces, or your students and/or your custodian and you can construct them. With some creativity, you and your students can arrange these cabinets in a variety of ways.

Small Items Storage

With an inquiry-based science program, you will constantly need to store many small items. Shoe, corrugated cardboard, cigar, and other small boxes provide space for collecting, organizing, and storing small, readily available materials for particular science areas. The following diagrams illustrate how to construct and store shoeboxes for small science items. Cardboard or clear plastic shoeboxes may be used. You may also use large cardboard boxes for storage, placing them in easily obtained wood or steel shelving units especially designed for this purpose. Your custodian can help with this.

Living Things Storage

Encourage your students to bring small animals (including insects) and plants into your classroom. To be well prepared, have the following kinds of containers available:

- Insect cages
- Small animal cages
- Aquariums
- Terrariums

SHOEBOX COLLECTION

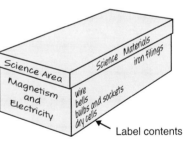

Label contents

Insect Cages.[1]

Use small cake pans, coffee can lids, or covers from ice cream cartons for the cage cover and base. Roll wire screening into a cylinder to fit the base and then lace the screening together with a strand of wire.

---

[1]For additional information about insects in the classroom, see: Laurel D. Hansen, Roger D. Akre, and Elizabeth A. Myhre, "Homes Away From Home: Observe Insects Indoors With These Creature Containers," *Science and Children 31*(1), September 1993, 28–31; Rebecca Olien, "Worm Your Way Into Science—Experiments With These Familiar Creatures Promote a Better Understanding of the Natural World," *Science and Children 31*(1), September 1993, 25–27.

STORAGE OF SHOEBOX COLLECTIONS

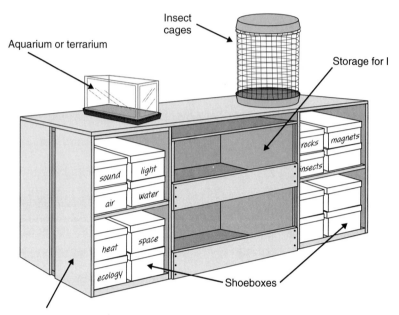

Four orange crates, two vertical, two horizontal

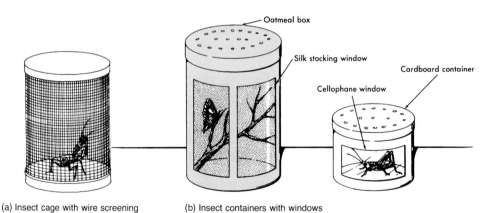

(a) Insect cage with wire screening   (b) Insect containers with windows

You can cut windows in a paper coffee container, oatmeal box, or another suitable cardboard or Styrofoam container. Cut out the window and glue clear plastic wrap, cellophane, silk, a nylon stocking, or some other thin fabric over the opening as shown.

Another home for insects such as ants that live in the soil can be made by filling a wide-mouthed quart or gallon pickle or mayonnaise jar with soil up to 2 inches from the top. Cover the jar with a nylon stocking and place it in a pan of water. Put the insects in and cover the jar with black construction paper to simulate the darkness of being underground.

Small Animal Cages.

You can also use some of the insect cages for other small animals. Larger animals can be housed in cages that you and your students construct from window screening. Cut and fold the screening as shown in the diagram. Use nylon screening or be very careful of the sharp edges of wire screening. Tack or staple three sides of the screening to a wooden base and hook the other side for a door.

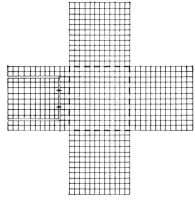

For housing *nongnawing* animals, you will need a wooden box and sleeping materials such as wood shavings. *Gnawing* animals need a wire cage. A bottle with a one-hole stopper and tubing hung on the side of the cage will supply water. Before proceeding, consult publications such as *Science and Children* and read some of the articles on the care and maintenance of various animals.

Terrariums.

The word *terrarium* means "little world." In setting up a terrarium for any animal, you should try to duplicate in miniature the environment in which the animal originally lived. You can make a terrarium with five pieces of glass (four sides and bottom) taped together. The top should be made of glass as well, but should have a section cut out to allow for access to the terrarium. Place the finished glass terrarium in a large cookie or cake pan. Commercially made terrariums are also available.

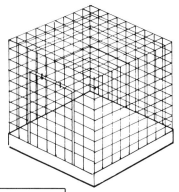

Another simple terrarium can be made from a two-liter, plastic soda pop bottle, charcoal, pebbles, topsoil, small plants, and scissors (see the diagram).

Constructing a 2L bottle terrarium

Soak the bottle in warm water to remove labels and glue. Carefully pry the bottom (a) from the bottle (b) so the bottom remains intact. Turn the bottle on its side. Rub your hand over it to find the ridge. With scissors, make a slit about 1.5 cm above the ridge. Cut all the way around the bottle at that level, staying above the ridge. Discard the top of the bottle and the cap.

Put layers of charcoal, pebbles, and topsoil into part (a). Select and arrange the plants in the soil. You can add moss, bark, or small ornaments to your terrarium. Moisten, but do not saturate, the soil. Invert bottle (b) upside down into (a). Push down gently to seal. Your terrarium is ready!

Source: Virginia Gilmore, "Helpful Hints—Coca-Cola® Bottle Terrarium." Reproduced with permission by *Science and Children* 16 (7), April 1979, 47. Copyright 1979 by the National Science Teachers Association, 1840 Wilson Blvd., Arlington, VA 22201.

Food Requirements for Various Animals

Food and Water	Guinea Pigs	Hamsters	Mice	Rats
Daily				
pellets		large dog pellets:		
or		1 or 2		
grain	corn, wheat, or oats		canary seeds or oats	
green or leafy vegetables, lettuce, cabbage, and celery tops	2 leaves	1½ T	2 tsp	3–4 tsp
		1 leaf	⅛–¼ leaf	¼ leaf
or				
grass, plantain, lambs' quarters, clover, alfalfa	1 handful	½ handful	—	—
or				
hay, if water is also given				
carrots	1 medium			
Twice a week				
apple (medium)	¼ apple	⅛ apple	½ core and seeds	1 core
iodized salt (if not contained in pellets)		sprinkle over lettuce or greens		
corn, canned or fresh, once or twice a week		1 T or ⅓ ear	1/4 T or end of ear	1/2 T or end of ear
water	¼ ear	necessary only if lettuce or greens are not provided		

Food and Water	Water Turtles	Land Turtles	Small Turtles
Daily			
worms or night crawlers	1 or 2	1 or 2	¼ inch of tiny earthworm
or			
tubiflex or blood worms and/or			enough to cover half the area of a dime
raw chopped beef or meat and fish-flavored dog or cat food	½ tsp	½ tsp	
fresh fruit and vegetables		1/4 leaf lettuce or 6–10 berries or 1–2 slices peach, apple, tomato, melon or 1 T corn, peas, beans	
dry ant eggs, insects or other commercial turtle food			1 small pinch
water	always available at room temperature; should be ample for swimming and submersion		
	¾ of container	large enough for shell	half to ¾ of container

Food and Water Plants (for Fish)	Goldfish	Guppies
Daily		
dry commercial food	1 small pinch	1 very small pinch; medium-size food for adults; fine-size food for babies
Twice a week		
shrimp—dry—or another kind of dry fish food	4 shrimp pellets or 1 small pinch	dry shrimp food or other dry food: 1 very small pinch
Two or three times a week		
tubifex worms add enough "conditioned" water to keep tank at required level	enough to cover ½ area of a dime allow one gallon per inch of fish; add water of same temperature as that in tank—at least 65°F	enough to cover ⅛ area of a dime allow ¼–½ gallon per adult fish; add water of same temperature as that in tank —70° to 80°F
Plants:		
cabomba, anacharis, etc.	should always be available	

Food and Water	Newts	Frogs
Daily		
small earthworms or mealworms or	1–2 worms	2–3 worms
tubifex worms or	enough to cover ½ area of a dime	enough to cover ¾ area of a dime
raw chopped beef	enough to cover a dime	enough to cover a dime
water	should always be available at same temperature as that in tank or at room temperature	

Note: See also: *Using Live Insects in Elementary Classrooms for Early Lessons in Life,* available from Center for Insect Science, Education Outreach, 800 E. University Blvd., Suite 300, Tucson, AZ 85721.

Source: Grace K. Pratt, *How to . . . Care for Living Things in the Classroom,* Arlington, VA: National Science Teachers Association, 11.

Safety Suggestions for Elementary and Middle School Inquiry Activities

1. Review science activities carefully for possible safety hazards.
2. Eliminate or be prepared to address all anticipated hazards.
3. Post appropriate safety rules in the classroom, review specific applicable safety rules before each activity, and provide occasional safety reminders during the activity.
4. Do not allow students to handle equipment, supplies, and chemicals until they have been given specific information on their use.
5. Maintain fair, consistent, and strictly enforced discipline during science activities.
6. Be particularly aware of possible eye injuries from chemical reactions, sharp objects, small objects such as iron filings, and flying objects such as rubber bands.
7. Require students to wear American National Standards Institute approved safety goggles (with Z87 printed on the goggles) whenever they do activities in which there is a potential risk to eye safety.
8. Consider eliminating open flames; use hot plates where possible as heat sources.
9. Prevent loose clothing and hair from coming into contact with any chemicals, equipment, flame, or other sources of heat.
10. Consider eliminating activities in which students taste substances; do not allow students to touch or inhale unknown substances.
11. Warn students of the dangers of handling glassware; be sure proper devices for handling hot objects are available.
12. Warn students of the dangers of electrical shock; use small dry cells in electrical activities; be aware of potential problems with the placement of extension cords.
13. Instruct students in the location and proper use of specialized safety equipment, such as fire extinguishers, fire blankets, or eye baths, when that equipment might be required by the science activity.
14. Instruct students in the proper care and handling of classroom pets, fish, or other live organisms used as part of science activities.
15. For students with handicapping conditions, assure safe access and use of equipment and materials.
16. Instruct students to report immediately to the teacher
    - any equipment in the classroom that appears to be in an unusual or improper condition,
    - any chemical reactions that appear to be proceeding in an improper way, or
    - any personal injury or damage to clothing caused by a science activity, no matter how trivial it may appear.
17. Provide practice sessions for safety procedures.

Sources: The University of the State of New York, *Elementary Science Syllabus, 49*, 1985, Albany, NY: The State Education Department, Division of Program Development; Ralph E. Martin, Colleen Sexton, Kay Wagner, and Jack Gerlovich, *Teaching Science for All Children*, 1994, Boston: Allyn and Bacon.

Measuring Tools, Measuring Skills

In elementary and middle school science and mathematics, students should have many opportunities to

- use a variety of types of measuring instruments;
- measure length, area, volume, mass, and temperature; and
- make comparisons using different systems of units.

Metric Prefixes

milli = .001 (one thousandth)
centi = .01 (one hundredth)
kilo = 1000 (one thousand)

Measuring Length

Length is a linear measure.

Metric Units

millimeter = 0.001 meter (one-thousandth of a meter; the thickness of about 20 pages)
centimeter = 0.01 meter (one-hundredth of a meter; width of a little fingernail)
kilometer = 1000 meters (about 10 city blocks)

Some Conversions

1 inch = 2.54 centimeters
1 centimeter = 10 millimeters
100 centimeters = 1000 millimeters = 1 meter
1 meter = 39.37 inches = 3.28 feet
1000 meters = 1 kilometer = 0.621 mile
100 meters = 109 yards
1 yard = 3 feet

Use the ruler to convert lengths between units.

1 inch   = _____ cm = _____ mm
3 inches = _____ cm = _____ mm
10 cm   = _____ mm = _____ inches
140 mm   = _____ cm = _____ inches

Use the ruler to measure lengths.

Length of dollar bill = _____ inches = _____ cm = _____ mm
Diameter of quarter = _____ inches = _____ cm = _____ mm
Thickness of quarter = _____ inches = _____ cm = _____ mm

Measuring Area

Area is a surface measure.

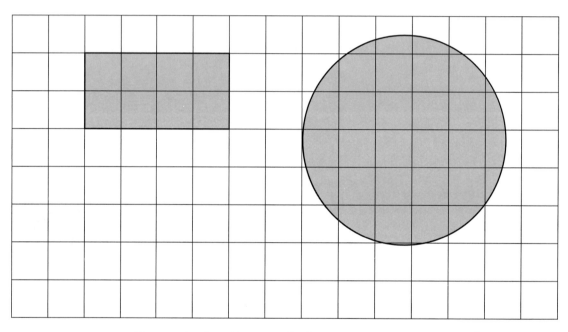

The area of each small square in the figure is 1 square centimeter = 1 cm^2.

Determine the area of the shaded rectangle

- by counting squares. _____
- by formula ($A = L \times W$). _____

Determine the area of the shaded circle

- by counting squares. _____
- by formula ($A = \pi r^2$). _____

Measuring Volume

Volume is three-dimensional.

1 cubic centimeter (cm^3 or cc) is the volume of a cube that is 1 centimeter on each side.

Some Conversions

$1 \text{ cm}^3 = 1 \text{ cc} = 1$ milliliter (ml)
$1000 \text{ cm}^3 = 1000 \text{ ml} = 1$ liter
1 liter = 1.06 quarts

Determine the volume of the large solid in the figure

- by counting unit cubes. _____
- by using the formula, $V = L \times W \times H$. _____

Estimate the volume of a golf ball in cubic centimeters. A golf ball has a diameter of about 4 cm.
[*Answer*: Estimate how many unit cubes (1 cm^3) might fit inside a golf ball if it were hollow. A good estimate of its volume might be between 25 and 40 unit cubes. By formula, the volume of a golf ball is about 33.5 cm^3]

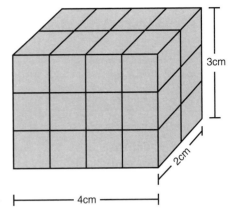

3cm

2cm

4cm

Measuring Mass and Weight

Mass is a measure of the amount of matter in an object and, also, a measure of the inertia of an object. Mass is measured in grams, milligrams, or kilograms using a balance. Weight is a measure of the gravitational pull on an object, measured with a spring scale. Mass and weight are not the same thing, but the weight of an object can be found from its mass.

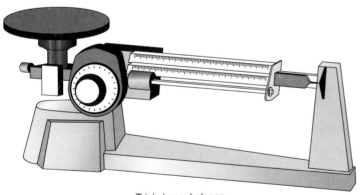

Triple beam balance

Some Conversions

1000 grams (g) = 1 kilogram (kg)
1 milligram = 0.001 gram (one-thousandth of a gram)
1 gram = 1000 milligrams (mg)
1 kg-mass weighs 2.2 pounds on the surface of the earth

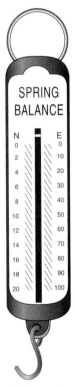

SPRING BALANCE

Spring scale

Nutrition Facts

Serving Size 2/3 cup (55g)
Servings Per Container 12

Amount Per Serving

Calories 210
   Calories from Fat 25

	% Daily Value*
Total Fat 3g	**5%**
Saturated Fat 1g	**4%**
Polyunsaturated Fat 0.5g	
Monounsaturated Fat 1.5g	
Cholesterol 0mg	**0%**
Sodium 140mg	**6%**
Potassium 190mg	**5%**
Total Carbohydrate 44g	**15%**
Other Carbohydrate 23g	
Dietary Fiber 3g	**13%**
Sugars 18g	
Protein 5g	
Vitamin A	0%
Vitamin C	0%
Calcium	2%
Iron	6%
Thiamine	10%
Phosphorus	10%
Magnesium	10%

* Percent Daily Values are based on a 2000 calorie
diet. Your daily values may be higher or lower
depending on your calorie needs.

	Calories	2,000	2,500
Total Fat	Less than	65g	80g
Sat Fat	Less than	20g	25g
Cholesterol	Less than	300g	300g
Sodium	Less than	2400mg	2400mg
Potassium		3500mg	3500mg
Total Carbo		300g	300g
Dietary Fiber		25g	30g

Calories per gram:
Fat 9   •   Carbohydrate 4   •   Protein 4

Some Masses and Weights

Mass of nickel = 5 g
Mass of small child weighing about 60 pounds on earth = 27.3 kg (divide 60 by 2.2)
Weight on moon of small child of mass 27.3 kg = 10 pounds (⅙ of weight on earth)

Food labels tell how many grams and milligrams of different substances are in a food product.

Measuring Temperature

Temperature is a measure of how hot or cold a substance is. Temperature is measured with a thermometer in degrees Celsius or degrees Fahrenheit.

Some Equivalent Temperatures: Use the Fahrenheit/Celsius thermometer to convert from one temperature unit to the other.

Boiling point of water	100°C =	_____ °F
Normal body temperature	_____ °C =	98.6 °F
Room temperature	22°C =	_____ °F
Freezing point of water	0°C =	_____ °F
Slush of crushed ice, water, and ice cream salt	_____ °C =	10°F
A really cold day in Alaska	_____ °C =	−15°F

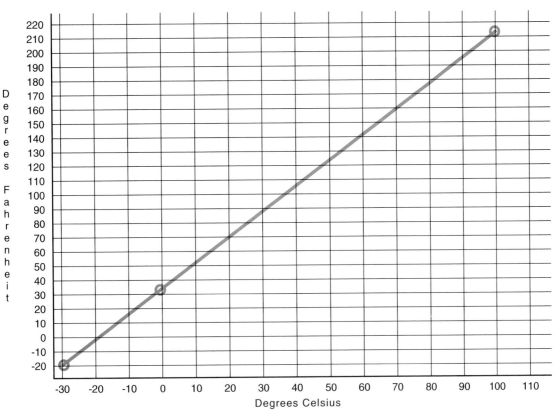

Temperature in °C and °F

Degrees Fahrenheit (y-axis), Degrees Celsius (x-axis)

Use the graph to find equivalent temperatures.

0°C   = _____ °F
212°F = _____ °C
40°F = _____ °C
180°F = _____ °C
50°C = _____ °F

Selected Science Education Periodicals for Teachers and Children

American Biology Teachers

The National Association of Biology Teachers
11250 Roger Bacon Drive
Reston, VA 20190-5202
Toll Free: 800-406-0775
Phone: 703-471-1134
Fax: 703-435-5582
Email: NABTer@aol.com

Audubon Magazine

The National Audubon Society
613 Riversville Road
Greenwich, CT 06831
Phone: 212-979-3000
Fax: 212-691-7483

Cornell Rural School Leaflets

New York State College of Agriculture
& Life Sciences
Rural Schools Program
114 Kennedy Hall
Ithaca, NY 14853
Phone: 607-255-8056

Discover Magazine

114 5th Avenue
15th Floor
New York, NY 10011
Toll Free: 800-829-9132

Journal of Research in Science Teaching

John Wiley & Sons
605 Third Avenue
New York, NY 10158
Toll Free: 800-225-5945
Phone: 212-850-6000
Fax: 212-850-6049

Junior Natural History

American Museum of Natural History
Central Park West at 79th Street
New York, NY 10024-5192
Phone: 212-769-5000
Fax: 212-769-5511

National Geographic/National Geographic Society

1145 17th Street NW
Washington, DC 20036
Toll Free: 800-647-5463,
800-638-6400
Phone: 202-857-6112
Fax: 202-775-6141
Email: natgeo1@aol.com

Natural History/American Museum of Natural History

American Museum of Natural History
Central Park West at 79th Street
New York, NY 10024-5192
Phone: 212-769-5000
Fax: 212-769-5511
Email: nhmag@amnh.org

Nature Magazine

American Nature Association
529 14th Street NW #968
Washington, DC 20045
Phone:202-737-2355

OMNI/OMNI Publications International Ltd.

277 Park Avenue
New York, NY 10172

Ranger Rick/National Wildlife Federation

8925 Leesburg Pike
Vienna, VA 22182
Phone: 703-790-4544
Web site: www.nwf.org

Readers Guide to Oceanography

Woods Hole Oceanographic Institute
Woods Hole, MA 02543
Phone: 508-289-2865
Fax: 508-289-2156
Email: apaul@whiu.edu

School Science & Math Association/Donald Pratt, Exec. Sec.

Bloomsburg University
Department of C & F
400 E. 2nd Street
Bloomsburg, PA 17815-1301
Phone: 717-389-4915
Fax: 717-389-3615

Science/American Association for the Advancement of Science

1200 New York Avenue NW
Washington, DC 20005
Phone: 202-326-6626
Fax: 202-289-4950

Science & Children/NSTA

1840 Wilson Boulevard
Arlington, VA 22201-3000

Science Education

John Wiley & Sons
605 Third Avenue
New York, NY 10158
Phone: 813-253-3333

Science Newsletter/Science Service, Inc.

1719 N Street NW
Washington, DC 20036
Phone: 202-785-2255

Science Scope/NSTA

1840 Wilson Boulevard
Arlington, VA 22201-3000

Science Teacher/NTSA

1840 Wilson Boulevard
Arlington, VA 22201-3000

Science World/Scholastic

555 Broadway
New York, NY 10012
Phone:212-343-6100
Fax: 212-343-4535
Web site: www.scholastic.com

Scientific American

415 Madison Avenue
New York, NY 10017
Phone: 212-754-0550
Fax: 212-355-6245

Sky & Telescope/Sky Publishing Corp.

49 Bay State Road
Cambridge, MA 02138
Toll Free: 800-253-0245
Phone: 617-864-7360
Fax: 617-864-6117

Your Big Backyard/National Wildlife Federation

8925 Leesburg Pike
Vienna, VA 22182
Phone: 703-790-4544

Weekly Reader Corp.

3001 Cindel Drive
Delran, NJ 08075-1182
Toll Free: 800-446-3355
Web site: www.weeklyreader.com

Professional Societies for Science Teachers and Supervisors

AAAS (American Association for the Advancement of Science)

Education Department
1333 H Street NW
Washington, DC 20005
Phone: 202-326-6605
Fax: 202-371-9849

AAAS (American Association for the Advancement of Science)

Project on Science, Technology, and
   Disability
1333 H Street NW
Washington, DC 20005
Phone: 202-326-6630
Fax: 202-371-9849

American Chemical Society

(*To order periodicals*)
P. O. Box 3337
Columbus, OH 43210
Phone: 800-333-9511
Fax: 614-447-3671

Association for Supervision and Curriculum Development

1259 N. Pitt Street
Alexandria, VA 22314-1403
Phone: 703-549-9110
Fax: 703-549-3891

Association of Science-Technology Centers

1025 Vermont Avenue NW
Washington, DC 20005
Phone: 202-783-7200
Fax: 202-783-7207

Council for Elementary Science International (CESI)

c/o Dr. John Penick, Publications Co-
   ordinator
789 Van Allen
Iowa City, IA 52242
Phone: 319-335-1183
Fax: 319-335-1188

International Society for Technology in Education (ISTE)

1789 Agate Street
Eugene, OR 97403-1923
Phone: 503-346-4414
Fax: 503-346-5890

National Association of Biology Teachers

11250 Roger Bacon Drive
Reston, VA 22090
Phone: 800-406-0775
Fax: 703-435-5582

National Geographic Society

Educational Services
1145 17th Street NW
Washington, DC 20036-4688
Phone: 800-368-2728
Fax: 301-921-1575

National Science Teachers Association (NSTA)

1840 Wilson Boulevard
Arlington, VA 22201-3000
Phone: 800-722-NSTA
Fax: 703-522-6091

Contemporary Elementary Science Project—
Developed Programs

Name	Grades	Address	Characteristics
AIMS	K–10	AIMS Educational Foundation P.O. Box 8120 Fresno, CA 93747	*Activities for Integrating Math and Science Project:* Integration of math skills with science processes into a series of enjoyable investigatory activities; accompanying teacher booklets.
BSCS	K–6	BSCS 5415 Mark Dabling Blvd. Colorado Springs, CO 80918-3842	*Biological Science Curriculum Study:* Name of project, "Science for Living: Integrating Science, Technology, and Health." Integrated curriculum designed to relate what children know with their exploration and evaluation of new knowledge. Designed around concepts and skills for each grade level: order and organization (grade 1); change and measurement (grade 2); patterns and prediction (grade 3); systems and analysis (grade 4); transformation and investigation (grade 5); balance and decisions (grade 6). Each investigatory lesson has five sequenced phases: engagement, exploration, explanation, elaboration, and evaluation.
ESS	K–6	Delta Education 80 Northwest Blvd. Nashua, NH 03063	*Elementary Science Study:* A program of 56 nonsequential, open-ended exploratory activities that are not grade-level specific. Student worksheets, booklets, and teacher's guides. Most units are accompanied by kilts of materials. Films and film loops also available. Although designed for regular students, ESS units have been shown to be useful in teaching science to children who have language deficiencies, learning difficulties, or other learning disadvantages.
FOSS	K–6	Lawrence Hall of Science University of California 1 Centennial Drive Berkeley, CA 94720 Available from: Delta Education 30 Northwest Blvd. Nashua, NH 03063	*Full Option Science System:* Designed for both regular and special education students, 12 modules with lab kits are available. Lessons are in earth, life, and physical sciences with extension activities in language, computer, and math. Can be integrated with textbook programs and state frameworks.

Contemporary Elementary Science Project—Developed Programs *(continued)*

Name	Grades	Address	Characteristics
GEMS	1–10	Lawrence Hall of Science University of California 1 Centennial Drive Berkeley, CA 94720	*Great Explorations in Math and Science:* Developed at the Lawrence Hall of Science, this is a series of more than 30 teacher's guides for activities using easily obtained materials.
SAVI/SELPH (Designed students with disabilities)	2–10	Center for Multisensory Learning Lawrence Hall of Science University of California 1 Centennial Drive Berkeley, CA 94720	*Science Activities for the Visually Impaired/Science Enrichment Learning for the Physically Handicapped:* Teacher activity guides in nine modules, student equipment kits.
SCIS 3+	K–6	Delta Education 80 Northwest Blvd. Nashua, NH 03063	*Science Curriculum Improvement Study:* Originally developed by a team at the University of California, Berkeley, there have been several generations of SCIS developed, with the most recent being SCIS 3+. The SCIS programs are built around a hierarchy of science concepts. Science process skills are integrated into the materials-centered programs, which use an inductive instructional approach and a three-phase learning cycle: (1) student exploration, (2) teacher explanation of concepts, and (3) student application of the old with new.
STC	1–6	Carolina Biological Supply Co. 2700 York Rd. Burlington, NC 27215	*Science and Technology for Children:* This program consists of units of hands-on instruction that integrate science and mathematics with other disciplines. A primary focus of program developers is to interest more females and minority children in science.

Source: Richard D. Kellough, *Integrating mathematics and Science for Kindergarten and Primary Children,* 1996, Englewood Cliffs, NJ: Merrill/Prentice Hall, 396–397.